CW01019758

ISBN: 9781290547543

Published by:
HardPress Publishing
8345 NW 66TH ST #2561
MIAMI FL 33166-2626

Email: info@hardpress.net
Web: http://www.hardpress.net

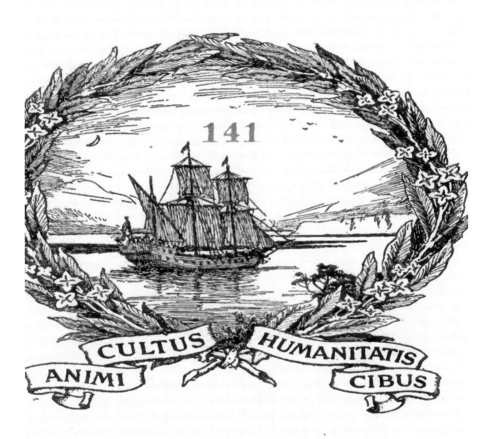

141

CULTUS ANIMI HUMANITATIS CIBUS

Griffing Bancroft

presented to the

UNIVERSITY LIBRARY
UNIVERSITY OF CALIFORNIA
SAN DIEGO

by

Mrs. Griffing Bancroft

THE COLLAPSE OF THE KINGDOM OF NAPLES

THE COLLAPSE OF THE KINGDOM OF NAPLES

By H. Remsen Whitehouse,
Lately of the United States Diplomatic
Service. ❧ ❧ ❧ ❧ ❧ ❧ ❧
Author of the "Life of Amadeus of
Savoy, King of Spain," Etc.

NEW YORK
BONNELL, SILVER & CO.
1899

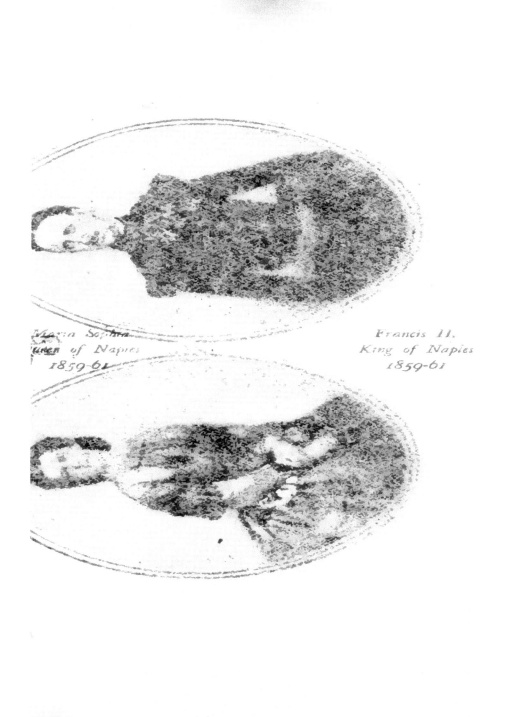

Maria Sophia
Queen of Naples
1859-61

Francis II.
King of Naples
1859-61

THE COLLAPSE OF THE KINGDOM OF NAPLES

By H. Remsen Whitehouse, Lately of the United States Diplomatic Service. ❦ ❦ ❦ ❦ ❦ ❦ ❦ ❦ Author of the " Life of Amadeus of Savoy, King of Spain," Etc. ❦ ❦ ❦

VINCIT OMNIA VERITAS

NEW YORK

BONNELL, SILVER & CO.

1899

Copyright, 1899, by

BONNELL, SILVER & CO.

All rights reserved.

TO

JUDGE AND MADRÉ

IN LOVING GRATITUDE I DEDICATE

THIS STUDY.

"THE LARCHES,"
OCTOBER, 1899.

CONTENTS.

PAGE

Preface.. 11

CHAPTER I.

Mr. Gladstone's letters from Naples.—Their effect on Europe and in Naples.—Traces of the reign of Murat.—Ferdinand I. grants Constitution.—Conference of Laybach.—Revocation of Franchise.—Political persecution.—Ferdinand II. and his relations with Liberalism.—The Bandiera brothers. —Revolutions of 1848.—Ferdinand II. grants Constitution. —Sicily in 1848.—Offer of Crown to Duke of Genoa.—Dismissal of Liberal Ministry—Filangieri in Sicily.—Bombardment of Messina.—Fall of Palermo.—Lord Minto intermediary in subsequent negotiations......................... 15

CHAPTER II.

Ferdinand II. attempts to free himself from Parliamentary restraints.—Disorders in Naples.—Flight of Pius IX. to Gaeta.—Revolution in Rome.—Grand Duke of Tuscany seeks refuge at Gaeta.—Charles Albert's offer of assistance.—Gioberti's policy misrepresented in Piedmont.— French intervention.—Ferdinand meets Garibaldi's forces at Palestrina.—Defeat of Neapolitans at Velletri.—Restoration of the Pope.—International relations of Kingdom of Naples.—England and France during Sicilian revolution.—Mazzini and "Young Italy."—Parliamentary complications in Naples.—Mr. Morrison's letter to Daniel Webster.—Ferdinand seeks to abolish Franchises.......... 35

CHAPTER III.

Factors which undermined Neapolitan Throne.—Idea of National Unity.—Characteristics of lower classes.—Educational opportunities.—University of Naples.—Colleges of the Jesuits.—Their sphere of influence.—Measures to check spread of Liberal theories.—Newspapers and the Press.—The Aristocracy and its relations to Public Affairs. —Diplomatic service.—The Army and Navy, and their relations with the Crown.—The Swiss Guard.—Politics in the Army.—Arsenals and Shipyards.—Taxation.—Police system.—International influences.—Recall of English and French diplomatists.—Napoleon III. and Prince Murat.— Decline of Neapolitan Diplomacy......................... 53

CHAPTER IV.

Count Cavour's projects for alliance with Naples.—The Plombières' interview. — Plans of Napoleon III. and Cavour.—Dynastic ambitions.—Proposed partition of the Peninsula.—Attempted assassination of Ferdinand II.— Milano and "Young Italy."—Political significance of attack.—Pisacane's expedition.—The "Cagliari" incident. —British claims.—Lord Malmesbury on transportation of political prisoners. — Diplomatic interference —Ferdinand's policy from 1856–59 reviewed.—His reactionary measures.—His bigotry and superstitions.................. 82

CHAPTER V.
PAGE

Marriage of Crown Prince.—Ceremonies in Munich and Trieste.—Ferdinand starts for Adriatic coast.—Incidents of the journey.—The suspicious illness at Ariano.—Accusations against the Bishop.—The Court reaches Bari.—Arrival of Maria Sophia.—Her meeting with Francis and members of his family.—Ferdinand's illness increases.—The Count of Syracuse arrives.—The return to Naples.—Alarming news from Turin.—Napoleon III. and Victor Emmanuel.—Opinions of foreign royalty visiting Naples.—Details of Ferdinand's last days.—His death............. 102

CHAPTER VI.

Expectations of a change of policy.—Events in Northern Italy.—Their influences on Naples.—Accession of Francis II.—Ferdinand's second marriage.—Education of Francis.—Life at the Neapolitan Court during his youth.—His character and early training.—The religious influences.—Want of political training.—The "Camarilla"; its composition and objects.—Influence of the Queen-Mother.—The Count of Syracuse.— His surroundings and political ambitions. — Palace intrigues. — Conspiracy in favor of Count of Trani.............................. 121

CHAPTER VII.

An envoy from Turin.—Proposals for alliance between Naples and Piedmont.—French and English diplomatic relations are resumed.—Royal proclamation eulogizing Ferdinand—Filangieri at the head of the Government.—His previous career.—Political problems confronting him.—Count Salmour's mission.—Opposition to alliance.—Mazzini's schemes.—Action of Swiss Government.—Revolt of Swiss Guard.—Massacre of same.—Swiss regiments disbanded.—Kossuth on situation in Naples.—Court functions and etiquette.—Abstention of aristocracy.—Their sympathies for Murat.-... 135

CHAPTER VIII.

Filangieri's political sympathies.—Napoleon III.: his aims and policy.—Cavour's policy.—Plan for partition of Papal States.—Count Salmour's failure.—Villafranca.—Cavour resigns.—Rumors from Sicily.—Filangieri's resignation.—His retirement at Sorrento.—Blunders of the Administration.—Cavour to Marquis d'Azeglio.—Lord Palmerston on Cavour.—An Italian Confederation.—Napoleon's embarrassments.—Sir James Hudson and his associates.—English policy in Italian question.— Opinions of Prince Consort.—Diplomacy at Turin.—Marquis Villamarina goes to Naples.—His instructions.—His report on situation at Naples.. 154

CHAPTER IX.

Efforts to secure alliance.—Cavour returns to office.—His correspondence with Villamarina.—Prudential policy.—Cession of Nice and Savoy.—The reasons for same.—Villamarina's reports.—Distrust and opposition excited by cession of territory.—Cavour's relations with Kossuth and Hungarian patriots.—Cavour and European Diplomacy.—Victor Emmanuel's letter to King of Naples.—Determined opposition to alliance................................ 176

CHAPTER X.

PAGE

Revolutionary plotting.—Morelli in Calabria.—Garibaldi and Tennyson.—Preparations for Garibaldi's expedition.—Mazzini indorses Unity and Victor Emmanuel.—Conspiracy and Massacre of La Gancia.—Risings in Sicily, their repression.—Diplomatic protests.—Nunziante's mission.—Rumors of Garibaldi's expedition.—Plans to frustrate same.—Garibaldi lands at Marsala.—Lanza sent to Sicily.—His methods of combating revolution.—Sicily welcomes Garibaldi 191

CHAPTER XI.

Cavour and the Sicilian expedition.—His relations with Garibaldi.—Diplomatic perils.—Garibaldi a Republican.—His letter to Victor Emmanuel.—Cavour to d'Azeglio concerning expedition.—He explains position of Piedmont.—Cavour is blamed.—His defence of his policy.—A Russian protest.—Cavour and European Diplomacy.—Anecdotes from his private correspondence.—His relations with French and English politicians.—Louis Napoleon's entanglements.. 212

CHAPTER XII.

Anxiety at Naples.—Filangieri's counsels.—He leaves Naples.—Francis sends De Martino to Paris.—His reception by French Emperor.—The Emperor's advice and warning.—The "Camarilla's" accusations.—Francis grants Constitution.—The Pope antagonistic to Piedmontese alliance.—The Franchise coldly received by Liberals.—Riots in Naples.—The application for alliance.—Cavour's embarrassments.—His conditions.—Arrival of Neapolitan Envoys at Turin.—Their demands.—Victor Emmanuel writes Garibaldi.—The General refuses obedience.—Cavour confides to D'Azeglio details of his policy..................... 227

CHAPTER XIII.

Promulgation of Constitution.—Preparations for elections.—Amnesty of political prisoners.—Tumultuous reception of exiles.—Action of troops.—Disorders in the capital.—Romano's influence.—Romano; his character and antecedents.—The Queen-Mother goes to Gaeta.—Intrigues of the "Camarilla."—Romano's further demands.—Insulting resignations. — The Press embarrasses the Government.—Schism in Revolutionary Committees.—Romano's revelations.—His political memoirs.—Cavour's opportunity.—His despatch to Envoy at St. Petersburg.—His remarks to Nisco.—Disaffection in Neapolitan Army.—The Ministerial programme.—The elections postponed .. 250

CHAPTER XIV.

Garibaldi crosses the Straits.—Preoccupations of Cavour.—Plan to neutralize Garibaldi's prestige.—The mission to Chambéry.—Napoleon's encouragement.—Conspiracy of the "Camarilla."—Seizure of arms.—Expulsion of Count of Aquila.—Francis amidst conflicting counsels.—Romano's memorandum.—Letter of the Count of Syracuse.—Francis addresses himself to Garibaldi.—Indecision of King.—Energetic policy of Cabinet.—Resignation of same.—Garibaldi at the gates.—Francis decides to leave Naples. 270

CHAPTER XV.

PAGE

Farewell proclamation and protest.—Suspicions of treachery.—Preparations for departure.—The gunboat "Messagero."—Reception of Ministers and Diplomatists.—The
Sovereigns leave the Palace.—Refusal of Neapolitan war-
ships to follow King.—The voyage to Gaeta.—The King
and Queen during journey.—Arrival at Gaeta......... ... 294

CHAPTER XVI.

Naples remains calm.—Offer to land Piedmontese troops
refused.—Commission appointed to meet Garibaldi.—His
communications with Romano.—An officious Provisional
Government.—Garibaldi enters Naples.—His reception by
populace.—Evacuation by Royalist troops.—Garibaldi's
loyalty suspected at Turin.—Romano's attempts at reconciliation.—Mistakes of Dictator's Government.—The Piedmontese ultimatum to the Pope.—Cavour's justification.
—Piedmontese troops enter Papal States.—Diplomatic
protests.—Napoleon privately approves.................. 300

CHAPTER XVII.

Francis at Gaeta.—He forms a Ministry.—Instructions to
local officials.—Address to the Army.—The battles of the
Volturno.—Garibaldi's submission.—Political excesses in
Naples.—Piedmontese troops enter Neapolitan territory.—
Cavour's audacious counsels.—His belief in non-interven-
tion of France and England .—Austrian hostility.—Victor
Emmanuel at Ancona.—His proclamation to Southern
populations.—The "Times" on situation.—Appointment
of Pro-Dictator at Naples.—The Plebiscite.—Meeting of
Victor Emmanuel and Garibaldi.—Fall of Capua.—Victor
Emmanuel in Naples.—Departure of Garibaldi.—Honors
and rewards offered him.—Alexander Dumas in Naples.
—His opinion of Garibaldi................................. 317

CHAPTER XVIII.

Operations on the Garigliano.—Failure of fleet to co-operate.—Napoleon's enigmatical policy.—Conference at Varsovie.—Defeat of Royalists.—Retreat on Gaeta.—The fortress of Gaeta.—Its garrison.—Members of Royal Family
assembled there.—Early days of the siege.—Napoleon
proposes armistice.—Francis writes Emperor refusing to
capitulate.—Action of Powers.—Cavour's influence over
English statesmen.—Lord Palmerston's assertions........ 340

CHAPTER XIX.

The Siege of Gaeta.—Bombardment.—Diplomatic interference.—Cialdini makes unexpected attack.—Francis rejects proposals for capitulation.—His letter to the Emperor Napoleon III.—Departure of French fleet.—Action
of Royalist officers.—Heroism of Queen Maria Sophia.—
Typhus Epidemic.—Negative results of bombardment.—
Series of catastrophes —Renewed attacks.—Terrific explosions.—A truce.—General Milon negotiates surrender.
—Conditions of capitulation.—Departure of King.—
Francis addresses troops.—He goes to Rome.—His wanderings and death.—Surrender of Messina and Civitella.
—Victor Emmanuel proclaimed King of Italy.—Conclusion.. 354

PREFACE.

IN presenting the following study the author lays no claim to the discovery of recondite, or hitherto unpublished, documents. His aim has been to place before readers unfamiliar with the historical and biographical literature of Italy and France, a consecutive narrative of a curious episode of contemporaneous history, the true inwardness of which is little known outside a small coterie of students interested in the social and diplomatic undercurrents of this period of Italian political regeneration.

A great mass of confusingly conflicting material, treating of the Italian political renaissance, is at the disposal of students in Italy and France, as also in Germany and Austria; but the author is unacquainted with any work in English dealing exclusively with the national and international causes, political as well as social, which contributed to the collapse of the Kingdom of the Two Sicilies.

11

Most readers are, of course, aware that the direct result of Garibaldi's filibustering expedition to Sicily was the annexation of Naples, and of that island, to the recently extended dominions of King Victor Emmanuel II. ; but the circumstances which made it possible for this handful of adventurers to overturn the organized military, naval and civil institutions of a State numbering nearly eleven millions of inhabitants, are neither adequately understood nor appreciated by many professing an interest in the historical data of this century.

For this purpose a study of the life and times of the two Princes whose benighted policy contributed more directly to the collapse of their Dynasty (which had ruled nearly one hundred and twenty-six years) has been necessary.

In formulating his estimate of the characters and influences of Ferdinand II., and his son, Francis II., of Naples, the writer's authorities have been selected on the most eclectic principles.

Amongst Italian writers there exists, not unnaturally, a tendency to either pass the sponge over the blood-stained record of past years, or to magnify the evils of an abhorred system. Dispassionate criticism is looked for in vain amongst the authors who were witnesses of, or actors in, the drama, and whose prejudices or personal sympathies warped their judgment. Nevertheless such divergent testimony has been taken as offered by Nisco, "Memor," Bersezio, Chiala, Giampaolo, Rattazzi, Insogna, Villamarini, Romano, Zini, Garibaldi, Settembrini, Bianchi, de Cesare, White-Mario, and many others too numerous for mention here. Besides these, many ephemeral pamphlets and documents, published contemporaneously with the events criticised or recorded, have been perused and digested, with every endeavor to arrive at a just and unbiased appreciation of their value, and to reconcile widely diversified opinions, and statements, by the aid of a comparison of facts, and the light thrown upon them by the recent publication (in Italy) of confidential correspondence, hitherto inaccessible.

The author has, moreover, been fortunate in enjoying the privilege of personal acquaintance, or correspondence, with several of the minor actors in the drama he describes, and has thus been enabled to gather opinions and criticisms at first hand of a period which, although hardly remote, is yet sufficiently removed from the present generation to be endowed with the dignity of History.

The author desires to express his gratitude for the courtesies extended him by Commendatore Giacomo Malvano, Senator of the Kingdom of Italy, and General Secretary of the Italian Foreign Office ; and to the Duke de San-Martino di Montalbo, Agent of the Neapolitan Bourbons in Rome, whose constant fidelity, and indefatigable labors in the service of his late Sovereign, compel the admiration and respect of all parties.

THE COLLAPSE OF
THE KINGDOM OF NAPLES.

CHAPTER I.

Mr. Gladstone's letters from Naples.—Their effect on Europe and in Naples.—Traces of the reign of Murat.—Ferdinand I. grants Constitution.—Conference of Laybach.—Revocation of Franchise.—Political persecution.—Ferdinand II. and his relations with Liberalism.—The Bandiera brothers.—Revolutions of 1848.—Ferdinand II. grants Ccnstitution.—Sicily in 1848.—Offer of Crown to Duke of Genoa.—Dismissal of Liberal Ministry—Filangieri in Sicily.—Bombardment of Messina.—Fall of Palermo.—Lord Minto intermediary in subsequent negotiations.

WHEN Mr. Gladstone startled the world in 1851 by his famous letters to Lord Aberdeen, in which he described the administration of the Kingdom of the Two Sicilies as "the negation of God erected into a system of government," the catching phrase found a ready circulation throughout Europe and America.

The letters were speedily translated into many tongues, and as rapidly disseminated by

15

those who had for years been agitating, within
and without the realms of the Neapolitan
Bourbons, for reforms.   Now for the first time
the deeds of darkness enacted by a Government,
long known as the most retrograde and bigoted,
were brought under the searching light of
public opinion abroad.   The barbarous repression of the Liberalism of 1848 had passed
almost unnoticed at a moment when most European governments were engaged in struggling with, and in some instances succumbing
to, similar popular outbursts.   The government
of the Kingdom of Naples, or of the Two Sicilies, as it was officially termed, was known
to be despotic, and those people out of Italy
who thought about it at all were vaguely aware
that Ferdinand II. kept regiments of Swiss
guards for his protection.   Some of those who
had gone deeper into the affairs of the State
knew that Ferdinand after having had wrung
from him a Constitution which he solemnly,
and with unnecessary reiteration, had sworn to
uphold and defend, once the peril averted, had
quickly perjured himself, setting the inconvenient document aside, and devoted his energies to venting his fury upon all those who
had advocated its adoption.   But to what
extent the despotism was carried ; how rigor-
ously liberal ideas were crushed ; to what

degree of cruel repression all intellectual or moral progress was doomed, few, if any, had had the curiosity to inquire. The energies expended ; the principles involved ; the intellectual and social impulses, struggling for life and mastery ; the real political nullity of an obsolete system galvanized into a semblance of vitality by unreasoning abhorrence of liberal innovations were truths ignored by the world until the great English statesman and philanthropist indignantly flung the results of his investigations before the tribunals of civilization.

Lord Palmerston stated in Parliament that he had caused reprints of Mr. Gladstone's now famous letters to be sent to each of Her Majesty's Representatives in Europe, directing them to hand each government a copy of the pamphlet, with the hope that, by affording an opportunity for its perusal, their influence might be secured in promoting the distinguished writer's object.

On the government of the Two Sicilies, Mr. Gladstone's letters, emphasized and given official significance by Lord Palmerston's vigorous despatch, produced no impression whatever. The latter document was carefully withheld from Ferdinand by his ministers, who casually referred to the subject as " one of Lord Pal-

2

merston's usual impertinences." When, however, in spite of ministerial precautions, the King did become acquainted with the text of "Palmerston's impertinence," he dismissed the subject with the oracular remark that it was "an important and well written document."

It was not until some years later (1856), that Count Cavour, during the Congress of Paris, cleverly exploited the wide-spread indignation at the methods employed by the Neapolitan Bourbons in a memorable speech, which may be said to have dealt the death-blow to the ascendency of Austrian influence in the Peninsula, and thus prepared the way for the downfall of the obnoxious dynasty.

The French occupation and reign of Murat had left indelible traces of liberty, and had dowered the country with really progressive and liberally intentioned institutions, some of which were in many respects superior to those at that moment (1851) existing in other Italian States. The evil lay not in the laws and institutions themselves so much as in the fact that the administration thereof had become either a dead letter, or totally corrupt. Murat had done his utmost to model his new possessions on the lines established by his imperial brother-in-law in France. To him were due the reforms in the antiquated legal procedure ; the abolishment of class privileges ; the curtailment of ecclesiastical prerogatives and time-honored exemptions of Church property.   The City of Naples is indebted to him for its fine promenade ; the construction of the only military roads, and engineering works of public utility, were the result of his efforts.   When, after the fall of the Emperor Napoleon I., the Congress of Vienna recalled Ferdinand I. from his refuge in Sicily, and restored to him his dominions, he promptly set about abolishing or rendering innocuous all the reforms introduced during the reign of the French General, and speedily had the kingdom again under the despotic rule of the earlier years during which Lord Nelson and Lady Hamilton had been his intimates, and the latter his counsellor.   He did indeed, in dire distress, grant a Constitution to his subjects, and greatly impressed all who witnessed the imposing ceremony attending his taking the oath thereto, by solemnly adding of his own accord as his eyes sought the Cross over the altar : " Omnipotent God, who with infinite penetration lookest into the hearts of men and into the future, if I lie, or if one day I should be faithless to my oath, do Thou at this instant annihilate me."

Austria, however, soon aided him in ridding

himself of troublesome obligations, and his return from the Conference of Laybach was the signal for wholesale persecution of all who had been instrumental in influencing his decision to grant the odious franchise.   Farini computed at eight hundred those who suffered death in the cause of liberty during the years 1821 and 1822 ; but of the untold host who languished in dungeons or dragged out a miserable existence in the galleys ; and of those more fortunate who found safety in exile, no estimate can be formed.

Fortunately for his subjects, Ferdinand I. died in 1825.   The reign of his successor varied only in that it was considerably shorter, and consequently less onerous to this enslaved people.

Since 1830, when he succeeded his father, Francis I., Ferdinand the Second had been occupied at intervals in the suppression of revolutionary movements of greater or less importance both in Sicily and the mainland.   The expectations founded on his leanings towards Liberalism which had possessed some shadow of probability before he ascended the Throne, quickly evaporated when he assumed the Crown.   His first marriage, with a daughter of the House of Savoy, had given satisfaction to his subjects, but she was all too quickly succeeded by an

Austrian Princess with whose advent the influence of her native country once more became paramount.   Discontent and insubordination were rife throughout the realm, more especially in Sicily ; but the risings were sporadic, totally lacking in competent leaders or cohesive action, and therefore more easily trampled under.   That of the Bandiera brothers in 1844, owing to the romantic interest attached, succeeded for a moment in arousing the sympathies of Europe.   These two young Venetians of distinguished family, having deserted from the Austrian service, enrolled themselves under the banner of Mazzini's society of " Young Italy," and accompanied by a handful of followers, embarked upon one of the most heroic, but utterly fantastic, enterprises of modern times.   Having effected a landing in Calabria they were quickly captured, and perished miserably for the cause they represented.

The year 1848 was, however, to witness far more serious upheavals of the old order, not only in the Kingdom of Naples, but throughout continental Europe.

In Piedmont, Charles Albert became constitutional King of the nation which had welcomed him as the recognized head of Liberalism in 1821, when for a brief period he held the Regency.   Ten days later Pius IX. who had astounded conservative Europe a couple of years earlier by his sympathy with the abhorred creeds of reform, timorously yielded to the importunities of his subjects, and issued the Politico-ecclesiastical Franchise, paraphrased a Constitution, which was to prove his undoing.   The revolution of February had deposed Louis Philippe as King of the French ; and even Austria and Germany were in the throes of internecine strife.   Italy was ablaze from Sicily to the Alps ; and to add to the general conflagration Charles Albert declared war against Austria with public sympathy throughout the length and breadth of the Peninsula behind him.

On February 10, 1848, Ferdinand yielded to the popular clamor which threatened to sweep away his Throne, and promulgated a Constitution modelled on that given to the French in 1830.   Shortly after, an army, under General Pepe, marched bravely out of Naples amidst indescribable enthusiasm, on its way north to re-enforce the operations against Austria. This last astounding concession was, however, a mere feint to silence the obsessions of the Liberals, for its Commander carried in his pocket instructions not to cross the Po.   The subsequent events at Custozza and Novara furnished an excuse for its recall, and although General Pepe and a few of his followers refused to conform to this change of policy, and actually did join the Venetians, the main body of the troops obediently returned to Naples. In May of the same year, on the date fixed for the meeting of the Parliament which had been convoked in Naples, riots broke out in the city, and furnished a pretext to postpone the meeting of the Chamber, as well as to suspend the Constitution. There is small doubt but that the whole trouble was the direct result of intrigues and inspirations from high quarters. The King felt he could rely upon the Swiss regiments and knew that his friends the "lazzaroni" were always on hand when an opportunity for disorder and plunder presented. As a consequence barricades were erected, palaces were plundered and burned, while the streets were strewn with the dead and dying. True to his nickname, King "Bomba" ordered the guns of the forts trained upon the town, and Naples was quickly bombarded into subjection.

In Sicily the revolution was not so expeditiously disposed of. For over a year the island had been seething in suppressed fury, bursting forth, however, in local revolts where the blind tyranny of the oppressors goaded the miserable sufferers to madness : risings each in turn smothered with accompaniments of untold cruelty and barbarism. "Nothing is more

powerfully demonstrative of the inflexible brutality of the Bourbon rule," says Stillman,
" than this persistence, in the face of such terrible lessons, of the pleasure-loving people of the
southern provinces, in their efforts to escape
from their chains."

The inhabitants of the unfortunate island
demanded the Constitution of 1812 which had
been accorded them under the guarantee of
England, and impatient of delay had broken
out in insurrection with the opening of the
new year (1848). After protracted fighting
Palermo was evacuated by the royal troops who
fell back on Messina. Flushed with success,
and secretly trusting in aid from England, a
representative Sicilian Parliament, which had
been hastily convened, decided on the deposition of the Bourbon dynasty, and agreed to
offer the Crown to the young Duke of Genoa,
son of Charles Albert of Savoy, and younger
brother of Victor Emmanuel. This body, con-
sisting as it did of men of the highest standing
and influence in the land, both as regards birth
and education, gave conclusive evidence of the
universal character of the prevailing discontent.
The realization of the project was, however,
doomed to failure quite as much on account of
the grave local political complications to which
it would give rise, as by reason of the defeats

and abdication of Charles Albert, and the subsequent inevitable restoration of the predominance of Austrian influence from Milan to Naples. Although the offer of their Crown by the Sicilians was given a quasi-international significance from the fact that the members of the Commission charged to negotiate with Charles Albert were conveyed from Palermo to Genoa in English and French war vessels, which had recognized and saluted the tricolor flag, the support of these nations was purely moral ; while England immediately after the reverses of Piedmont, made it clearly understood that such it should remain. Furthermore it is doubtful if, in view of the modifications and exactions now introduced into the original Constitution of 1812, and by which the Sicilian Parliament had hedged about and cramped the royal prerogatives and dignity, Charles Albert would have consented to allow his son to accept the offer. Be this as it may, Ferdinand had notified the Piedmontese Court that a favorable consideration of the Sicilian offer must mean war with Naples, and neither Charles Albert nor his successor were in a position to force an issue hazardous at the best, and which under existing circumstances would have been suicidal. The Commission was therefore assured of the gratitude of the House of Savoy for the honor it sought to bestow on one of its members, but diplomatically informed that Charles Albert could neither accept nor refuse the Crown offered his son without a careful consideration of the highest interests of Italy.   The Duke of Genoa added personally that he would in any event obey his father, and be guided by the higher interests of the Italian cause before his own.   So the subject was allowed to lapse, while the Sicilians on returning to their island soon had their hands and hearts full with the far more momentous issues of the vengeance wreaked upon them by the monarch they had so lately declared " forever deposed."

It was hardly to be expected that Ferdinand would submit passively to the insulting decrees of the Sicilian Parliament, yet the disturbances nearer home both in Naples and Calabria were of such a character as to counsel prudence. Then again the early achievements of the Sardinian arms at Goito and Milan, and Liberalist uprisings throughout Europe decided him to await as far as possible the issue of current events before committing himself irretrievably to a policy which might prove disastrous. Ferdinand had contrived to reassure Austria as to the true inwardness of the armed demonstration on the Po, while cunningly propitiating the tide of Liberalism he momentarily could not

stem. To this policy was due the procrastination of military operations against the revolted
island. Once it had become reasonably certain
which way the wind was going to blow as indicated by such straws as the Austrian successes in Hungary and at Custozza and Volta,
and the purely platonic attitude of England
and France in the Sicilian question, he began
the operations which had been secretly in
preparation during the period of uncertainty.

The Liberal Ministry was promptly dismissed,
its members and supporters being loaded with
chains and thrust into the prisons or galleys.
A reactionary Cabinet replaced the audacious
advocates of Liberty and Reform, and taking
their cue from their royal master, devoted their
energies to ferreting out the adherents to the
policy of their predecessors in office, and
suffocating liberal aspirations, even of the
mildest forms, in the dungeons of Nisida,
Procida, Ischia, or worse. Carlo Poerio and
Settembrini, the former a few months previously
the apparently valued counsellor of the King ;
the latter a distinguished and influential man of
letters, were amongst the most notable victims.

Having thus made atonement to Austria for
the temporary desertion of the principles of
Absolutism, Ferdinand was able to give undi-
vided attention to the Sicilian rebels.

Towards the end of August General Filangieri, a veteran of the Napoleonic wars, who had been entrusted by Ferdinand with the command of the expedition, started forth on the re-conquest of Messina, the key to successful operations in the island. Twenty thousand men had been massed in the neighborhood of Reggio, the Calabrian port facing Messina. Colonel Orsini, who commanded the Sicilian troops occupying Messina, had had frequent brushes with the Royalists who continued to hold the citadel of that town after the retreat from Palermo. He had repeatedly implored the Council of War sitting at Palermo to allow him reinforcements in order to dislodge the enemy from their stronghold, and free the island from Neapolitan occupation ; but his advice had been systematically disregarded, and consequently when the invading army landed the Sicilians found themselves between two fires, or rather three, for the fleet anchored before the town, as soon as Filangieri had accomplished a landing, began a furious bombardment. Under cover of this, General Nunziante brought his division to the shore, close under the citadel, and co-operated with its occupants in the attack on the town. Although speedily reduced to a mere heap of ashes the city defended itself stubbornly. The citizens had sworn to perish under the ruins of their homes rather than return to an allegiance they loathed, and were particularly infuriated by the participation in the struggle of the mercenaries of the Swiss regiments. The slaughter had become so terrible that the foreign Consuls implored Filangieri to grant a truce, hoping some mutual agreement might be reached. Filangieri replied that he would order his men to cease firing when the citizens returned to their allegiance to their lawful Sovereign. This the desperate defenders still stubbornly refused to do, and the struggle was resumed, the Sicilians disputing each inch of their soil, but yielding step by step, and street by street, until their every stronghold was surrounded and captured.

Heartrending accounts were published concerning the unqualified cruelty, and savage butchery, practised by the victorious troops on this occasion. Certain it is that the English and French admirals threatened active intervention should Filangieri not moderate the fury of his soldiers. It must be remembered, however, that Filangieri had dismissed the transports which conveyed his troops across the straits, thus cutting off all escape and making a complete and final victory imperative. On the other hand, as has been already stated, the Sicilians had taken oath to bury themselves beneath the ruins of their town rather than yield. Thus both parties were rendered desperate : a war to the death had been declared, and it became a question of killing or being killed. Undoubtedly barbarous cruelties were perpetrated on both sides ; unpardonable license being granted the victors by their officers ; but the sympathies of most European countries being undeniably with the oppressed, the contemporaneous published accounts are tinged with obvious exaggeration. The account given by an eyewitness, an officer of the Swiss Muralt regiment, who published his experiences in 1851, does not differ materially from the description of any battlefield of modern civilization. To the attacks made upon him later, both in his own country and abroad, for the enormities perpetrated by his soldiery, Filangieri replied with counter charges against the rebels, even going so far as to state that the inhabitants of Messina had quartered the dead bodies of the Swiss, and sold the flesh in the streets at a penny a pound.

The proclamation issued by Filangieri on taking possession of the town certainly conveys no intimation of undue vengeance. After inviting the former municipal officials to resume their functions, on September 10 he published an edict stating that His Majesty, "the loving father of his people, would forget the past madness, being persuaded that from henceforward his Sicilian subjects would return to the devoted and faithful allegiance to his sacred person." Of course it may be objected that the unfortunate inhabitants of Messina had small choice in the matter, while it may be further argued that the determination to make Messina a free port in order that its prosperity might be revived, was not altogether a disinterested action on the part of those who were to administer its ruined finances. If we would find a reason for such suspicious clemency we must seek a political motive. Ferdinand realized that with the fall of Messina the backbone of the insurrection was broken, and it was greatly to his interests to win back the remainder of the island by diplomacy should such a course be feasible, for already the French Republic, to say nothing of England, gave token of viewing the harsh repressive measures employed with none too favorable an eye. The next few months demonstrated the wisdom of the policy of procrastination, and conciliatory debate and discussion, pursued by the King. The attitude of Russia greatly influenced the pretensions of the French Government concerning the independent legislation of Sicily, while the Austrian victories made Lord Palmerston, who now remained practically alone in his opposition to Ferdinand's methods of dealing with his revolted subjects, still less inclined to become actively involved in the dispute.

The fall of Messina was closely followed by the capitulation of Milazzo, the garrison of which fell back on the capital.

Meanwhile Palermo still remained impenitent and unpunished. For the last seven months the island Parliament had been frittering away its time over protracted discussions, and the editing of magniloquent proclamations, which had led to little beyond the creation of personal jealousies and widening of party enmities. Provision for the troops under arms, or the levying of fresh recruits, there was scarcely any. The floating of a loan which had been attempted in Paris had proved a failure, and the Provisional Government had not been any more successful in the collection of a forced contribution at home. All idea of national cohesion of action, or scheme of federation with northern Italy, was lost sight of, and the struggle drifted into the narrow limits of insular independence ; which in its turn became more and more subjected to mere local interests. Ferdinand, pursuing the astute policy of discrediting the rebels in the eyes of European sympathies, continued to show a disposition to come to terms in spite of the Royalist advantages. Lord Minto, who acted as intermediary, was indefatigable in his efforts to reconcile the conflicting interests, and journeyed to and fro between the Island and Naples bearing draft after draft for constitutional reform, or concertive administrative concessions. Even when these appeared most liberal, trustworthy guarantees were lacking, or spurned as unacceptable by a people whose faith in royal promises had been so often and so rudely shaken.

Thus negotiations dragged on month after month until France and England, having exhausted both patience and influence, stood aside. Hostilities began afresh in March, 1849, and resulted in the capture of Taormina, and the bloody sack of Catania, surpassing by many degrees the cruelties and horrors of Messina. Again the foreign admirals intervened ; again came fruitless negotiations ; then again a resort to arms. The result was, as foreseen by the circumstances following the fall of Messina, and in view of the total lack of organization on the part of the leaders,—political and military,—the capture of town after town, and the final surrender of Palermo on May 15, 1849.

Filangieri, on taking possession of the capital, granted a general amnesty, which, however,

3

excluded some forty of the principal political and military offenders.

Thus ended the Sicilian revolution. The unhappy victims, however, soon found themselves again under their accustomed chains, which, despite all promises to the contrary, continued to be drawn tighter and weighted more heavily, until after a lapse of ten years the successful invasion of Garibaldi knocked the fetters from their limbs.

CHAPTER II.

Ferdinand II. attempts to free himself from Parliamentary restraints.—Disorders in Naples.—Flight of Pius IX. to Gaeta. —Revolution in Rome.—Grand Duke of Tuscany seeks refuge at Gaeta.—Charles Albert's offers of assistance.— Gioberti's policy misrepresented in Piedmont.—French intervention.—Ferdinand meets Garibaldi's forces at Palestrina.—Defeat of Neapolitans at Velletri.—Restoration of the Pope.—International relations of Kingdom of Naples. —England and France during Sicilian revolution.—Mazzini and " Young Italy."—Parliamentary complications in Naples.—Mr. Morrison's letter to Daniel Webster.—Ferdinand seeks to abolish Franchises.

FERDINAND now found himself free to enter frankly on the policy of reaction he had tentatively inaugurated in May of the previous year. He could afford to snap his fingers at the Parliament he had rendered innocuous, and which he only awaited a more favorable combination of circumstances to rid himself of entirely. On receiving the news of the fall of Messina the King sent Ruggiero, one of his Ministers, to inform the Chambers that the session was prorogued until the 31st of November. A howling mob, suborned by the reactionists, accompanied Ruggiero to the University where the deputies were assembled, shrieking, "Long live the King;" "Death to the Deputies." In the course of the day other demonstrations in favor of King and Constitution paraded the streets and put to flight the advocates of Absolutism. The police and troops, seeing their protégés in danger, now came upon the scene, and proceeded to arrest the newcomers. A part of the city was placed under martial law; numbers were imprisoned; several condemned to twenty-five years in chains. Thus was inaugurated the reactionary policy, and system of political persecution, which by reason of its excesses eventually compassed the destruction of the Dynasty it was formulated to uphold.

From the 7th of September, 1848, no opportunity was lost to weaken the National Guard. Under one pretext or another regiment after regiment was disbanded; sometimes the reason advanced was failure to repress Liberalist manifestations; at others, the accusation that the organization prevented free expression of public rejoicing over the return to paternal government. On the 27th of July, 1849, the destruction of the national militia was complete, and the Absolutist party was rid of this inconvenient instrument of popular manifestation.

Meanwhile fortune seemed to play into the

hands of the Neapolitan Ruler. On the evening of November 24, 1848, Pope Pius IX., dis-
guised as a common priest, fled from Rome,
in the carriage of the wife of the Bavarian
Minister to his Court, and crossing the Neapolitan frontier, took refuge in Gaeta, a sup-
plicant for his royal hospitality. The circumstances which had led up to this desperate action were complex. Voluntary concessions to
the Liberalism of the day on the part of the
most rigidly conservative Court in Christendom
had dumfounded Europe ; and had caused
the Pope to be looked up to and saluted as
the champion of Italian liberties and political
regeneration. But the incline on which the
Pontiff had thus rashly ventured, prompted
by personal convictions perhaps, but with a
total lack of political foresight or genius, soon
proved too steep for him to keep his footing.
Swept from one premature concession to another ; yielding when it would· have been
wiser to refuse, and as weakly withholding
what it would have been politic to grant ; the
Sovereign Pontiff was overwhelmed by the
flood too suddenly unloosed, and which, no
channel having been prepared for it, over-
flowed, submerged and devastated that which
it had been intended to cultivate and fructify.
Liberty too suddenly achieved, and without

training and careful preparation, by a people unaccustomed to political freedom, is as dangerous as a loaded weapon in the hands of a child. The Romans, for long centuries kept in political serfdom, considered Liberty and License as synonymous terms. When, with the assassination of Count Rossi, the swing of the pendulum indicated reaction, they were in no mood to passively accept restrictions placed upon its abuse, and the flight of their Sovereign, was the signal for a Mazzinian Utopia. Count Pasolini, the original initiator of Pius, then Cardinal Mastai-Ferretti, Bishop of Imola, into the mysteries of Liberalism ; and Marco Minghetti, had indeed foreseen the danger, and continually counselled moderation and caution. They had, however, merely succeeded in getting themselves distrusted by both parties.

The news of the Pope's flight and safe advent at Gaeta was carried to Ferdinand by Count Spaur in person, and transported the Neapolitan Court with joy. "Rejoice," cried the Government organs, "the representative of Jesus Christ is in the Kingdom ; and Ferdinand II., the descendant of Saint Louis, is the host of the most holy Father." And indeed Ferdinand had cause for rejoicing, for the utter failure of Liberalism, as illustrated in so strikingly prominent an example, could not fail to strengthen his own hand. Pius the Ninth ; the idol of the progressive party ; the declared champion of National Independence and Liberty ; the advocate of Constitutionalism and Federation ; a victim of the reforms he had himself instituted, was now a refugee within the realm of the Sovereign who, amongst all Italian despots, passed as the most antagonistic to the Liberal Creed erstwhile professed by the High-priest of Christendom !

A couple of months later (January, 1849,) Ferdinand was still further elated by the unceremonious arrival at Gaeta of another royal fugitive in the person of the Grand Duke Leopold II., of Tuscany, likewise a victim of the spread of Mazzini's theories for popular government. The old fortress and stronghold of successive Neapolitan dynasties became for the time being the centre of a brilliant Court, and the hotbed of reactionary intrigue. Hither hastened the diplomatists of the various European Courts accredited to the Holy See, together with the special envoys sent with offers of mediation, or more substantial aid, for replacing the Pope in the Chair of St. Peter. Nor did these offers come from the ultra-conservative rulers alone. The danger which must result from the ill-considered Roman insurrection was keenly felt by those who had the true interests of the national cause at heart. In spite of his conscientious espousal of the doctrines of Constitutionalism, or because of them, Charles Albert of Savoy quickly discerned the peril engendered by the excesses committed both in Rome and Florence, and recognized the injury to the Nationalist principles which would ensue should the Pope be successful in his appeals to Spain and Austria to regain for him his Crown. He therefore despatched his envoys to Gaeta to plead with him that he dispense with foreign aid, and accept that of Sardinia. Ferdinand was, however, too astute to allow the prestige of aiding the dethroned Pontiff to regain possession of his dominions to be alienated. He was fully alive to the fact that should this end be accomplished by the Moderate Liberals who formed the vast majority of the national party, and of whose policy Cavour was later a notable exponent, their cause would be immediately enhanced in the eyes of European conservatism. It was obviously to his advantage to discredit them abroad, and encourage the prevalent misapprehension which confused the advocates of Constitutionalism and liberal reforms with those rabid republicans inoculated with the virus of Mazzini's irredentist principles. Even at this early date, and in spite of his recent military reverses, Charles Albert had achieved a popularity throughout the Peninsula which gave umbrage to his fellow-sovereign. It was consequently with considerable satisfaction that Ferdinand witnessed the success of Neapolitan influence and diplomacy which secured for him the advantage of co-operating with Austria and Spain.

The Neapolitan official newspapers accused Charles Albert of insatiable cupidity, insinuating that having failed to obtain either glory or additional power in his attempts to set himself up as the champion of Italy against Austria, or by encouraging the unitarian conspiracies directed against the Princes of the Peninsula, he desired to try his fortune once more by appearing as the defender of the Holy See. Gioberti, the originator of the proposed policy, does not appear to have been in thorough sympathy with his colleagues in office, or with a considerable portion of the Piedmontese and Italian political world. The scope of the proposed intervention in Tuscany and at Rome which he considered essential to safeguard national independence threatened by foreign invasion, was wilfully misconstrued by his enemies at home and abroad ; and branded as a traitor by those he sought to serve, he was made to pay the penalty of his zeal. It is, of course, an open question whether his influence with France, then under the fascination of Lamartine's eloquence, would have saved Rome the humiliations she was to undergo.   But the plan possessed at least an undeniable patriotism, coupled with a plausible political hypothesis, which makes it difficult to clearly understand, when stripped of petty personal jealousies, the tremendous opposition of statesmen whose names eventually became synonymous with patriotism and energetic action.

Pio Nono was disinclined to owe his restoration to the bayonets of the French Republic; while Ferdinand was equally apprehensive concerning the ideas which might be imported by those who had so recently taken part in the Revolution of February.   Initiative was, however, taken from him by the appearance of General Oudinot under the walls of Rome; and no alternative offered but for Naples to co-operate against Garibaldi who was in command of the Roman forces, with all possible haste. This Ferdinand proceeded to do, marching to the frontier of the Papal States with an army ten thousand strong.   At Palestrina, Garibaldi, himself at the head of about four thousand men, met the Neapolitans, and although both parties claimed the victory the Bourbon forces found it advisable to fall back upon Velletri.

A few days later (May 16, 1849), Garibaldi having been considerably reinforced, attacked the King at Velletri and inflicted a signal and final defeat upon his arms.

From a military point of view the Neapolitan expedition had been a failure ; but its political and diplomatic advantages were manifest. By his action Ferdinand had allayed the rancor and suspicions of Austria, which his armed demonstration on the Po had given rise to, and at the same time convinced the conservative Princes that his apparent sympathy with the Italian movement in Northern Italy had been wrung from him by force of circumstances, and was not in accord with personal convictions. Austria signified the desired approval ; styling him the "Initiator of the restoration of order in Europe." The Pope, who might now be relied upon to abandon the anomalous position he had assumed with the Tiara, became his debtor and his ally. There remained France and England. Of the former he was also in a sense the ally, since the nominal object of the presence of the two armies on Roman territory had been the same, namely,—to replace Pio Nono on his throne. Yet Ferdinand could not forget that the coming man in France, Louis Napoleon, had fought for the Italian cause in 1831, and had bound

himself by solemn oath to assist its furtherance.
He could hardly expect the new French Republic, whose birth was founded on revolutionary principles, to openly acquiesce in his meditated return to Absolutism.   In regard to
England his anxiety was less, for he thoroughly
understood the sentimentalism underlying an
only apparently vigorous policy of intervention
in his affairs.   And here we find the key to his
otherwise inexplicable clemency and toleration
in Sicily—a policy almost Machiavelian in its
astute proficiency.   England and France both
became his dupes for the time being ; and in a
sense, almost his accomplices, since their
squadrons passively followed his operations,
their commanders acting somewhat in the relation of seconds in a prize fight, and calling
time when the Sicilians were too roughly
handled.   His line of diplomacy was fixed.
None could question his right to lead his legitimate but revolted subjects to an appreciation
of their error.   At the same time, that there
was serious cause for the revolt few would deny;
while the fact that the tendencies of the age
demanded reform, and radical reform, was dis-
tressingly evinced on all sides.   Concessions
must be made, but he determined they should
be concessions of such a character that, while
satisfactory to the self-constituted protectors of

Sicilian interests, when their moment of usefulness had passed, the empty shell might be cast away, none but the victims being the wiser that the kernel had never existed.

In this Ferdinand was successful, and when the British Government reminded him of the pledges given and the rights of his Sicilian subjects, his Minister replied, under date of September 20, 1849 : "Sicily enjoys perfect tranquillity, and the inhabitants are happy to have returned to the protection of their legitimate Sovereign."

Although open resistance to the government had been trampled down, the effervescence by no means subsided ; and both in Sicily and on the mainland we find the agents of Mazzini particularly active in keeping it alive. In spite of the visionary and often crudely impracticable nature of the great agitator's schemes, to his soul-inspiring enthusiasm is due much that was afterwards accomplished by cooler heads. His society of "Young Italy" appealed directly to the hearts of the generous youth of the country, and aroused in them fervent patriotism, intense hatred of their foreign rulers, together with an irrepressible yearning for glory and martyrdom. Neither Mazzini nor Garibaldi possessed any genius for, or sympathy with, the cold, calculating science of Diplomacy ; the skill and pa-

tience of the manipulator of political opportunities ; the prudence of the statesman who
looks beyond the immediate result, and carefully weighs and calculates the ultimate consequences of the action, were to them incomprehensible, when not absolutely contemptible.
Both frequently imperilled the cause they devoted their lives to by this utter contempt of
international complications.   Both possessed
unparalleled magnetic influence over the majority of those who came within their orbit ;
both labored for the doctrines they professed
with purely disinterested motives, and total
abnegation of self.   Of Garibaldi's tangible
achievements, the record is writ large, yet there
can be no doubt but that to the dogged perseverance despite every form of persecution, to
the consummate skill in conspiracy and intrigue, as well as to the miraculously inciting,
though often bombastic, eloquence of Mazzini,
Italy owes as much.

Meanwhile in Naples, Parliament, after having
been prorogued a second time, was finally allowed to meet on February first (1849).   As the
deputies entered the hall they were greeted
with applause and cries of encouragement, for
the people knew the occasion to be one in
which their rights were in grave peril.   From
the outset the representatives found themselves

in open conflict with the Government, and on the horns of a dilemma. During the enforced recess the Government had taken upon itself to collect taxes unauthorized by Parliament ; thus violating a constitutional prerogative of that body. The Chambers consequently found themselves in the unfortunate position of either passing over in silence a proceeding fundamentally illegal, or of placing themselves in overt opposition to the Crown, and thereby running the risk of dissolution. To the surprise and anxiety of all when the session opened the Ministers made no reference to the matter, neither attempting to justify their illegal action nor to obtain authorization for its continuance. Evidently a trap had been laid, and a situation created expressly to embarrass the Assembly, and force an issue. In order to escape with a semblance of dignity from an intolerable position, it was decided to introduce a bill providing the Government with the temporary power of imposing taxes in order that the public service be not embarrassed ; and simultaneously present an address to the King praying for the dismissal of those Ministers whose actions, directed against the fundamental principles of the Constitution, rendered them unworthy of the confidence of the Crown, and whose continuance in office fomented discord and dissensions between the dynasty and the country. This proposition gave rise to prolonged discussion. Many were against the presentation of such an address, appreciating the friction which must result. On the other hand it was urged that the Chambers, by tacitly accepting measures so contrary to the Constitution, stultified themselves, and became the accomplices of those whose aim it was to annul constitutional franchises. Considerable personal courage was displayed by those taking prominent part in the debate, for none were ignorant of the risks they ran. On March third the address was finally voted, accompanied by the declaration that the Ministry no longer enjoyed the confidence of the Country.

Ferdinand, however, relying upon the reactionary current, which had already set in throughout Europe, simply refused to receive the Commission nominated to present the address. Ten days later, having in the meantime allowed his dupes the empty satisfaction of passing laws to which he never gave official sanction, " Bomba " put an end to the " Constitutional Comedy " by dissolving Parliament.

With the subjugation of Sicily, the fall of the Roman Republic, and the victory of Austria at Novara, followed by the restoration of the Pope and the Grand Duke of Tuscany to their respective Thrones, the return of the good old days of paternal government, maintained by militarism and assisted by a police system ubiquitous and supreme, seemed assured. Yet Ferdinand had been badly frightened, and was besides too close and intelligent an observer of the psychology of a movement so universal and deep-rooted to be wholly at ease. To one so thoroughly versed in the subtleties of dissimulation the supposition that all danger had disappeared was absurd. Although Vesuvius might not be in active eruption it would be folly to suppose the hidden flames would not on occasion burst forth afresh. Of Italy he could be reasonably certain—that is with the possible exception of Piedmont, whose young Sovereign, Victor Emmanuel, was as yet untried ; but France, who had become in a sense his immediate neighbor, her troops being quartered in Rome, was an unknown quantity. Russia was his friend, and had given him moral support in the late Sicilian crisis, and Russia looked with not unnatural aversion on the growing power of the Bonaparte at the head of the French Government.

Home affairs, however, claimed his diplomacy quite as urgently as his interests abroad. It was obviously imperative to purge the Kingdom of the germs of Liberalism and disaffection.

4

This he promptly set about doing in the manner most congenial to his nature ; namely, executions, imprisonments and banishments. The Sicilians, protected to some extent by amnesties and guarantees, suffered relatively less than their unfortunate fellow-citizens of the mainland ; but on Naples the King vented his displeasure unchecked.

Mr. Morrison, United States Chargé d'Affaires at the Neapolitan Court, writing to Daniel Webster under date of April 19, 1851, says : . . . "It is apprehended that the peace of the Kingdom may be disturbed by the congregation of revolutionary chiefs at the London Exposition of Universal Industry. Possessed of such an opinion the government has refused to grant passports to native artisans proposing to exhibit their specimens of Neapolitan manufactures. The policy of the present Cabinet, I fear will, sooner or later, produce another insurrection. No reforms of any description are being made, while a system of military terror everywhere prevails. The islands around the Bay of Naples, as well as the prisons and galley-hulks, are filled with unhappy beings legally condemned, or held on suspicion, for participation in the revolution of 1848. The expected amnesty at New Year's was not granted, and hundreds of men of refined, intellectual tastes, and lately high in position, are laboring in the galleys side by side with the most infamous and abandoned criminals. The most earnest appeals and representations on the part of the representatives of friendly foreign powers have thus far been ineffective to induce the King and his Ministers to change their policy. The consequence is that, with the first opportunity, there will be a general rising throughout the Kingdom, particularly in Sicily, the inhabitants of which are entirely estranged from the reigning family."

The "general rising" anticipated by Mr. Morrison did not take place for many years; yet, in spite of the fearful expiation of the recent attempts, the sullen discontent and wretchedness continued to be evinced by sporadic demonstrations in Naples and Calabria at not infrequent intervals.

As we have seen, Parliament had been dissolved, the halls where the rare sessions had been held being actually dismantled. The official journal had modified its title, and got rid of the "constitutional" prefix; but the crafty King had not deemed it prudent to openly revoke the obnoxious Chart, fearing that by so doing he might lend a color of illegality to his government. He was nevertheless firmly determined that all should be in readiness for its disavowal when the opportune moment arrived. This he proposed to hasten by means of popular petitions—a method equally ingenious and original, and which could be relied upon not to lead to complications with foreign States.   Already, in August, 1849, emissaries had been despatched throughout the various provinces with instructions to sound those in authority, and to suborn communes and municipalities with promises of grants for public works, railway concessions, remission of local taxes, or simply the bestowal of honors, or pecuniary remuneration ; thus gradually and stealthily paving the way for the withdrawal, or consignment to oblivion, of the last vestige of public liberties.

Ferdinand II.

Ferdinand II.

Maria Teresa

CHAPTER III.

Factors which undermined Neapolitan Throne.—Idea of National Unity.—Characteristics of lower classes.—Educational opportunities.—University of Naples.—Colleges of the Jesuits.—Their sphere of influence.—Measures to check spread
of Liberal theories.—Newspapers and the Press.—The Aristocracy and its relation to Public Affairs.—Diplomatic service.—The Army and Navy, and their relations with the
Crown.—The Swiss Guard.—Politics in the Army.—Arsenals
and Shipyards.—Taxation.—Police system.—International
Influences.—Recall of English and French diplomatists.—
Napoleon III. and Prince Murat.—Decline of Neapolitan
Diplomacy.

THUS far we have considered the political
institutions and aspirations of the Kingdom of
Naples, but it would be manifestly unfair to
confine the investigations to this field alone, or
to attribute the causes for the collapse entirely
to the influence of the revolutions of 1848 and
1849. Although the great revolutionary period
finished with the latter year, the following decade was fraught with issues at home and
abroad, which, while less important individually and separately, formed in the aggregate
the determining weight in the oscillating scales,
and swayed the Dynasty to its ruin.

Yet notwithstanding the undeniable influence of these factors, the destruction of the Throne of the Two Sicilies was the result of an Idea : nay ! more, the advent of a Man whose personality gave substance to a Theory centuries old—a combination fraught with such colossal potentialities that even had that Kingdom enjoyed a less unsatisfactory government, it must inevitably have succumbed. The Idea was Italian Unity : the Man, Victor Emmanuel II., "the Honest King." Slow of growth ; often crushed out of sight, or overlooked in combinations calculated to defeat its accomplishment ; plotted against, misrepresented, and maligned ; it nevertheless constituted the fundamental principle on which all political creeds, all national aspirations and ambitions, were based.

Although this is essentially true, yet is it equally a fact that the subjects of King Ferdinand, and later of his son, Francis II., were, as a whole, not dominated by this desire for national unity. To use a paradoxical, but expressive, phrase, the upheavals came from above, not below. That is to say, they were fomented and carried out by the upper and educated classes ; government officials, literary and professional men ; not to mention a royal Prince or two. The mass of the population stood aloof, apathetically interested but not sufficiently educated to be actively concerned with questions outside their daily routine. To them it was all an affair of taxation : should unity mean a lightening of their burdens, they were unionists ; if not, " Bomba " was good enough for them. This was perhaps not equally true of Sicily, where a peculiar system of land tenure, combined with other local idiosyncrasies, had familiarized all classes with insurrection ; and where, although the peasant was certainly no less ignorant, he was nevertheless more alert to grasp any chance of bettering his material position, and quick to note the value of the political enfranchisement which would enhance his importance as a factor in local interests. Beyond these, however, his concern was as apathetic as that of his brother across the water. He might belong to a secret society —as a matter of fact, he rarely did—but if so, its political creed was generally so vague and confused, or so transcendental, as to be totally beyond his ken ; although this did not render him a less dangerous instrument in the hands of his leaders, or less docile if called upon to fight. But on such as these the doctrines of Mazzini had little hold. They could, in fact, only be reached and influenced by their immediate superiors, and were not generally avail-

able for purposes of purely political revolt.   In
a study of the social and political regeneration
of Southern Italy the peasant class constitutes
an unimportant factor.   He fought when made
to fight, or defended himself when cruelly
attacked ; but the ethics of the cause he served,
or combated, were nothing to him, and victory
or defeat left him where they found him.
Italy can point to no Andreas Hofer in her
struggle for independence.   Rome produced a
Ciceruacchio, it is true, but he was no peasant,
but a wine-carrier of the Trastevere.

Although the lower classes were left in a
state of almost complete ignorance, it being
the exception for a peasant to be able to sign
his name, the educational opportunities were,
for the times, of no mean order, and in many
respects superior to those offered in other parts
of Italy.   The University of Naples enjoyed
a wide-spread reputation in the middle of the
century, and although the curriculum appears
meagre in our days, it was on a par with, if
not ahead of, many similar institutions in the
Peninsula.   It supported six Chairs, or Facul-
ties : Theology, Mathematics, Natural Sciences,
Jurisprudence, Literature, and Medicine.   It
is characteristic of the detestation entertained
by Ferdinand of the vulgarization of the
Science of Government that after 1849, the

University Chair of Political Economy was officially styled " Public Economy."

Good as it was, the University of Naples was
alone of its class in the King's dominions north
of Sicily. For this reason, as well as owing to
the great difficulties of communication between
the capital and the provinces, was due the relatively restricted number of students who attended its lectures. This number was further
diminished by the vexations of a meddlesome
police, constantly interfering, and not infrequently disbanding the classes on account of
some imaginary political conspiracy. The
authorities looked with unconcealed aversion
upon any considerable congregation of students,
fearing the dissemination of liberal ideas, or
even an interchange of local subjects for discontent. For this reason a Sicilian was denied
access to the University of Naples. Even in
that island a choice of the three Universities
was not permitted. Natives of the provinces
of Palermo, Trapani and Girgenti must pursue
their studies in the University of Palermo.
Those of the provinces of Catania, Caltanissetta
and Noto, at Catania ; while the youth of Messina were obliged to frequent the institution
maintained in the capital of that province.

Although Naples alone of the cities on the
mainland possessed a University, several of the

royal colleges, invariably under the control of the Jesuits, supported chairs of Law, Civil, Penal and Roman ; of Anatomy and Physiology ; of Theoretical and Practical Surgery ; of Chemistry and Natural History ; and, in one or two instances, of Mineralogy and Geology. The Jesuits themselves undertook the instruction of Literature, Philosophy, and Physical and Mathematical Sciences : the professors of other branches being usually laymen. The colleges of Salerno, Bari, Catanzaro and Aquila, provided more or less complete courses. These institutions also issued diplomas in Law, Medicine, Mathematics and Physics, thus making it possible for the less ambitious student to dispense with the honors conferred by the University at Naples.

The Royal College of Theology enjoyed special privileges, and claimed the Sovereign Pontiff as Honorary Rector. This establishment was naturally under the direct supervision and control of the Clergy, and was devoted to ecclesiastical and classical studies. There existed also a number of more or less private institutions, generally in the hands of the Jesuits, and frequented by the sons of the lesser nobility, and professional classes.

The Council of Public Instruction was, during the last decade of Ferdinand's reign, under

the presidency of Don Emilio Capomazzo, a
man of vast culture whose Voltairian sympathies and open detestation of the Jesuits,
were in noted contrast with the majority of his
colleagues. It is to be observed, however, that
Ferdinand himself had no leaning towards the
followers of Loyola, fearing and mistrusting
their special aptitude for political intrigue.
Nevertheless the Order had strong advocates
at Court, headed by the Queen. All works intended for the press must pass the censorship
of this Council not once but twice; for although permission might be granted to print,
a second scrutiny was necessary, before publication, in order that the members might be assured that there existed no surreptitious inex-
actitude between the original manuscript and
the printed pages. The staff of officials charged
with this supervision, as well as that of books
imported from abroad, was composed, with but
three exceptions, of ecclesiastics.

Yet guarded, supervised, and purged of all
dangerous seditious taint, as were the publica-
tions provided for the subjects of the Neapolitan King, the seeds of revolt were wafted
over the frontiers, and found congenial soil in
university, college, and school. By no such
puerile constraint, irksome and irritating to a
degree, could it be hoped to erect a barrier

between the Kingdom and the thought of the outer world ; or to quash legitimate aspirations for the political rights of which the nation had been defrauded.   The exiles and conspirators beyond the frontiers were able, despite all precautions, to keep in touch with the revolutionary element at home, and by means of clandestine presses, or manuscripts circulating from hand to hand, keep alive the fires which burned sullenly beneath an apparently tranquil surface. The chronicles of those years (1849–1859) teem with the condemnations and martyrdom suffered by the would-be patriots caught redhanded, or ferreted out by the ubiquitous police.   The possession of an illicit printing press meant long years in the galley-hulks or prisons, or death,—the latter by far the least appalling form of punishment.

Newspapers were published in the capital and some of the larger towns, but journalism, in the modern sense, can scarcely be said to have existed.   All foreign news items, or happenings within the realm, of a political significance adverse to the government, when not suppressed, were so misrepresented or manipulated to harmonize with the royal policy, as to lose all value or interest.   The editors had to content themselves and their readers with purely literary articles : criticisms of the plays performed at

the various theatres, or opera ; poetry and
charades, by means of which latter bits of
political information were not infrequently conveyed to the initiated. The literary articles
were often of a remarkably high standard of
excellence, and served as illustrations of graceful writing ; but naturally under these circumstances the Press had no weight with public
opinion, and furnished no indication of the
political pulse of the nation. The Neapolitan
of those years took up his paper in search of a
competent verdict on last night's play, or an
exhaustive analysis of the latest fashionable
romance. Or he eagerly scanned the list of
apartments to let ; or yet again, if socially inclined, glanced at the names of foreigners of
distinction who had recently arrived. Should
he chance to be one of those to whom the trend
of public affairs abroad, or information affording some clue to the political regeneration of
his beloved Italy, was of interest, he had recourse to the dangerous expedients already
mentioned.

Although several members of the aristocracy,
and, as has been hinted, even connections of
the royal family, were actively concerned in
revolutionary intrigues, and in sympathy with
the Italian movement, they as a class took little
interest in politics, and an insignificant part in

the administration of the government. Even the diplomatic posts were, with one or two exceptions, filled by men not of noble birth. This can be partly accounted for by inferiority of education, owing to the system which confided the sons of the aristocracy to the Jesuits, and ignored the higher branches, but is also to be attributed to indolence and love of pleasure.

Paris, and after the accession of Victor Emmanuel II., Turin, were the most important diplomatic posts ; but as Ferdinand allowed his representatives no initiative, their mission was merely one of observation. The King of Naples was his own Foreign Minister, as he was his own Inspector of Police. The entire mechanism of government, down to minute details of administration, centred in his hands. Even his military commanders took no action except under explicit orders ; while the police made their reports directly to the Royal Chancery. With his genius for diplomacy, his undeniable intelligence, as well as his marvellous capability for work, the King cast in the shade all those surrounding him, and dwarfed even their most ambitious efforts.

As was to be expected Ferdinand's interest was centred in the army : a broken reed, alas ! which served the dynasty ill. Before 1848 the Neapolitan troops numbered sixty thousand,

on paper ; but in reality mustered scarcely
forty thousand fighting men.   After the events
of that and the following year the army was
gradually increased to one hundred thousand.
Of the revenues of the State which did not
reach thirty millions of dollars, eighteen millions
were spent on this supposed bulwark of the
Throne.   In this profession also the aristocracy
were conspicuous by their absence.   The tradi-
tion which surrounded the king with the flower
of the youth of the highest nobility had vanished, their places being filled by the sons of
the provincial gentry, government officials, or
military families.   Many of the chiefs were old
warriors of the days of Murat ; " Men without
political creed, who served the Bourbons whom
in secret they despised ; men who in private
were the friends of liberty, in public the brutal
instruments of servitude."   Notable exceptions to these were found in Filangieri, Ischitella, and Castelcicala : men of high moral
principles and noble antecedents.

   In spite of the sarcastic words of his grand-
father, who, coming upon Ferdinand, still a
youth, occupied in selecting designs for new
uniforms, savagely muttered :   " Dress them
as you will, they will always run away," the
latter, who, while without any pronounced tal-
ent, yet possessed considerable military knowl-

edge, continued to identify himself personally with his army. He invariably appeared in uniform, in private as well as on public occasions ; assisted at all reviews or annual camps, and frequently inspected the barracks and military establishments.   With the men he entertained cordial relations, conversing with them in dialect and addressing numbers of them by name. In spite of this condescension and ingenuous affability his presence inspired a cringing fear. Discipline, although extremely strict, almost cruel, in non-essentials, was of such a nature as to increase the dread of the soldier for the results of transgression, rather than instill a spirit of reasoning obedience to his superiors.   Flogging was of frequent occurrence ; often inflicted for insignificant breaches of military etiquette, and was moreover carried out with most brutal and degrading accessories.   The prevalence of the " Camorra " was the curse of the army ; even the most terrible forms of punishment never succeeding in eradicating this national scourge. As has been said the superior officers were almost without exception men far past the prime of life, but the military college of the Nunziatella turned out well-educated and efficient men who filled the lower grades.   Amongst the latter there existed a decided *esprit de corps,* unfortunately totally absent in their superiors, who were for the most part men without convictions and of purely expedient loyalty to the dynasty they served.   Several of these had served King Murat, and are said to have looked back with thinly concealed regret to that régime.   The younger men, however, conscious of the deficiencies of their service and fully alive to the dangers arising from the low moral standard they deplored, made earnest though ineffectual attempts at reform.   But reform of any description, even when it so nearly touched the interests of his own salvation, was insuperably repugnant to Ferdinand ; and the advice and admonitions of the more far-seeing of his officers were allowed to pass unheeded. All material of war, including guns, cannon, and powder, was manufactured in the Kingdom ; the home industries also providing everything necessary for the clothing and maintenance of the soldier.   Poor and ill-cared for the latter undoubtedly was, but not exceptionally or conspicuously so for the times in which he lived.

If we judge the Neapolitan soldier by his conduct in Sicily, and his precipitate retreat at Velletri, we should be apt to stigmatize him as pusillanimous.   It should be borne in mind, however, that on these occasions enthusiasm for the cause for which he was made to fight was totally lacking ; and that he was called

5

upon to wage a fratricidal war absolutely abhorrent to his convictions ; in itself a sufficient explanation for an undeniable faintheartedness.

When in later years the forlorn hope of defending a dynasty, discredited by perjury, and covered with odium, was offered, the handful of troops which remained faithful to their King, displayed a heroism and self-abnegation at Gaeta which compelled the admiration of their political enemies, and the sympathy of the civilized world.

In earlier days Napoleon and Murat had entertained the highest opinion, and expressed the warmest praise for the Neapolitan troops under their command. In Spain with Murat ; in the Russian campaign and retreat from Moscow with the Emperor ; at the battle of Lutzer and before Danzig, their bravery and endurance of hardships and privations had been especially commended by the Emperor and their various chiefs.

Given an incentive worthy of his courage, and led by chiefs in whom confidence could be reposed, the Neapolitan was fully equal to any demands made upon him. This trust was never given to Ferdinand ; while the devotion displayed in the lost cause of his successor was more the result of fortuitous circumstances than any conviction, or loyalty, for the principles involved. How little real confidence Ferdinand had in the affection of his troops, or what illusions he entertained as to their loyalty in an emergency, is strikingly evinced by the treatment of the pampered Swiss Guard to whose especial care the safety of the Throne was entrusted. These consisted of four regiments, recruited for the most part in the Catholic cantons, and had taken the place of the Austrians after the Congress of Vienna had definitely arranged the political status of what Count Metternich described as the various "geographical expressions" of the Peninsula. By virtue of their origin, rather political than military, the Swiss Guard became a purely dynastic institution, and as such the recipient of marked attestation of royal predilection. The remuneration was two-thirds greater than that of the Neapolitans, while they enjoyed besides numerous privileges and indulgences denied their native-born comrades. Although in the ranks might be found men of questionable antecedents and more than doubtful character, they were officered exclusively by representatives of the oldest and most distinguished Swiss families, of both the German and French Cantons, and included some of the proudest names in the Confederation. The

cost of the maintenance of this body exceeded
six hundred thousand dollars annually ; but
the value of their service to the Crown was inestimable. Naturally enough the Neapolitan
viewed this favored outsider with envy and
hatred ; and looking upon him as a barbarian,
lost no opportunity for stirring up trouble and
making bad blood. On the other hand the
privileged mercenary was not slow to retaliate,
assured of the indulgence if not the open
approval of his royal master. Thus native
and foreigner led a cat and dog existence
which only terminated with the dissolution of
the Swiss regiments resulting from their mutiny
in 1859.

During Ferdinand's lifetime, in spite of
manifest cause for discontent, the army remained passively indifferent to the blandishments of the advocates of Liberalism and
Nationalism. That proselytes abounded in
the higher grades is proved by the sudden success of the propaganda immediately following
the death of the Despot. The personal influence of the Sovereign, the intense fear he
inspired, and the dread of his vengeance,
coupled with the belief in the fidelity of the
Swiss Guard, were, strange as it must appear,
sufficient to keep the latent forces down. With
his death the whole edifice crumbled and fell ;

destroyed not merely by its own inherent rottenness, but swept by the irresistible political avalanche from beyond the frontiers.

When the peculiar configuration of the Kingdom is considered it must be acknowledged that the Neapolitan marine forces were in no way proportionate to the requirements of the country. Surrounded on three sides by the sea, with the greatest and most populous island of the Mediterranean an integral part of the realm, and numerous smaller islands dependent on it, the resources of the Neapolitan Crown as a sea power were insignificant. The fleet, although neither numerous nor powerful in armament or tonnage, was, however, well manned and officered, the organization being far superior to anything of the kind in Italy. Count Cavour, always vigilantly alert for improvements in the Sardinian service, borrowed from it the drill practice, and flag signal system. Had Ferdinand displayed the same amount of interest in his navy as he lavished on his land forces the material was at hand wherewith to have built up a peculiarly efficient service. But he was no sailor himself, and had moreover made the grave mistake of appointing as Vice-Admiral, and President of the Admiralty Board, his brother, the Count of Aquila, who cared even less for naval matters.

This branch of the national defence was consequently left in the hands of officers, who although individually thoroughly efficient were, nevertheless, powerless to procure the royal protection necessary to advance the best interests of their service. This neglect was keenly felt, and in his hour of trial was the cause of bitter humiliations to Ferdinand's successor. The Royal Marine College, and the school for the education of non-commissioned officers, sailors and gunners, were ridiculously insufficient for the demands of the service. The former accommodated forty pupils who graduated as officers and naval constructors; the second institution made provision for only fifty. The High Military Court was common to both services, and was composed of military and naval officers. It was designed as a species of Court of Appeal, more especially charged with the revision of courts-martial, with the object of defining whether the law of procedure had been violated. Unfortunately this institution, calculated by virtue of its composite character to stand as a healthy corrective of bureaucratic abuses, was, like every other branch of the administrative service, poisoned by Court influences, and its efficiency destroyed by obsequious subservience to the royal will.

The arsenals and ship-yards at Naples and

Castellammare, where all the vessels of the fleet were constructed, were amongst the best of their kind in the Mediterranean, and vastly superior to any others in Italy.

The financial system of the Kingdom was admirably conceived but detestably administered. Scialoia, who undertook in 1857 a parallel between the State Budgets of the Piedmont and Naples, demonstrated that the subjects of Victor Emmanuel II. paid a mean annual tax of twenty-six lire (about five dollars) per capita, while those of King Ferdinand were called upon to furnish the State with but twenty-one lire. The former had, however, as compensation for their slightly heavier burden, greater security for individual liberty and protection of property ; besides economical advantages resulting from the ready and convenient modes of intercommunication, works of public utility, and an honest administration. None of these advantages were enjoyed by the Neapolitan, whose taxes went to support an oppressive, corrupt and unprogressive government. The roads throughout the Kingdom were wretched, and for political considerations purposely kept so. It was a journey of twelve days from Reggio to the capital. A short line of railway connected Naples with Castellammare on the bay, and another ran to the Royal Palace at

Caserta; a total of perhaps eighty kilometres for the two lines.   Besides these no others existed in the Kingdom.

No description, however summary, of the salient features of that period of Ferdinand's reign embraced between the return to the reactionary and absolutist policy in 1849, and his death ten years later, would be complete without a glance at its most prominent characteristic—the Police.

It has been said with truth, that Ferdinand was his own Prefect of Police.   He received the reports of the official chiefs under whom worked an army of inspectors, detectives and rapacious spies, whose unholy zeal was stimulated to the utmost by the knowledge that they in turn were tracked and spied upon by secret agents in every class and walk of life.   The demoralization engendered by this odious espionage permeated every crevice of the social fabric, turning to fear and hate the relations between officials and those in private life, and making every species of familiar intercourse a danger few cared to incur.   Politics, local, national or international, formed the quarry of this pack of voracious sleuth hounds.   To hold political opinions contrary to those dictated by the theories of Absolutism, or any opinions not in accord with a blind subservience to the will of the Despot, constituted treason. The expression of such opinions, even in private, branded the speaker as a dangerous demagogue ; a source of peril to organized society, and consequently legitimate prey for the police. As a matter of course this branch of the administration became omnipotent not only in the affairs of the general public but even in the Palace. Ferdinand himself became their victim, for realizing their power the various chiefs soon began to play upon the credulous timidity of the King, exaggerating, contorting, or even inventing plots which should redound to their personal advantage, or increase their influence. Under this system the police became the greatest and most powerful institution of the Kingdom, and it is hardly to be wondered at that such a practically limitless sphere of authority should have engendered intolerable abuses and acts of unwarranted violence. Under police control were placed : excavations and archæological research ; bands of music ; railways ; the census ; the national archives ; the telegraphs ; the Official Journal ; the importations of horses from abroad ; the post-office ; suppression of smuggling ; and, of course, the supervision of university students and those attending all schools. Even diplomatists and Consular agents were not exempt from their inquisitorial vigilance ; while they kept a careful eye on the Guard of Honor ; the reserves ; the prisons ; and the pharmacies throughout the realm.

The events of 1848 and 1849 had determined King Ferdinand to surround his subjects with a moral Chinese Wall which should effectually shut out the dreaded Liberalism which had made such giant strides abroad. Knowing full well the vigorous campaign kept up beyond the frontiers against his reactionary policy, his chief dread of the dissemination of seditious theories was centred in the foreign Press. He had succeeded in muzzling, and rendering innocuous the journals of the Kingdom, but his police was powerless to prevent the surreptitious introduction of newspapers from the north, in spite of an army of censors. These journals circulated in the universities and schools, being forbidden fruit, were read with greedy eagerness. Had the police confined themselves to unearthing revolutionary plots and bringing the conspirators to judgment they would have been performing a manifest duty, necessary for the preservation of public order and the safety of the State. But by their unparalleled brutality, by their frenzied despotism, constituting a form of tyranny of which the King himself was a victim, the legitimate

ends were smothered in a heterogeneous maze
of oppression, cruelty, deceit, and senseless
persecution ; arousing the defiant irritation,
the madness of despair, of a populace which
would have formulated no complaint under a
reasonable system.   To be arrested because the
brim of a hat was too large, and might signify
conspiracy ; to be arraigned as a demagogue on
account of a pointed beard, were the pin-pricks
of a policy which provoked even the most
phlegmatic citizen who sipped his coffee, or
toyed with his " granita " under the awning of
a café.   But when it came to dragging honest
men from their beds in the dead of night on
the merest shadow of a suspicion of complicity
in a plot which had no more substantial existence than that of a figment conceived in some
police inspector's brain ; and leaving the victim
to languish, untried, for months in one or other
of the horrible, pestilential prisons, the thirst
for revenge engendered the organism of revolt.

Salvatore Giampoalo, a Neapolitan of conservative tendencies who published his memoirs
shortly after the annexation of Naples to Italy,
says that the police system of those times constituted the real conspiracy against the State
and against the Dynasty, and was the direct
cause of the events of 1860.   Those who peruse
the long list of victims, and the sickening

details of the refinements of cruelty and torture inflicted—often on absolutely innocent men— will agree with him.

It would be unfair to cast the whole odium of the police misrule on King Ferdinand.   Yet he originated the system, and if the vast machine got beyond his control, the responsi- bility was still his, and the curses of his sub- jects, together with the indignation of the civilized world, were hurled at the Dynasty which tolerated such anacronisms.

In as great a measure as was possible Ferdi- nand had isolated himself and his people from the political influence of all States beyond his frontiers, excepting the Court of Rome.   We have seen that his diplomacy, as a service, was reduced to mere watchfulness on the part of his representatives ; they being allowed to take no part in the alliances or political combina- tions of the years succeeding the events of 1849. The atrocities perpetrated within his realms were, however, noised abroad, and formed the subject of frequent diplomatic warning, and attempts at amicable intercession.   The storm raised by the publication of Mr. Gladstone's letters threatened for a time serious compli- cations, only averted by the impossibility of accord amongst the European Powers, and the adroit diplomacy of Austria.   Then came the

Crimean war which engaged the attention not only of France and England, but also of Piedmont. The subsequent Congress of Paris gave Count Cavour his long awaited opportunity for drawing official notice to the condition of the Italian States under Austrian influence. Cavour's insinuations and censure had the desired effect on public opinion ; but until Austria could be humbled it was useless to attempt to strike at the root of the evil. Napoleon's : "Que peut-on faire pour l'Italie," set Cavour on the track of an eventuality to be patiently schemed for, and laboriously cultivated until the propitious moment for joint action arrived, and Magenta and Solferino opened up a vista of dazzling possibilities.

In the meanwhile the storm-clouds continued to gather. Diplomatic notes reached Naples in May, 1856, in which the Cabinets of London and Paris intimated, in no ambiguous language, that it would be advisable that an amnesty be granted to political prisoners, and that radical reforms be undertaken in the judicial administration of the Kingdom. Ferdinand replied that he considered himself the only competent judge of what was necessary within his realm ; and reminded Count Walewsky and Lord Clarendon that he recognized the right of no government to interfere in the administration of a foreign State ; and especially in questions affecting the dispensation of judicial authority. Although undoubtedly strictly within his rights as the legitimate ruler of an independent State, Ferdinand would certainly have hesitated a few years earlier before despatching so categorical a reply to such powerful counsellors. But his diplomatic astuteness had become blunted, and he who had been a past master in the crafty art of dissimulation and intrigue in his younger days, now rashly assumed an inflexible attitude of obstinate defiance in the face of the disapprobation of the better half of Europe. In spite of the unsatisfactory political conditions existing at home, and the open hostility this abrupt repudiation of advice must entail, he discarded · the equivocal assurances which would at least have temporarily silenced his inopportunate admonishers ; thus placing himself in direct antagonism with the Emperor whose star was so greatly in the ascendant, and whom he had been the first to recognize on his assumption of the Imperial purple. The inevitable result was the rupture of diplomatic relations, the English and French representatives demanding, and receiving, their passports.

October twenty-first, 1856, was a gala day for the Liberals who recognized in the depar-

ture of the representatives of powers friendly
to their cause the forerunner of the dawn which
should usher in their triumph. Sympathetic
demonstrations greeted the diplomatists as they
drove through the streets of Naples, in spite of
the precautions taken by the police. The incident had, however, no tangible result beyond
the temporary cessation of official intercourse,
and in due time the respective Legations were
reoccupied by their former tenants. Nevertheless Count Cavour and the Liberal Party were
right in estimating the occurrence as a triumph
for the Italian cause. Although Austrian influence had apparently scored a victory, Ferdinand's lack of political foresight, or insuperable
distrust, threw the omnipotent French Emperor
into the outstretched arms of the House of
Savoy ; a circumstance Cavour had foreseen
and prepared for. By this ill-considered policy,
while he secured the isolation his timorous soul
craved, he encompassed his own ruin, and fur-
thered the political combinations of the enemies
of the only foreign State whose influence he
tolerated. It appears incomprehensible that a
man who had displayed such marked political
ability, especially amongst the tortuous paths
and pitfalls of diplomacy, should become so
blinded by prejudice. That Ferdinand was
convinced that the consummation of a united

Italy was not at any moment contemplated by
Napoleon III., and that the inviolability of the
Papal States was assured, is not improbable.
Cavour himself had at that time no plan beyond
the expulsion of Austria ; and even the later
promise of the French Emperor to free Italy
"from the Alps to the Adriatic" was not interpreted to embrace Southern Italy.   Theoret-
ically this reasoning was correct.   Yet at the
same time Ferdinand had ample and frequent
demonstration of the deep-rooted discontent
amongst the more intelligent and cultured
classes of his subjects, and of the wide-spread
unpopularity of his Dynasty.   He was not ignorant of the sympathies, insignificant and restricted to a small circle, it is true, entertained
for Prince Murat, but which, nevertheless,
owing to the relationship existing with the all-
powerful Emperor, were not unworthy of consideration under conditions so essentially unsatisfactory at home and abroad.   A more
plausible explanation, but one for which, while
frequently advanced there exists absolutely no
reliable authority, is that the misguided King
had come to a mutual personal understanding
with Austria and Russia, although no formal
treaty or league existed.   This theory, which
is cited merely as an historical legend, is not
necessarily invalidated by the fact that Ferdi-

nand refused an avowed alliance with Russia, or by the subsequent efforts of his successor to obtain the support of Piedmont and the good offices of the French Emperor. However this may be, the conduct of the Neapolitan Court in 1856 drove another nail into the coffin of the Bourbon dynasty, while it strengthened the Liberalist cause, gaining for it the service-able forbearance of powerful neutrals, perhaps not in complete sympathy with the funda-mental creed of the movement.

6

CHAPTER IV.

Count Cavour's projects for alliance with Naples.—The Plom-
bières' interview.—Plans of Napoleon III. and Cavour.—
Dynastic ambitions.—Proposed partition of the Peninsula.—
Attempted assassination of Ferdinand II.—Milano and
"Young Italy."—Political significance of attack.—Pisacane's
expedition.—The " Cagliari " incident.—British claims.—
Lord Malmesbury on transportation of political prisoners.—
Diplomatic interference —Ferdinand's policy from 1856–59
reviewed.—His reactionary measures.—His bigotry and
superstitions.

IT is now very definitely substantiated by the
recent publication of political documents and
diplomatic despatches, that Count Cavour had,
up to the period of Garibaldi's unexpected
achievements, formed no concrete plan for the
annexation of the Kingdom of the Two Sicilies
to the House of Savoy.   His opposition to the
Bourbons of Naples, and his attacks on the flagrant misrule existing within their realm, were
prompted by the Austrian influences paramount there and so detrimental to his projects
for the emancipation of northern Italy.   Prior
to Magenta, and for a considerable period there-
after, we have irrefutable evidence that he
would have urged his Sovereign to welcome an
82

alliance with the southern Kingdom for purposes of united action in driving out the foreigner. Had this been accomplished the sacrifice
of Nice and Savoy might have been avoided,
for Napoleon, after Villafranca and the consequent non-fulfilment of his engagements, had
himself absolved Victor Emmanuel and Cavour
from the obligations previously contracted :
although it is certain that France would in this
case have considered herself entitled to some
compensation for the (at that moment unforeseen) annexation of Tuscany. The political
unity of the Peninsula must thereby have been
retarded, although its ultimate accomplishment was inevitable. Yet again, the unfortunate chaotic interval after the fall of Gaeta
would have been avoided by allowing the Neapolitans time and opportunity to themselves
throw off the yoke, as the Tuscans had done.
Cavour realized this : and being perfectly
satisfied that the plum must eventually fall into
his royal master's lap, was content to let it
ripen thoroughly on the tree ; having no relish
for green fruit. This philosophic nonchalance
was, however, attended by a systematic solicitude
that the warm sunshine of Liberalism, as evinced
by the Constitutional Government of Piedmont,
should be given every opportunity to hasten the
maturity of the luscious southern fruit. Too

wise to show his hand so early in the game, while apparently falling in with the Emperor's never very definite plan for a restoration of the Murat régime at Naples, he kept his official and non-official agents actively employed in disseminating an essentially Pan-Italian propaganda.

During the famous Plombières interview, in July, 1858, when Napoleon III. and Count Cavour were casting about for a plausible pretext for a joint declaration of war on Austria, the difficulties of a satisfactory re-arrangement of the Italian chessboard came under discussion. The Pope and the King of Naples caused the Emperor considerable embarrassment : the first on account of the fact that the Catholic sympathies of France, with which he would have to reckon, must be with the Head of the Church ; the second because any attack on King Ferdinand would arouse the susceptibilities of Russia, who made a point of honor of protecting him. Cavour, equal to the occasion, pointed out to the Emperor that it would undoubtedly be advisable to leave the Sovereign Pontiff in the possession of Rome, protected as he was by the French garrison, but that on account of the notoriously bad government of the Romagna provinces under Papal rule, there could be no objection to *allowing* them to revolt. As for the King of Naples, he might be left undisturbed, unless he took sides with Austria. Nevertheless his subjects might also be *permitted* to revolt if they considered the moment opportune for casting aside the paternal domination of the Bourbons.

This arrangement being satisfactory to the Emperor, the following map of Italy was decided upon. The Valley of the Po, Romagna and the legations (Bologna and Ferrara) would constitute the Kingdom of Upper Italy, and would be governed by the House of Savoy. The Pope would retain Rome, and the territory surrounding it. The rest of the Papal states, together with Tuscany, would form the Kingdom of Central Italy. The States of the Kingdom of Naples would not be interfered with. These four Italian States would constitute a Confederation similar to the Germanic, the Presidency of which would be given to the Pope.

Cavour, in transmitting an account of this conversation to Victor Emmanuel, adds : " This arrangement seemed to me quite acceptable. According to its provisions Your Majesty being already by right Sovereign of the richest and strongest portion of Italy, would become the effective sovereign of the whole Peninsula."

During this same conversation Napoleon III. spoke openly of the pleasure it would afford him could he return to Murat the throne which had been occupied by his father.

The price of this compact, which Bismarck sneeringly styled "la politique de pourboire," was to be : as a retainer, the hand of Victor Emmanuel's eldest daughter, Princess Clotilde, for the Emperor's cousin Prince Jerome ; and, on execution, the cession of Savoy and Nice to France.

The conditions were onerous, but the immense advantages which would accrue to his royal master caused Cavour to eloquently urge their acceptance.

In forming a judgment of the third Napoleon's policy and actions in Italy it is of importance that what may be termed dynastic pride be not overlooked. The Emperor may, or may not, have been sincere in his avowed sympathy with national aspirations in the abstract ; in practice a united Italy was manifestly detrimental to French interests, and could not fail to be so considered by French Statesmen. The treaties of 1815 not only humbled France while overturning the Napoleonic dynasty : the maintenance of their stipulations lessened the prestige of the Second Empire. Austrian supremacy over what had been one of the brightest jewels in his uncle's sceptre constituted an unquestionable check to the nephew who sought to revive the lustre and traditions of that brilliant epoch. Cavour with penetrating insight, and thorough understanding of the foibles and ambitions of the new Cæsar, encouraged this policy to the best of his ability, at the same time bringing into play every subterfuge by which the Italian cause might profit without a corresponding advantage being reaped by his Imperial ally within the boundaries of the Peninsula. We have witnessed his acceptance of the Plombières compact by which the political geography of Italy was to be transformed, and it is known that Napoleon had on this occasion hinted at the desire that his cousin Jerome might be intrusted with the administration of Tuscany. But to neither this scheme nor the proposal that Murat be given the throne of Naples, did Cavour commit himself, although he bowed before the expression of the Emperor's wishes. Help to drive out the foreign invader was imperative, and the price coveted for such aid he could offer. Once this accomplished, the famous " Italia farà da se " would suffice for the decisions concerning the occupancy of the vacant throne or thrones, and the signs of the times left little doubt as to who would be elected. Villafrance came nigh to destroying all these patiently elaborated plans, while the hastily convened congress at Zürich still further darkened the horizon.   In the meanwhile portentous events neutralized the significance of the resolutions adopted by the diplomatic Congress assembled in Switzerland, and swept the prudently prepared combinations of Cavour himself, not to ruin, but towards unlooked-for success.

The meeting at Plombières, although the drift of the conversations between the Emperor and Cavour could only have been surmised by him, left Ferdinand uneasy.   The close amity existing between France and Piedmont foreboded no good for Naples, and must be considered in the light of encouragement by the Liberals, who turned to the French Emperor for the furtherance of their plans.

The Neapolitan King had been much impressed by the political significance of the desperate attack upon his life made by Milano, on December 8, 1856.   The assassin, one Agesilao Milano, a private in one of the regiments stationed at Naples, would appear to have nursed the plan of ridding his country of the enemy of national regeneration for a considerable period, and certainly displayed great cunning and perseverance in putting himself in a position to accomplish his object.   A blind and unreasoning adherent to the teachings of Mazzini, he had become affiliated with the society of "Young Italy" during his sojourn in Naples, and had proclaimed to the companions to whom he owed his initiation his determination to sacrifice his life for the cause. In vain his sponsors warned him of the futility of such isolated action, and urged him to wait until arrangements could be made for a general uprising to follow a successful assassination. His thirst for martyrdom was not to be overcome by any arguments of prudence or expediency, although when the moment he had chosen arrived, he led them astray by feigning to have postponed his intention.

Mazzini, while he never actually advocated assassination for the attainment of the political aims of his sect, did not on the other hand oppose extreme measures when brought to his notice. On such occasions he evasively argued that the responsibility rested upon the individual, not on the society or its doctrines. If he did not actually place the knife in the hands of his disciples, he was nevertheless disinclined to disarm, or even discourage, the individual avenger of political wrongs whose lower instincts led him to adopt assassination as a means to his ends. In the present instance Milano appears to have been guided by the spirit if not the letter of the doctrines he had imbibed, act-

ing on his own initiative in as far as the moment
to be selected, but in obedience to the moral
suasion of at least two of his fellow-associates.
At a review which Ferdinand was holding at
Naples on the above mentioned date, Milano,
selecting the opportunity when in the march
past he found himself within a few feet of the
King, suddenly left the ranks and rushing upon his victim aimed a violent bayonet thrust,
which must inevitably have been fatal had not
the pistol-case at the bow of the saddle turned
aside the weapon, which glancing off inflicted
but a slight wound.   Before Milano could
make the second lunge which he attempted, he
was seized and overpowered by those surrounding the King.   Ferdinand, in spite of his wound,
is said to have displayed the greatest calm and
courage.   The review was not interrupted,
many close at hand being unaware that an attempt on the King's life had been perpetrated.
To Count di Montemolino who witnessed the
assault, and rushed to the King's aid, Ferdinand
whispered : "Stand back.   Keep silent." This
presence of mind undoubtedly saved Naples a
bloody conflict.   Had the attempted assassination been generally observed it would immediately have been attributed to a military conspiracy, and the Swiss regiments have been
called upon by their officers to fire on the native

troops then and there. General Sigrist, commanding the Swiss regiments, has asserted that had he witnessed Milano's assault he would unhesitatingly have given such an order ; and it has also been stated by officers in the Neapolitan army that they would have retaliated with their artillery. Under these circumstances the populace must inevitably have become involved, and the slaughter been enormous. It has been suggested that Milano may have had this eventuality in view ; and counted on a civil war to facilitate a general rising of the Liberals throughout the Kingdom.

The review over, Ferdinand, surrounded by his Bodyguard, was driven rapidly to the Palace, and immediately summoned his physician. The possibility having been suggested that the weapon was poisoned, the Queen threw herself on her knees and sucked the wound.

During the inquiry which was immediately instituted, Milano indignantly repudiated the plea of insanity advanced by his advocate, and repeatedly maintained that his act was premeditated and unrepented. A Court-martial in due time condemned the would-be assassin to death by hanging. When the sentence was read to him he raised his eyes to Heaven, and exclaimed : "My God, I die like a thief for Italian Liberty."

Many arrests were made in connection with this affair, and numerous expulsions from the army followed, but no actual accomplices were discovered.   Ferdinand is credited with the desire to spare the man's life, but is said to have been overruled by the protests of the members of the Government and his Household, as well as by the advice of certain foreign representatives at his court.   Of course the police redoubled their activity in the search for possible accomplices or conspirators ; no portion of the Kingdom being exempt from their fiendish machinations and brutal despotism.

Milano's crime, despite the precipitancy of its author which had made collective action impossible, nevertheless aroused the Liberals to an appreciation of the necessity for cohesion. Many of the revolutionary clubs and associations dated their organization from this event. The malcontents waxed bolder notwithstanding the vigilance of the police ; clandestine printing presses sprang up and issued seditious literature   which   found   ready   circulation throughout the realm.   On several occasions the walls of Naples were placarded with revolutionary posters, to the delight of the populace and fury of the authorities.   Tricolor cockades were secretly distributed ; and in the theatres the audiences clamored continually

for Verdi. The significance of the sudden
enthusiasm for this composer lay in the discovery that the letters spelling his name also
formed the anagram : "Vittorio Emmannuele
Re D'Italia." Nor were the Unionists alone
in their efforts to foment agitation ; the adherents of Prince Murat, and the followers of
Mazzini were also in the field, ready to take
advantage of any opportunity which might offer to raise the standard of revolt.

Mazzini himself came to Genoa to settle, with
Carlo Pisacane, the details of the plot, afterwards celebrated in the annals of diplomacy as
the "Cagliari" incident. This expedition,
which vied in audacity with that of the heroic
Bandiera brothers in 1844, was undertaken by
a handful of brave but misinformed enthusiasts ; and included besides the leader Pisacane,
Giovanni Nicotera, afterwards one of King
Humbert's Cabinet Ministers. The lines on
which the expedition was planned were simple
enough, but the links of the chain became dis-
jointed at the outset through failure to meet
Rosolino Pilo as had been arranged, and to receive from him the arms and men deemed necessary to take possession of the steamer "Cagliari," on which the conspirators had embarked.
Pisacane, however, succeeded in winning over
the captain and crew of the steamer without

the use of force, and induced them to steer for the convict station on the island of Ponza. Here they surprised the small garrison and released the eight hundred prisoners confined there. Reinforced by three hundred and twenty-three of these, and having collected arms and ammunition, they again set sail and effected a landing at Sapri, on the Calabrian coast, on June 28, 1857. In the meanwhile Mazzini having heard that the junction with Rosolino Pino had failed, and, taking it for granted that the whole scheme had miscarried, neglected to prepare his agents for the arrival of the conspirators. In addition to this the information as to the readiness of the populace to welcome their deliverers proved grossly erroneous, and the invaders soon found themselves arrayed not only against the Royal troops, but in actual conflict with the very peasants they had come to emancipate from the yoke of the Bourbon. Defeated and hunted for days amidst the mountains, where the inhabitants slaughtered all on whom they could lay hands, the leaders were finally arrested and condemned to death : a sentence afterwards commuted by Ferdinand.

Meanwhile the " Cagliari " in attempting to leave the Gulf of Policastro, after landing Pisacane's band, was boarded by a Neapolitan frigate, "Tancredi," and declared a lawful prize. This action gave rise to the diplomatic controversy which really lent importance to a singularly romantic, but otherwise not uncommon revolutionary, incident. It would seem impossible to absolve the vessel of the charge of pure and simple filibustering ; and thus the case appeared to most people. But Count Cavour took a different view, and encouraged the demand of the Rubattino Company that their vessel be returned to them. Backed by the British Minister at Turin, who seized as a pretext to interest himself in the dispute the fact that two of the engineers of the captured steamer were English subjects, Cavour insisted that the vessel was protected by the Sardinian flag, and had, moreover, been illegally boarded in waters beyond the limits of Neapolitan jurisdiction. Notwithstanding this very debatable point and the unquestionable object of the voyage, Lord Derby, on May 25, 1858, caused a threatening note to be written, declaring the capture of the "Cagliari" a violation of maritime law, and that it behoved Great Britain, in the interests of such regulations, to insist on the liberation of the crew and the return of the vessel to her owners. There was no alternative for the unfortunate Ferdinand, in view of this energetic intervention, but the payment of three thousand pounds as indemnity to the two foreign engineers, and the restitution of the captured vessel.

Arbitrary as the ruling of the British Government undoubtedly was in the present instance, and bitterly humiliating to the Sovereign, Ferdinand dared not protest. Universal indignation had been aroused abroad by the recent negotiations opened with the Argentine Republic seeking to arrange for the exportation to that country of political prisoners under guarantees that they should be so provided for as to relieve the Kingdom of the Two Sicilies from all fear of further molestation. These stipulations, stigmatized in the English Parliament as a revival of the slave trade, and which practically sold the victims into bondage under a foreign and half-civilized State, offended the humanitarian instincts of Europe. Owing to the violent denunciations this proposal elicited, especially the campaign waged by the London "Times," it was decided to embark the more notorious of the prisoners on a man-of-war, and transship them in a Spanish port to a merchant vessel bound for New York. The first half of the programme was successfully carried out, but the exiles having prevailed upon the captain of the merchantman to land them in England, were speedily enabled to renew their conspiracies, enhanced by the halo of martyrdom acquired by their recent, and loudly heralded experiences.

Lord Malmesbury, writing on January 23, 1859, to the Prussian Minister in London, says :* "Having received notice that several of the political prisoners were to be sent to America, I was led to hope that our official relations with the Government of Naples might be resumed. But my illusion was short-lived. Unfortunately the Neapolitan Government accompanied this act of mercy by a decree which curtails for the future the civil liberty of millions of subjects. This policy is as incomprehensible as it is distasteful to the English Government. The decree of December 27, 1858, is a permanent violation of Neapolitan laws : consequently it is worse than the temporary state of siege. It is therefore impossible for the Government of Her Majesty, after having broken off diplomatic relations with the Neapolitan Government in 1856 because its proceedings were tyrannical, to resume them in 1859, when Ferdinand II. still further restricts the civil and political guarantees of his people, and entrusts to Courts-martial the jurisdictions over political misdemeanors."

The Emperor of the French protested in

* Translated from the Italian version.

7

like manner ; but Ferdinand turned a deaf ear
to warning and entreaty.   Almost his last
official act (May 16, 1859) was an intimation
that his Ambassador would only be permitted
to return to Paris with the explicit understanding that no demands be made relative to the
internal administration of the Kingdom.   And
this after the declaration of war upon Austria
by France and Sardinia !

The last three years of Ferdinand's life
(1856–1859) were marked by an increasingly
persistent endeavor to collect and maintain
every detail of the Administration within his
own grasp.   At the same time, appreciating
the immense power of the Church, he aimed at
a closer community of interests between the
Altar and the Throne.   The Council of Bishops
held at Caserta, had in view the elaboration of
a system by means of which the Clergy would
be placed in a position not unlike that which
they held in the Middle Ages ; the power and
prerogatives of the Crown, far from being sacrificed, being still jealously guarded, or increased.   It was, in fact, a compact between
the Church and Crown directed against the
interests and liberties of the State.   By his
rescripts of May 3 and August 15, 1856, Ferdinand ordered that the organized charitable institutions should hand over to the Bishops a

portion of their revenues, or of the capital donated by testators. Successive decrees issued in 1857 restored to ecclesiastics, in violation of the fundamental laws of the Kingdom, privileges of which they had been deprived in the middle of the last century as being incompatible with the advance of civilization. The decree of May 6, 1857, granted the privilege to priests and monks of trial for penal offences in secret audience, and of expiating the correctional sentences inflicted in religious houses. The Bishops were intrusted, in May of the same year, with the revision and censorship of the Press ; thus annulling the law of August 13, 1850, which provided for the execution of this duty by the Council of Public Instruction. The law which forbade priests to bless a marriage before it had been sanctioned by the civil authorities was abolished. Amongst other retrograde concessions the Bishops were proclaimed inspectors by right of office of all public and private schools.

While placing the country under the heel of the Clergy, Ferdinand nevertheless maintained his despotism in all essentials. Although the influence of the Jesuits was extended, Absolutism was strengthened by placing the educational institutions under the guidance of men devoted to his person, and presumably to his dynasty. Yet herein lay the unconscious error of his system. It has been already pointed out that Ferdinand mistrusted the Jesuits ; not only on account of their leaning to political intrigue, but by reason of the very capabilities in educational matters he now professed to admire. Under no circumstances would he admit a member of the confraternity to his confidence, or to his private confessional. The explanation of the undoubted mutation of the policy of his earlier years when contrasted with that followed during the months immediately preceding his death, can be traced to two sources : the influence of the Queen, increasing in proportion to her husband's intellectual and physical decline ; and the bigotry and childish superstitions to which he became subjected. These would appear to have increased with the expansion of his religious fervor. Nisco cites many examples, most noticeable amongst which was the King's deadly terror of the " jettatura," or evil eye ; a peculiarity he shared, however, with millions of his subjects. Did it happen that he came face to face with a monk, or a lame, bald or squinting person, when setting out on a journey, the dread of pending misfortune kept him in constant apprehension. He is said to have attributed his illness during his last journey to the Adriatic to welcome his son's wife, to the encounter with two Cappucine monks as the carriage passed out of the gates of the Palace ; while the aggravation of his sickness was caused, he believed, by the persistent stare of a bald man in the cathedral at Brindisi.

CHAPTER V.

Marriage of Crown Prince.—Ceremonies in Munich and Trieste.—
Ferdinand starts for Adriatic coast.—Incidents of the journey.—The suspicious illness at Ariano.—Accusations against
the Bishop.—The Court reaches Bari.— Arrival of Maria
Sophia.—Her meeting with Francis and members of his
family.—Ferdinand's illness increases.—The Count of Syracuse arrives.—The return to Naples.—Alarming news from
Turin.—Napoleon III. and Victor Emmanuel.—Opinions of
foreign royalty visiting Naples.—Details of Ferdinand's
last days.—His death.

DISQUIETED by the warlike rumors and preparations in the north, Ferdinand, towards the
end of 1858, shook off his political lethargy to
the extent of opening negotiations for a matrimonial alliance for his son, the Duke of Calabria, later Francis II. Policy, as well as incli-
nation, pointed to the advantages to be secured
by strengthening the family ties which already
bound him to the Austrian Court. The struggle against the ever increasing tide of Liberalism had become complicated by the aspirations
of the Murat party, to which color was given
by the thinly veiled sympathies of Napoleon III.
A matrimonial alliance which would bring him
into closer relationship with the mighty Haps-

burgs might at least serve as a check to the latter evil.

With these objects in view the Neapolitan Minister at Munich was instructed to make proposals for the hand of the young Princess Maria Sophia, daughter of Duke Maximilian, of Bavaria, and cousin of the reigning monarch. A sister of the beautiful Elizabeth who had recently become Empress of Austria, Sophia, although not endowed with the marvellous loveliness of her radiant sister, was nevertheless an exceedingly handsome and charming young woman, while the subsequent misfortunes and cruel humiliations she was called upon to suffer gave evidence of a strength of character amounting on occasions to heroism. Under less pernicious influences, even in spite of her extreme youth and inexperience, this ardent and courageous woman might have done much to avert the disasters which overtook the Throne she shared.

The inevitable preliminary negotiations having been satisfactorily disposed of, and the formal demand accepted, the marriage by procuration took place in the royal palace at Munich on the evening of January 8, 1859. Prince Luitpold of Bavaria personified the bridegroom ; the King of Naples being represented by his special Ambassador, Count Ludolf.

On the thirteenth the new Duchess of Calabria set forth on the journey to her future home. At Vienna she was joined by her sister the Empress of Austria who accompanied her to Trieste, where the final ceremony of handing over the bride to the royal commissary, charged to escort her on board a Neapolitan frigate, was to take place. The great hall of the Palace at Trieste was for this occasion divided by a line simulating the demarcation of the frontiers of the two States, Bavaria and Naples. On the Neapolitan side stood the Duke of Serracapriola, Ferdinand's Commissary, and the ladies and gentlemen of the Court of the new Princess; on Bavarian territory the commissary of King Maximilian, Count de Rechberg, the ladies of honor of the Princess, and the civil and military authorities, awaited the entrance of the bride. When Maria Sophia appeared the respective Commissaries, and their suites, advanced to the line of demarcation, and formally exchanged their credentials. Count Rechberg having bid the Princess an official adieu, advanced with her to the dividing line, and handed her over to the Duke of Serracapriola. Once within Neapolitan territory the bride received the homages of her new Court, and of the admiral and officers of the squadron which was to accompany her to Bari, where her husband was awaiting her. On the conclusion of this interesting ceremony Maria Sophia, attended by her sister the Empress and the combined courts, proceeded to the Neapolitan frigate "Fulminante," on board of which the private farewell greetings with the members of her family and personal friends were gone through.

Meanwhile Ferdinand had quitted his capital and undertaken the journey to the Adriatic coast to attend the official welcome and reception of his daughter-in-law. The Queen, Maria Theresa, an Austrian by birth, and the bridegroom with his half-brothers and sisters accompanied the Sovereigns, who were attended by a numerous suite of Court dignitaries.

The original plans for the journey had been made with Manfredonia as the port where the meeting was to take place. This town was to be reached by a circuitous route embracing the cities of Taranto, Lecce, Brindisi and Bari, visited under the impression that a royal sojourn would do much to cement the loyalty of those provinces. Nothing can better demonstrate the mistrust with which the Sovereign looked upon his liege subjects than the avoidance of any refreshment at the hands of the provincial and municipal dignitaries within whose jurisdiction he might travel or seek rest.

All food or refreshment for the royal table was prepared and served by the trusted servants attached to his person.   The trip began under particularly trying circumstances : the cold was intense, and deep snow made the roads in the mountainous districts well-nigh impassable. On several occasions the danger resulting from the ice-bound condition of the highways made it necessary for the royal travellers to descend from their heavy coaches and traverse consider able distances on foot.   Extraordinary precau- tions had been taken for the safety of the King, who must needs travel through districts infected with brigands, and political malcontents, of every condition.   On the evening of the second day, which had been an unusually fatiguing one, owing to the steepness and abominable condition of the roads, the cortége arrived after nightfall at Ariano.   Tired out, and will- nigh frozen, Ferdinand was fain to accept the hospitality of the Bishop, Monsignor Michel Caputo, and to sup and spend the night at the Episcopal Palace.   It would appear that the political convictions of Monsignor Caputo were not altogether above suspicion from a Bourbon's point of view.   Be this as it may, all authorities agree in dating the illness which was to carry the Monarch to the tomb from the night passed at Ariano.   Shortly after the King had retired for the night his faithful body-servant, Galizia, who slept in an adjoining room, was roused by a violent noise ; and on rushing into his master's presence found him, with his pistols clutched in his hands, in a state of great excitement. The King asserted that an assassin was concealed in the chamber, and insisted on four sailors of his guard, together with Galizia, remaining with him. The servant declared that the attempted assassination was purely imaginary, and that he found the King suffering from violent fever, attended with pains in the body, and more particularly the bones. In spite of the fact that he was still suffering considerably the King insisted on resuming the journey next morning ; yet notwithstanding the unavoidable fatigue no alarming symptoms became manifest until after their arrival at Lecce. Although at the time no suspicions were aroused, after the King's death three months later, the wildest rumors were circulated. It was then currently affirmed that Monsignor Caputo had poisoned Ferdinand, and the fact that the Bishop ultimately became officially connected with Garibaldi lent a semblance of plausibility to such assertions, which, the adherents to the Bourbon Dynasty were not slow to seize upon as exemplifying the iniquity of their political foes.

There is not, however, a particle of evidence to substantiate so monstrous an accusation. The probabilities are that Ferdinand, unaccustomed to the severe exposure he had undergone, and which he rashly faced the day after his mysterious sickness, developed the seeds of the malady which, first from neglect, and later owing to inefficient medical treatment, became complicated by pre-existent disorders. Certain it is that on his arrival at Lecce on January 14, 1859, Ferdinand became so ill that the Court physicians were hastily summoned from Naples, while the plans for the journey were so altered as to provide for the reception of the bride at Bari, instead of at Manfredonia. For over a fortnight the royal patient lay grievously ill at Lecce ; then, a slight improvement having manifested itself, the Court hurried on to Bari which was reached the same evening. Greatly exhausted by the unavoidable fatigue of the rough journey, Ferdinand with difficulty mounted the stairs leaning heavily on the Queen and Doctor Romaglia, who assisted him to his bed.

On the second of February, the " Fulminante," having on board the young Duchess and her suite arrived off Bari, and was received with great ceremony and public rejoicings. Ferdinand, who was now suffering intensely

from inflammation of the lower intestines, complicated by an internal trouble the exact nature
of which the doctors failed to diagnose, was
unable to leave his bed to welcome the new
member of his family. The festivities were
consequently limited to the religious service
which completed the interminable nuptial ceremonies the young Duchess had already submitted to, and which was performed in the
great gallery of the Palace, converted for the
occasion into a chapel. "Memor," who has
preserved for us a most minute account of all
the circumstances attending the last months
of Ferdinand's life, in relating the meeting of
the Duke of Calabria with his wife, mentions
the fact that conversational intercourse between the bride and groom was rendered somewhat embarrassing as the Duke failed to understand the French used by Maria Sophia,
and comprehended not a word of the German
she addressed to his stepmother. The King
was greatly taken by the charm of his
daughter-in-law's manner, who in turn recip-
rocated his affection with warm sympathy.

Meanwhile Ferdinand's condition grew steadily worse and his sufferings became intolerable.
Doctor after doctor was summoned, but as
none were allowed to see the patient, and had
to content themselves with the diagnosis which

Romaglia, repeated to them, their services were negative.   In vain was the King's room hung with the pictures of all the most celebrated Saints of the Kingdom ; in vain did the patient imbibe waters and potions to which miraculous properties were attributed ; the disease resisted all treatment, physical and spiritual. Certain symptoms now began to appear which left no doubt in the minds of his physicians that a surgical operation would be necessary. Romaglia, having discovered the existence of pus, became greatly alarmed, and declining the responsibility of an operation in a small provincial town such as Bari, urged an immediate return to Naples by sea.   The Neapolitans from whom Ferdinand's condition had been concealed, now began to murmur at the prolonged absence of the Court, all the ceremonies attending the bride's reception being over. Strange rumors were circulated, and owing to the presence at Bari of the Austrian Archdukes Ranieri and William, it was asserted that an offensive and defensive alliance with Austria was being secretly negotiated.   This aroused the Liberals who were eagerly anticipating the armed intervention of the Emperor of the French for the liberation of northern Italy from the hated Austrian rule.   The King's brother, the Count of Syracuse, credited with liberal sympathies of a militant order, and who never ceased to urge an alliance with Piedmont and an understanding with the Nationalists, posted off in haste to Bari, to dissuade the King from such a course should it be under contemplation. The news of the landing of the political prisoners destined for America, and of their enthusiastic reception by the British public and press, had created considerable excitement in Naples. The facts were not concealed from Ferdinand, who in addition to the anger he felt, and weakened by suffering and disease, was disinclined to return to Naples and face the malicious triumph of the Liberals in his capital. With one pretext or another the departure was postponed until the seventh of March, on which date the royal family embarked on the " Fulminante " and set out for Naples. A fresh examination of the King, made at his request by the naval surgeons on board, confirmed the existence of pus, and counselled an immediate operation. To this the Queen would not listen. Palliatives were resorted to and the journey of fifty hours accomplished without undue suffering. A special train hurried the royal party from Naples to the Palace at Caserta, where the acute agony of the unfortunate Sovereign was to drag on for long weeks to come.

In spite of his physical sufferings and the knowledge that the only probable release was death, and that at no distant date, Ferdinand continued to give his personal attention to the affairs of State.   Carafa, who under the immediate supervision of the King discharged the duties of chief of the Bureau for Foreign Affairs, assiduously communicated the alarming despatches received from Count Antonini dated from Brussels, where he had established himself after the rupture of diplomatic relations between France and Naples, for the purpose of watching the progress of events.   The news received from this diplomatist, as well as from the representative at Turin, the Chevalier Canofari, left little doubt of the intentions of Napoleon III. and Victor Emmanuel.   The Congress, proposed by Russia and nominally accepted by all the great Powers, which was to deal with the Italian question, gave a momentary respite.   Few believed the French Emperor to be sincere in his professed willingness to refer the questions at issue to such a Congress ;   and while Ferdinand still preserved confidence in the ability of Austria to maintain by force of arms the " statu quo " in Italy, he could not but be impressed by the gravity of the political situation.   In Piedmont, and above all in the Liberal and Nationalist prin-

ciples prevailing there, he recognized the direst
foe to the institutions his personal influence
had, up to the present, been able to force upon
his subjects. That Cavour was a party to the
schemes for Italian Federation as conceived by
Napoleon III. he was assured ; but to what
extent the Emperor had committed himself in
connection with the disposition of southern
Italy he could only surmise. Such speculations
were not of a nature to procure repose for the
King who, tortured in body, and keenly aware
of his approaching dissolution, was forced to
passively witness the transformation of the
political creeds he so tenaciously clung to.

The visit of the Russian Grand Duke Con-
stantine, and that of King Frederick William
of Prussia, during the month of March, bringing with them assurances that peace would not
be disturbed, did not tranquillize the King,
who fully appreciated the significance of the
preparations so actively carried on within
the dominions of his cousin of Savoy. And
indeed the optimism of his royal guests was
rudely shattered before they had shaken the
Neapolitan dust from off their shoes. On
April sixteenth the Austrian ultimatum calling
upon Piedmont to disarm furnished the long-
awaited pretext, and its indignant refusal ten
days later swept the scheme for a Congress, as

8

proposed by Russia, into the limbo of diplomatic absurdities.   The military revolution at Florence of April 27th, resulted in the ignominious flight of the Grand Duke of Tuscany, and the establishment of the Provisional Government of Ricasoli.   Almost simultaneously the Duchies of Parma and Modena freed themselves of their rulers ; the Papal Legate retired from Bologna ; and the first successes of the French and Sardinian allies gave rise to the wildest exultation amongst the Liberals of Naples in the very face of the police, who, dazed and almost paralyzed by the rapidly shifting events enacted in Upper Italy, seemed utterly inadequate to cope with the added responsibilities thus bewilderingly thrust upon them.

Meanwhile in the great Palace of Caserta the long-drawn agony of the Sovereign was nearing its fatal termination.   The various doctors called to relieve the sufferings of the distracted Ferdinand were powerless to arrest the progress of general decay.   The purulent corruption had infected the entire organism of the patient, relentlessly invading external and internal organs : the lungs became congested, and horrible sores broke out on various parts of the body.   Every breath was agony : every movement an indescribable torture.   An operation afforded temporary relief, but confirmed the diagnosis, and convinced the physicians that all hope must be abandoned. The King spent much of his time in prayer : Maria Theresa, his faithful Consort, on her knees at his bedside. Continual recourse was had to so-called miracle-working remedies ; and as at Bari the royal bedchamber was littered with all the accessories of superstitious devotion ; relics, images of the Saints and Madonna, holy waters, or the fantastic preparations of ecclesiastic quacks. Although the King had lost all confidence in the power of doctors to aid him, he turned with simple faith to each new image, each holy relic, or miraculous picture, for the consolation denied him by human science. Although the condition of the King was an open secret in Naples, the doctors issued no bulletin until April 12th, in deference to the desire of the Queen, who feared the effect the alarming news might have upon the hostile political elements in the Kingdom. The administration of the last rites of the Church on this day made further concealment of the patient's desperate condition impossible. In sign of sympathy the theatres were ordered to close their doors, public entertainments of all sorts being forbidden.

These last weeks of suffering and anxiety furnish us with a side view of the character of the extraordinary man who for twenty-nine years swayed the destinies of the Kingdom of the Two Sicilies.   The tyrant whose will alone governed eleven millions of his subjects ; the despot who had unhesitatingly condemned hundreds of the brightest intellects of his realm to death, and worse than death, now showed a touching consideration for those who attended him in his hour of need.   The suspicion that the point of the bayonet with which he had been wounded by Milano was poisoned, had never been eradicated from Ferdinand's mind.   Shortly before his death he inquired of his surgeon, Capone, if there were any suppuration from the scar of the old wound, on which, since the attempted assassination, he had always worn a little stone supposed to possess miraculous qualities.   Capone having examined the scar, assured the King that the wound was completely healed, and at the same time gave vent to bitter vituperation of the would-be regicide.   Ferdinand gently rebuked this outburst, saying :   "I called you to examine the wound, not to judge the crime.   God has judged that ; and I have pardoned it ; so that is enough."   Yet this apparent softening was attended by no corresponding leniency or faltering in the political course he had so relentlessly pursued.   Cruel and barbarous this had undoubtedly been ; but

if his policy was shortsighted and bigoted, it
was at least consistent. Personal ambitions he
had none ; although his assumption of the exclusive control of matters of State is liable to
be construed as such. Nevertheless his aspirations aimed no higher than handing to his successor the integral inheritance which had been
his. He is asserted to have claimed, only a few
days before his death, that the Crown of Italy
might have been his, could he have reconciled
his conscience to the necessary spoliation of the
various Italian Sovereigns. This it may be permitted to doubt ; but the fact remains that territorial aggrandizement had no place in his political programme. When, on November 8, 1830,
he had succeeded his father, Francis I., his first
official proclamation savored of an aspersion on
the policy of the late government. "We do not
deny," he said, "the existence of profound evils
which merit redress, and that our people look to
us for the alleviation of the burdens which a
troublous past has placed upon them." The
next day his brother, the Count of Syracuse,
was appointed Viceroy of Sicily, and the Marquis delle Favare, whose cruel administration
had driven the islanders to desperation, was
given twenty-four hours' notice to quit. This
action, taken in conjunction with his own past
record, and the reform of certain administra-

tive abuses which had long oppressed his subjects, contributed to excite the wildest enthusiasm and most ardent expectations. But those
who founded their hopes on the liberal effusions
of his irresponsible youth were doomed to
speedy disappointment once the reins of government were well within his grasp. The few
half-hearted reforms granted in the first flush
of accession to power had, however, merely
whetted the appetites of the Liberals greedy
for more extended franchise, and Ferdinand
soon realized that this path must inevitably
lead not only to a very considerable infringe-
ment of the Absolutism dear to his Bourbon
soul, but also to the open antagonism of Austria, and, be it noted, the disapproval of the
King of Sardinia. Thus began the lifelong
struggle with the principles with which as Heir
to the Throne he had felt some latent sympathy,
but for which, as the love of power increased
with age, he conceived a loathing which blinded
him to any true appreciation of the spirit of
the times in which he lived, and wrecked the
political fabric he had counted on a quasi-
Chinese isolation to preserve.

This much can be said in extenuation of the
political excesses of which he was guilty. Of
the charge of infamous perjury ; and the iniquitous juggling with the sacred vested rights

of his people, nothing can absolve him. The utter disregard of all humanitarian obligations is equalled, if not surpassed, by the ferocious treatment of the patriots of the Italian provinces under Austrian rule ; but martyrs of the Spielberg revolted against a power which, if oppressive, was at least legally instituted, while the crime attributed to their unhappy brethren of Naples was, subsequent to the concessions of 1848, passionate adherence to the Chart which had been freely granted them under sacred oath, and of the privileges of which, through no fault of their own, they had been treacherously deprived. The sequel to the events of the fifteenth of May, 1848, must for all time brand Ferdinand the Second of Naples a perjured King, and a traitor to the liberties he had of his own free will (as he explicitly stated in his proclamation announcing the Constitution) accorded his subjects. No satisfactory explanation, no valid claim of expediency, can be brought forward in extenuation of the accusation of deliberate and conscious fraud.

On his death-bed Ferdinand, when recommending his soul to his Creator, added, that he craved the pardon of his subjects, both as Sovereign and as a man, for his wrongs towards them. When taken in conjunction with his final admonition to his son to change nothing in the policy he had himself pursued, the words quoted can hardly be construed as an expression of regret for the political course so persistingly and relentlessly pursued.

Surrounded by his family, attended to the last by the faithful Maria Theresa, whose constant devotion during the many weeks of sickness is beyond all praise, Ferdinand passed away a little after midday on the twenty-second of May, 1859.

CHAPTER VI.

Expectations of a change of policy.—Events in Northern Italy.
—Their influences on Naples.—Accession of Francis II.—
Ferdinand's second marriage.—Education of Francis.—Life
at the Neapolitan Court during his youth.—His character
and early training.—The religious influences.—Want of
political training.—The "Camarilla"; its composition and
objects.—Influence of the Queen-Mother.—The Count of
Syracuse.—His surroundings and political ambitions.—
Palace intrigues.—Conspiracy in favor of Count of Trani.

WITH the death of Ferdinand an alleviation
of many of the vexatious and antiquated forms
of administration was confidently looked for ;
while it was further anticipated by the more
sanguine that reforms more in accord with the
altered conditions of political life throughout
Italy, and the exigencies of international public
opinion, would be granted.

A great cry of relief and yearning expectation
went up from the exiles in Florence, Turin,
Genoa, Paris, and London. Hope, long crushed
and oft deferred, sprang up anew in the breasts
of those who had suffered weary years of banishment and poverty. Even the most ferocious
revolutionists, the Irredentists themselves,
paused awhile to see what use the new King

would make of his power. The opportunity was a golden one : who can say, had it been intelligently employed, what the consequences might have been ! Those personally acquainted with the young Sovereign did not, however, entertain illusions concerning the cessation of political abuses ; much less credit the rumors of imminent or radical reforms. The immense influence of the Queen-Mother, together with the opposition and jealousies of what was known as the " Camarilla," or Court reactionary clique, forbade optimistic surmises.

The last moments of the dying Despot had been embittered by the news from .northern Italy. Ferdinand lived just long enough to know of the success of the allied armies of France and Sardinia against the Austrians at Montebello, while he looked in vain for signs of the anticipated intercession of Russia and Prussia. That Ferdinand realized the grave significance of the political events of the last few months of his life none can doubt. But that he considered them of a nature to imperil his Dynasty seems improbable from the fact that his political instructions to his heir contained no suggestions for a modification of the system of political apathy which was hurrying the Crown to destruction. There was time, even now, to arrest the disintegration : and had

Ferdinand urged the alliance with Sardinia it is conceivable that his son would have respected his counsels and done his utmost to secure the goodwill of an already powerful neighbor, in spite of the emphatic disapprobation of Pius IX. As has been intimated, however, Ferdinand trusted more to the geographical conformation of his country, and to the buffer afforded by the Papal State to the north, than to shifting political alliances. In spite of the experiences of 1848, when he had entertained the fugitive Pope at Gaeta, the possibility of this protective buffer-State being removed seemed to him as inconceivable as that the sea which surrounded the other portions of his realm should evaporate.

Francis the Second, born on January sixteenth, 1836, was just over twenty-three years of age when he succeeded his father. His mother, Queen Maria Christina, a Princess of the House of Savoy, had, during her short career, made herself generally revered and beloved. The "Saint," as she was styled by the impressionable Neapolitans, did not live to watch over and guide her son. Barely a fortnight after his birth she died, never having recovered, it is said, from the effects of a brutal jest of her husband, who pulled a chair from under her shortly before her confinement.

After nine months of widowhood Ferdinand had given his subjects a new Queen of a very different stamp in the person of Maria Theresa of Austria, who, for reasons rather political than personal, he had preferred to the Princess Maria Christina of France, a daughter of Louis Philippe, for whose hand he had also been in treaty. Diametrically the opposite of the lamented " Saint " in disposition, character and physique, Maria Theresa, although possessing such sterling qualities as courage and determination, very speedily became an object of distrust and aversion to the subjects she ruled over. Of an intensely jealous temperament, descending even with her petty suspicions to those employed in menial positions in her bedchamber and household, she eliminated all social element from her husband's Court. With the aspiration to govern she rapidly acquired great authority and influence over her husband, while she completely dominated her step-son, who never freed himself from this baneful subjection. To her jealousies and machinations, rather than to any organic sloth of intellect, can be traced the deplorable lack of education, and total absence of political preparation for the duties he must one day assume, which proved so disastrous to his reign. During Ferdinand's lifetime, and even after Francis had ascended the throne, she constantly conspired against him in favor of her own son, Louis ; yet so skilfully were her intrigues woven, and so complete was her ascendency over the insipid Francis, that she retained her influence to the very end. Intensely superstitious and bigoted she was instrumental in greatly increasing the power and despotism of the Clergy, to whose bishops were conceded attributes usually allotted to the police.

Life at the Court of Naples since Francis had been of an age to participate in it had been neither brilliant nor diverting. After 1848, and especially after the attempted assassination by Milano, the Court had resided as little as possible in Naples. The palace of Caserta was the favorite residence of Ferdinand and his family, although annual visits were made to Gaeta, especially during the summer months. Once out of Naples, the family life differed very little from that of any well-to-do Italian household. The King hated pomp and ceremony of all kinds, and infinitely preferred the quiet domestic circle. All this had been very different in the early years of his married life ; but the anxious and painful experiences of 1848 would seem to have cast a gloom over his whole nature. In place of the pleasures or distractions of a Court which possessed all the elements for social brilliancy, there was gradually developed that intense absorption in State business, to its minutest details, which formed one of the most curious characteristics of this remarkable man.   Strange to say, Ferdinand at no time seemed to recognize the expediency of initiating his son into the mysteries of personal government.   As has been said, the education which Francis received was conspicuously insufficient and elementary at a Court where learning, or even the ordinary accomplishments or pursuits of a gentleman were held in disdain.   Not only was the heir to the Throne left with a mind absolutely uncultivated, and unprepared for the onerous duties and responsibilities of his position, but he was not even made proficient in the sports or pastimes of royalty.   Ferdinand's own education had been extremely imperfect ; but he was by nature endowed with a hard common-sense ; a shrewd knowledge of men; a prodigious memory; and above all a dose of self-assurance sufficient to compensate in no small degree for the absence of ordinary book-learning.   Surrounded, by preference, with men of very ordinary mental attainments, his natural brilliancy, combined with a certain essentially Neapolitan "esprit," made his educational shortcomings the less observable. He expressed himself most easily in the Neapolitan dialect, as also in the Sicilian idiom ; but his Italian was pure, if not eloquent, while his French was fluent and graceful. In Ferdinand, the king and the man were widely separated and distinct. If as a Sovereign little can be advanced in his favor, as a man, as a husband, and as a father, no criticism would be justifiable. Seated at his family table, loaded with the maccheroni and plebeian national dishes, the predilection for which he shared with the meanest of his subjects, the dreaded Monarch appeared the most benign and guileless of men. The family circle was a large one, for Maria Theresa had had nine children of her own, and the visits of relations from Tuscany or Austria were frequent. Each child had its diminutive, or pet name, and by such was invariably addressed by the King. A not uncommon sight in the environs of Caserta was a huge wagonette, driven by the King himself, and filled with children of all ages.

If the lay-education which Francis received was meagre, it may be added that his religious instruction could have fitted him for the priesthood. Exceedingly timid and retiring by nature, the conditions prevailing at his father's Court, and especially the treatment he received

at the hands of his stepmother, were not calculated to inspire self-assurance. Dominated by
his social surroundings, he became the more
readily subjected to fanatical religious influences. Unfortunately religion was synonymous
with superstition of the most gross and degrading character at the Neapolitan Court. One
of the principal duties of the troops garrisoned
in Naples was to swell the constant religious
processions to the various miracle-working
shrines for miles around the capital : which
functions were devoutly attended by the King
and his household. Ferdinand had caused the
church bells to be melted down for cannon in
1848 : ten years later the defences of the country
were remodelled for ecclesiastical purposes. Yet
in spite of the most minute observance of trivial
rites, and notwithstanding the haunting superstitions to which he was a prey, Ferdinand never
permitted the increased political power of the
prelates, whose hands he reverently kissed, to
degenerate into license. He was the Master :
and although advantage might be taken of his
subjects by those he placed in authority over
them, he personally insisted on implicit obedience and subservience in matters clerical as
well as secular. Even his dealings with the
Pope were conducted on a strictly business
basis, and no favor shown. While this was

possible to a nature which combined strength
of will and obstinacy of purpose, with craft,
and no mean intelligence, it stood to reason
that the yielding, vacillating and unformed
character of his son must be as wax to the
influences which surrounded him. And so it
was, for after his father's death we find Francis
ever the dupe and tool of interested and unscru-
pulous advisers ; swayed this way and that by
the conflicting factions in Palace or Council
Chamber : to-day completely dominated by the
Queen Mother ; to-morrow convinced by the
persuasive arguments of Liborio Romano ; only
to hark back again to the obsolete pretensions of
the " Camarilla." The antithesis of his father,
Francis had not even " les qualités de ses dé-
fauts " to redeem him from insignificance.
Like Charles the First of England and Louis
XVI. of France, it is by virtue of his misfortunes
that he will live in history. His tutors in child-
hood were General Ferrari and Admiral Spina,
the latter sleeping in the Prince's room, and
being charged with the supervision of the most
trivial occupations of his daily existence.
With the exception of the religious works, to
which his reading was confined, his instruction,
such as it was, was carried on by word of mouth,
history being so purged that accounts of revolutions, or constitutional liberties, might not
9

disturb his mind, these being represented to him as condemned by the Church. Later we shall find him gravely warning his erring subjects that revolt against his authority constitutes revolt against God, and consequently entails eternal damnation. Yet when driven to bay at Gaeta we shall have to record acts closely allied to heroism ; followed by a dignified resignation in adversity, which demands our respectful sympathy. The Duke of Sperlinga, a Sicilian nobleman, cites a dialogue which may be taken as illustrative of the theories instilled into the mind of the youthful Prince. Standing beside Ferdinand one fête-day and looking into the great square before the Palace thronged with pleasure-seekers, Francis asked his father : " What can the King do with all these people ? " To which the King made answer : " He has the right to cut their heads off ; but he doesn't do it out of respect for our holy Religion."

Another anecdote descriptive of the fatalism, or mystical resignation of the young King is related by " Memor." During a conference with the director of the Ministry of Finance, De Liguro, the accidental trembling of the table at which they were seated was immediately interpreted by the King as an omen that his reign would be short. De Liguro remonstrated with his sovereign for allowing such thoughts

to haunt his mind ; but Francis sadly replied :
" Dear Sir ; I hold neither to my life, nor to
my throne, because I remember what is written :
'Dominus dedit, Dominus abstulit,' and I say :
God gives, God takes away."

By the " Camarilla," of which mention has
been made, is understood that party in the
Court circle which professed the principles of a
pure Absolutism, and was consequently irreconcilable to any concessions of a liberal or constitutional nature. The Queen Mother was conspicuously the leader of this faction, whose
influence with the new King was not unnaturally
preponderant, for to its doctrines most of the
members of the royal family also adhered. A
notable exception was the Count of Syracuse,
Francis' uncle, who was, and had for some time
been, in open sympathy with the Liberals, and
the Nationalist cause. It is certain that when
the Count first advised his nephew concerning
the expediency of political concessions, urgently
demanded by his subjects, and counselled an
alliance with Piedmont, his conviction in regard
to Liberalism and Nationalism went no further
than Louis Napoleon's " Italy for the Italians,"
and embraced no scheme for national unity.
In a note dated May 11, 1859, and consequently before Ferdinand's death, Count
Gropello, Chargé' d'Affaires of the Sardinian

Legation at Naples, advised his Government
that the King's brother was in favor of such
an alliance for the purpose of freeing Italy
from foreign rule. Cavour at this period
strongly advocated such a course, fully appreciating the advisability of the two greatest Italian powers being at one on this point. His
agents therefore had special instructions to
cultivate intimate relations with the Count of
Syracuse, and through this Prince attempt to
influence the King. The house of the Count of
Syracuse was notoriously the political "rendezvous" of men of professed Liberal tendencies;
and as such was closely watched by the police.
Ferdinand called his brother's salon "the
antechamber of Hell," in allusion not only to
the political plots hatched therein, but also to
the not always strictly immaculate moral
character of its frequenters. As a matter of
fact it was one of the rare Neapolitan houses
where artists and literary men were received on
their intellectual merits; and where diplomatic
representatives of foreign powers congregated
for the interchange of the political news of the
day. By rabid advocates of the Bourbon
régime the Count of Syracuse has been termed
a traitor to his family; an accusation substantiated in the minds of many by his subsequent
conduct. Yet prior to Garibaldi's Sicilian

incursion, the Count certainly nourished no
more extended projects of reform than those
which have been already mentioned.   That he
should be hated and distrusted at Court was
not to be wondered at : nor can we feel surprise
that Maria Theresa should have done all in her
power to destroy his influence with his nephew,
and to poison the King's mind, through the
medium of his confessor, with insinuations that
the Count aspired to the Regency.   In reality
his supposed influence amounted to little or
nothing with Francis, although owing to his
high position at Court, and to his noted
sympathies, he was appealed to, flattered and
cajoled, by those who possessed the confidence of the steadily growing party whose political convictions he was understood to share.
Thus he became a very monster of iniquity in
the eyes of the " Camarilla," who poured out
upon him the vials of their wrath ; branding
him traitor, and tracing to his machinations
the downfall of the old order.   This odium he
shared later with his brother, the Count of
Aquila, who was subsequently banished by
Francis for lending countenance to an administrative transaction, open to the interpretation
of treason ; but banished with such tender
solicitude for public opinion, that his disgrace
was adroitly concealed beneath the intimation

of the advisability of his acceptance of an important political mission abroad.

Nor was the Palace itself free from intrigues to dispossess the unfortunate Francis, and place his half-brother, the Count of Trani, upon the Throne. Such a plan was currently reported to have received the sanction of Maria Theresa ; and one or two insignificant demonstrations in favor of her own son actually took place in the province of Bari. Certain incriminating documents are said, by " Memor," to have been brought to the notice of the King by Filangieri. Francis, however, on being informed of the nature of the accusation, threw the papers unopened into the fire, exclaiming with touching simplicity to his Minister : " She is the wife of my father." Be this as it may, there is no trustworthy evidence of the direct participation of the Queen Mother in any of these intrigues, which may be safely attributed to the over-zealous adherents of the " Camarilla." Nevertheless such incidents, proving as they did the existence of a spirit of rebellion against his authority amongst those to whom he would most naturally turn for support, could not but increase the suspicious timidity and constitutional lack of self-confidence of the young King.

CHAPTER VII.

An envoy from Turin.—Proposals for alliance between Naples and Piedmont.—French and English diplomatic relations are resumed.—Royal proclamation eulogizing Ferdinand—Filangieri at the head of the Government.—His previous career.—Political problems confronting him.—Count Salmour's mission.—Opposition to alliance.—Mazzini's schemes.—Action of Swiss Government.—Revolt of Swiss Guard.—Massacre of same.—Swiss regiments disbanded.—Kossuth on situation in Naples.—Court functions and etiquette.—Abstention of aristocracy.—Their sympathies for Murat.

THE accession of Francis II. furnished the pretext for the despatch, in accordance with the usages of diplomatic courtesy, of a special Ambassador from Turin, who, while he carried the official condolences of his Sovereign for the recent bereavement of the Neapolitan Court, was in addition charged by Cavour to improve the opportunity afforded for a mutual political understanding. Count Salmour's confidential instructions leave no doubt as to the nature of Cavour's preoccupations at this date. "There are sound arguments," he writes on May 27, 1859, "for the belief that in undertaking the war for Italian independence Napoleon III. entertains no dynastic ambitions ; if, however,

135

with the progress of events, such were to be developed, an alliance between the two Italian Powers would be useful as a check." Cavour then proceeds to state that the Sardinian Government would be disposed to go to the length of a compact, reciprocally guaranteeing the inviolability of the territories of the two realms, in the form of an offensive and defensive alliance. At the same time he urges the necessity of inaugurating the new reign with broad and liberal reforms, which, together with the prestige acquired by a league with Piedmont, could not fail to bear good fruit at home and abroad.

England and France had also resumed diplomatic relations with Naples on the death of Ferdinand, and their representatives bore instructions which, although the ends to be served were necessarily divergent, coincided in the main with the views entertained by Sardinia, and laid stress on the advisability of a radical departure from the system of government so persistently adhered to by the young King's predecessor. The British Cabinet, which looked with distrust on the ascendency of French influence brought about by the success of the Franco-Sardinian arms, was inclined to favor the preservation of the Bourbon Dynasty, provided such support be rendered consistent with the nation's unvarying attitude as the advocate of Constitutional liberties. Russia and Prussia viewed with alarm the eventual destruction of the treaties of 1815, and the dangers of Napoleonic supremacy in the Peninsula, should the upholders of Murat be triumphant. Napoleon III. himself, realizing that the sentiment of Europe must be against him in such an attempt to emulate the Imperialism of his uncle, and desirous of preserving the confidence of England, instructed his Minister at Naples to join his diplomatic colleagues in urging Francis to recognize the altered conditions of the political arena, by spontaneously granting his subjects the desired reforms. Such an understanding was, however, supremely distasteful to the advanced Liberals, who looked to National Unity, and to that alone, for the alleviation of the existing evils in the Peninsula. Nor was such a solution any more acceptable to the Republicans of whom Mazzini was then still the revered and magnetic leader.

Glancing at the political situation in Europe at this moment (May and June, 1859), it seems incredible that Francis and his advisers should have hesitated to adopt a course so patently indicated for the preservation of the Throne. Yet Francis hastened his fate with

the committal of an initial error which could
but alienate the sympathies of well-wishers,
and destroy the prospects of substantial support either at home or abroad.

In a proclamation issued almost immediately
after the funeral ceremonies, the young King
lauded to the skies the political and administrative wisdom of his father, "that great
and pious Monarch whose virtues could never
be sufficiently extolled," and gave it to be
clearly understood that no modifications, in a
Liberal sense, would be made in the line of
policy hitherto pursued. It is claimed by
apologists of the Bourbon Dynasty, that Francis
had indeed contemplated a different programme, and that he actually laid before his
Ministers on the occasion of their first meeting
the draft of a proclamation providing for the
convocation of the electoral colleges ; the
special conditions under which his august
father had deemed it advisable to suspend the
Constitution having, in his estimation, now
ceased to exist. Francis is represented, by
these same apologists, as reluctantly yielding
such personal inclinations " to the wider experience in affairs of State " possessed by his advisers, to whom such a course was distasteful,
as involving the disapproval of Austria. There
is no valid historical authority for such asser-

tions, which are, moreover, totally at variance with the irresolute and timid character of the young Sovereign.

Acting on the advice of his father, Francis, after some hesitation, and the temporary employment of Troja as chief of the Government, called to his councils the aged General Filangieri, Prince of Satriano. The advantages of a wide experience were certainly not lacking to the hoary old soldier, when, at the age of seventy-five, he undertook the guidance of the destinies of a discredited and tottering Dynasty, surrounded by enemies and undermined by dissensions affecting its very vitals. Filangieri had fought at Austerlitz, and upon the glorious fields of France, Italy and Spain ; had served Joseph Bonaparte in Naples and in Spain ; had been aide-de-camp to Murat, and a representative of his diplomacy. To him Ferdinand owed the reconquest of Sicily in 1849 : a task he had undertaken with considerable reluctance. Thoroughly imbued with the spirit of progress ; a modern, in his political convictions and sympathies, he was, nevertheless, devoted to the Bourbons, and loyal to his oath—a soldier's oath, untainted by partisanship. Unfortunately Filangieri found himself surrounded by colleagues in office whose influence over the King completely paralyzed the vigorous initia-

tive he realized as imperative to avert a catastrophe. Hampered on all sides by the jealous
bureaucracy of the military and civil adminis-
trations, which resented any interference with
abuses which had with long immunity come to
be considered as privileges ; openly antagonized
by the Court party, headed by the Queen
Mother ; and without possessing the real confidence of the King ; it is hardly surprising
that his efforts proved powerless to cope with
the complicated, and extremely grave, political problems demanding prompt solution. He
did indeed induce Francis to condone the sentences of a few of the political martyrs who
had not been included in the decrees of December 27, 1858, and March 18, 1859 ; but they
were immediately pestered by such unbearable
restrictions and vexations that a voluntary exile
alone remained possible.

Writing a few months later (March 17,
1860), Lord Malmesbury, in his " Memoirs of
an Ex-Minister," says : " Naples is in a dreadful state. The tyranny of the present King far
exceeds that of his father, and the exaspera-
tion is so great that a revolution may take place
at any moment. But events in the north of
Italy have much to say to these feelings, and
naturally encourage the Neapolitans to imitate
them."

Filangieri had from the outset realized the vast importance of the events taking place in the north, and was prepared to neutralize their consequences by concessions calculated to make comparisons between the two Governments less invidious. Consequently he would gladly have seen his Sovereign lay aside the injurious adherence to his father's system of isolation, and frankly accept the proffered friendship of Piedmont. The importance attached to Count Salmour's mission, and the sympathies of his subjects therewith, had been very clearly demonstrated to Francis through the public reception offered the Sardinian Envoy on his arrival at Naples. On the evening of his advent many thousands of cards were left at his hotel, while the enthusiasm of the crowds which thronged the adjacent thoroughfares broke all bounds in its wild exultation. Several arrests were made, but the weakness and indecision of the Government were manifest. Count Salmour's official reception was courteous, but every effort was made to deprive it of the significance attributed to it by the public. In order to avoid a monster demonstration, said to be in preparation, to greet the diplomat on the occasion of his visit of ceremony to the Palace of Capodimonte, Francis decided to meet his guest in Naples. Filangieri and Francis himself were

deeply impressed by the proposals formulated
by the Sardinian Envoy.   Palestro and Magenta
(June 4), which latter battle liberated Lombardy, had considerably shaken the confidence
professed by the Neapolitan Court as to the
ultimate success of the arms of the Dual Monarchy, and Francis showed signs of wavering.
The news of the victory of Magenta had called
forth an imposing demonstration at Naples,
and undoubtedly suggested the substitution of
Filangieri for Troja in the direction of affairs ;
which substitution might well be considered in
the light of a concession.   With the arrival of
Count Salmour and the knowledge of his frequent colloquies with General Filangieri, the
rumor spread that the alliance was practically
decided upon.   To defeat this end one of the
strangest, most incongruous, and withal unconscious, coalitions of history was forced into
existence.   Fighting for diametrically conflicting ends, both parties united with the sole
object of rendering impossible the conclusion
of the obnoxious alliance.   On the one hand
the Queen Mother, the Princes of the Blood,
the Court party and the powerful " Camarilla,"
contending for the principles of Absolutism,
and an alliance with Austria ; on the other the
Unionists at all costs, who saw in the projected
alliance the ruin, or at least the indefinite

postponement, of their cherished hopes. By the former irresistible pressure was brought to bear on the unhappy Francis, whose characteristic vacillation and suspicious timidity made him an easy prey, and who, thoroughly terrified by the dread consequences conjured up by the "Camarilla," allowed the golden opportunity to slip through his fingers. By the Unionists, and the whole swarm of revolutionary exiles congregated at Turin, Cavour was overwhelmed with bitter denunciation for the attempted abandonment of a policy they had been led to believe he vigorously advocated.

Before war had broken out between the Franco-Sardinian allies and Austria, and while European diplomacy was still frantically striving to avert the threatened crisis, Lord Loftus, Her Majesty's Ambassador at Vienna, in an interview with M. de Buol, had endeavored to persuade the Minister of the paramount necessity for the cessation of intervention in the affairs of such Italian States as were not under the political control of Austria—an intervention which could only encourage warlike sentiment and revolutionary intrigues. To all such arguments Count de Buol emphatically replied : "Do you suppose, my lord, that the option of peace or war is in the hands of the various Governments ? It is in the hands of the

Mazzinians, in the nets of whom England herself is taken ; without knowing it, she is playing the game of the revolutionary party."

How far this was literally true it is impossible to say ; certain it is, however, that in the present instance the Mazzinians, in conjunction with the Liberals, were able to secure the co-operation of one neutral State to the limited extent deemed necessary for the furtherance of their objects ; a co-operation perfectly legitimate, however, and in absolute harmony with the Liberalist theories officially in practice within its territory.   Yielding to the representations of the revolutionary commission which had been despatched to Berne, the Swiss Confederation requested of the Neapolitan Government that the title of Swiss Guards be withdrawn from the mercenary regiments in its pay ; at the same time forbidding the further use of the Cantonal arms which had ornamented their banners since 1829.   Major Latour, who was sent from Switzerland with these instructions, received the moral support, not only of the French and English Ministers at Naples, but also the native officers, who looked on the existence of the privileged Swiss regiments as a slur put upon their loyalty and valor.   The mercenaries were readily persuaded by interested parties that the decision of the Confederation implied, not only the loss of their ancient privileges, but even the forfeiture of their rights as citizens of the Republic.

This proved a sufficient incentive for insurrection. On the evening of June seventh, a company of the Second Regiment (there were four in all) mutinied, and reinforced by their infuriated comrades in the various barracks, seized their banners, and killing or wounding such of their officers as attempted to impede or restrain them, marched forth with beating drums and wild cries towards the Palace of Capodimonte. The noisy charge in the semidarkness through the silent streets, accompanied by reports of guns fired at random, and the din of hoarse voices vociferating in an unknown tongue, struck terror into the souls of the Neapolitans, who but vaguely realized that a military revolt was in progress. Rumors of the disturbance were carried to the Palace, but it was only when the mutineers reached the gates that the full import of the insurrection was understood. The portals were hastily closed, while Rear-Admiral Del Re, who was in command of the scant guard, prepared for the defence. Although it was about midnight the mutineers demanded to see the King, and insisted that their nationality as well as the preservation of the Cantonal arms on their banners be guaranteed them. The terror and confusion in the Palace was indescribable. The Queen Mother, who had been informed that a military revolt had broken out, quietly advised that the Swiss regiments be sent for ; but when told it was they who mutinied, turned pale and prepared for flight. It was believed that all four regiments had revolted, and that their object was to take the royal family prisoners. As there were no officers, or chiefs, a parley was difficult ; especially as the thousand or more fully armed men were in a state of the wildest excitement. Francis sent Admiral Del Re, accompanied by several officers of his household, to attempt to calm the men, authorizing him to inform the soldiers that, being favorably disposed towards them, he would consider their grievances, and meet them on the following morning on the Parade Ground.

Mollified by the royal assurances, the noisy band straggled off in the direction of Capodichino, discharging their guns in the air, and looting the wine shops along the route.

Meanwhile Generals Filangieri, Lanza, Garofalo and Nunziante were devising means to smother the dangerous outbreak and check the possible spread of an insurrection it was feared might become universal. Early next morning the mutineers were surrounded where they had encamped, and shot down by the artillery of the Thirteenth native regiment and that of their compatriots (the Fourth) which had remained loyal. Eighty were killed outright, about two hundred wounded, while two hundred sixty-two were taken prisoners. The rest having disbanded escaped to the outlying country. The impression caused by this massacre was tremendous and wide-spread. Nunziante was accused of having ordered the troops under his command to fire without giving the insurgents the option of surrender. This assertion was officially contradicted, and would indeed seem too barbarous for truth. The fact remains, however, that out of the attacking forces but two soldiers were wounded; this would seem to indicate that the mutineers were taken completely by surprise.

On the advice of Filangieri, and as a consequence of the incidents described, the Swiss regiments were declared disbanded, thus putting an end to an institution which had enjoyed the fullest confidence of the Throne for over thirty years.

That the disbanding of the Swiss Guards, rendered inevitable by the recent disaster, deprived the Crown of one of its most dreaded supports was universally and exultingly recognized by Liberals and revolutionists of every

shade.   The odium of the fierce carnage on the
Parade Ground was naturally laid at the door
of the hated Despot; although that Francis
was personally to blame for the excessive zeal
of Nunziante was not seriously credited even
by his foes.   The opportunity for making political capital out of the disgraceful occurrence
was, however, not one to be lost.   Undoubtedly
had Francis been consulted the brutal butchery
of an unofficered rabble of disgruntled mercenaries would never have been allowed, and the
incident would have passed unchallenged by
the world, or at most have excited a recrudes-
cence of protests from those who contended
that the Throne should dispense with a support
so derogatory to its dignity.

Shortly after the disappointing peace of Villafranca, Kossuth in a political memorandum,
in which he rapidly reviews the situation and the
possibilities it offers, wrote to Count Teleki in
reference to the neutrality of the King of
Naples : * " Would to Heaven that he moved !
It would not even be necessary to beat him,
because the mercenaries being abolished the
Neapolitan army within a fortnight would have
Garibaldi as its leader, and Italian unity would
be accomplished.   However, this intervention

* Chiala, Politica Segreta di Napoleone III. e di
Cavour.

of the Bourbon does not seem in the least probable."

Others besides Kossuth appreciated the significance of the revolt of the seventh of June. Francis had no more confidence than his father had entertained before him in the impeccable loyalty of the Neapolitan troops, while it was speedily made manifest to him that he individually was completely lacking in that personal prestige which had compelled unquestioning, if reluctant, obedience to Ferdinand's authority. The loss of the Swiss regiments was consequently an irreparable one, and although an effort was made to replace them by a wholesale importation of Bavarian and Austrian recruits, the defection was recognized as a serious menace to an authority already so deeply undermined by conspiracies extending to the domestic hearth, and permeating the family circle of the Sovereign.

Nevertheless the extreme youth and inexperience of the Sovereigns precluded the supposition that affairs of State, however weighty, should completely absorb them. It must be remembered that Francis was barely twenty-three, while his bride had but just passed her eighteenth birthday. The etiquette of Court mourning had enforced a period of seclusion and abstinence, which had now come to an

end.   On July 24 the ceremonies and festivities
attending the young King's accession to the
Throne were inaugurated with a State visit to
the shrine of San Gennaro, the Patron Saint of
Naples ; when the miracle of the liquefaction
of the Saint's blood was accomplished with
more than usual promptitude, and duly interpreted as a propitious omen for the prosperity
of the opening reign.   Then followed the solemn but gorgeous function of kissing hands,
which was carried out with all the rigorous
rules of the etiquette of a bygone age.   For
many years Court pageants of any description
had been rare.   Ferdinand, after the troubles
of 1849, had withdrawn more and more to the
comparative privacy of Caserta and Gaeta, and
dispensed with all superfluous official recep-
tions.   Deeply immersed in the business of
government, which, as has been described, centred in his hands, and to the most minute and
trivial details of which he gave his personal
attention, it was manifestly impossible to bestow much time on display, even had his tastes
lain in that direction.   Had Ferdinand so desired there is little doubt but that he could, in
the earlier years of his reign, have won back the
Neapolitan aristocracy, as a class, from the
isolation to which they had been self-con-
demned since the Bourbon restoration.   This

isolation, more apparent than real, had been brought about by the reception extended to Joachim Murat. Ferdinand, however, deemed it a prudent policy to hold aloof ; believing it expedient to foster the illusion that, dispensing with the support of the aristocracy, the Crown rested on the surer foundation of the popular suffrage of the masses, with whom it was thus brought in more democratic contact. The reasoning was subtle, if fallacious, and gave rise to misconceptions and confusion on the part of leaders of the Second Empire in their intrigues concerning the destinies of the Kingdom of Naples. Because as a class the Neapolitan aristocracy had welcomed Murat in the beginning of the century, it did not follow that Lucien would be similarly received forty odd years later, when the theory of national independence, and, above all, of Italian unity under an Italian Prince, had become a burning issue. That great discontent existed amongst the more enlightened members of the aristocracy was evinced by the popularity of the Count of Syracuse, whose open hostility to the Court made his salons the rendezvous of malcontents of all parties, and in which they rubbed shoulders with Liberals of such advanced opinions that they closely resembled Republicans. The fluctuating importance of the Neapolitan " Mu-

rattisti " was, however, regulated and controlled
by the rise or decline of French influences in
the Peninsula, despite the undoubted encouragement the movement received from a very
restricted circle of Italian sympathizers.   The
aristocracy was, however, without political
training or aspirations, and as completely out
of touch with popular sentiment as with Court
influence.

With the accession of Francis many individual aristocratic malcontents returned to
their allegiance, or at least took advantage of
the fêtes and gaieties to appear at Court.   Nevertheless the bulk of those attending the gala
performances at the huge San Carlo theatre, or
the ceremonies at the Palace, belonged to the
official world, the few exceptions being those
whose love of pleasure, or apathetic lack of
political convictions, made their surroundings
a matter of indifference.   To a great extent
the opposition of the aristocracy was traditional, having its origin in the loss of certain
privileges, of which with the return of the
Bourbons they had been deprived.   That political prejudices were not very deep-rooted is
evinced by the fact that many who would have
welcomed a Murat accepted Court positions
under Victor Emmanuel ; while several of
those who had occupied high posts under the

Bourbons were equally desirous of discharging similar functions in connection with the House of Savoy. This is not only true of the aristocracy, but applies also to many leading Neapolitan statesmen, as well as army and navy officers of all ranks, and lends a semblance of truth to the cry of "Treason" raised by the Absolutists who remained staunch to their allegiance to the fallen Dynasty. In Sicily this generalization did not hold good; many of the most ancient and aristocratic families were also foremost in their intelligent eagerness for the political welfare of their country. In 1848 and 1849 the flower of the nobility fought side by side with the representatives of the humbler classes for the ·freedom of the island. The Sicilians, although availing themselves of every occasion for revolt against the Bourbon yoke, never having been under the dominion of Murat, were impervious to the blandishments of the conspirators who sought the re-establishment of Bonapartist supremacy. Given a Murat and a Francis II., they remained Legitimists by force of habit; but when a third alternative was presented in the person of the "Honest King" of Savoy, there was no doubt in which direction their sympathies lay.

CHAPTER VIII.

Filangieri's political sympathies.—Napoleon III.: his aims and policy.—Cavour's policy.—Plan for partition of Papal States. —Count Salmour's failure,—Villafranca.—Cavour resigns. —Rumors from Sicily.—Filangieri's resignation.—His retirement at Sorrento.—Blunders of the Administration.— Cavour to Marquis d'Azeglio.—Lord Palmerston on Cavour.—An Italian Confederation.—Napoleon's embarrassments.—Sir James Hudson and his associates.—English policy in Italian question.—Opinions of Prince Consort.— Diplomacy at Turin.—Marquis Villamarina goes to Naples. —His instructions.—His report on situation at Naples.

THE glorious adventures and triumphs of his youth had imbued Filangieri with very pronounced Bonapartist sympathies. As a veteran of the Napoleonic wars he was cosmopolitan, in the broadest and best sense of the word ; as a politician and a statesman he clearly foresaw that a change of front and the abandonment of the narrow principles of the internal and foreign policy followed by Ferdinand, could alone save the Dynasty and insure the autonomy of the Kingdom. For the accomplishment of this end the friendship and support of the Western Powers, especially France, was of prime importance. It needed but a modicum

154

of statesmanship to appreciate the fact that
the interests of Napoleon III. could profit
neither by the obliteration of the Kingdom of
Naples from the map of Europe, nor its absorption, under the pretext of suppressing revolutionary anarchy, in the all-devouring maw
of Piedmont.   To secure the support of Louis
Napoleon, deeply committed to the principle
of Italian nationalization (not unity), two concessions were imperative : the total and unconditional severance from Austrian influences ;
and the immediate grant, or revival, of a Constitution framed in accordance with the liberal
theories of the day.   General Roguet, sent by
Napoleon III. to congratulate Francis on his
accession, had special instructions to urge the
acceptance of this programme, and was ener-
getically seconded by the French Minister who
had returned to his post on the resumption of
diplomatic relations.

Reference has already been made to the alliance with Piedmont, which Count Cavour
desired not only as a protection against Austrian supremacy but also as a check to Bonapartist ambitions in Tuscany.   After Magenta
a territorial manipulation involving the transformation of the political geography of Italy
was suggested, and received, it is said, the
sanction of Napoleon III. and Lord Palmerston.

Piedmont was to be allowed to annex Lombardy, the Duchies and the Legations as far south as the River Cattolica; while to the King of Naples would be given Umbria and the Marches. The Pope would thus be relegated to the so-called Patrimony of Saint Peter; a dominion considered ample for the exercise of his temporal prerogatives.

In the Council of Ministers Filangieri could count on no majority to advance his proposals, and he was fully aware of the insurmountable repugnance Francis would oppose to any project involving a rupture of friendly relations with the Holy See. Tempting as was the bait offered, and thoroughly convinced as he was of the advantage of gaining the good-will of his powerful accomplices, Francis, who had been prepared by Troja for the proposed spoliation of the Papal dominions, indignantly refused to become a party to so " sacrilegious a scheme," and promptly reported the iniquitous proposal to Rome. Bearing in mind the quasi-sacerdotal education Francis had received, together with his mysticism and the apathetic fatalism of his character, it is difficult to understand how such a programme could ever have been expected to receive his support.

The rebuff administered to Count Salmour on this occasion destroyed all probability of his success in the negotiations for an offensive and defensive alliance, and he took his departure amidst the enthusiastic plaudits of the advanced Liberals and Unionists, who had looked upon the possibility of such an alliance with considerable alarm.

Meanwhile portentous events were rapidly succeeding each other in Northern Italy. The Legations rose in rebellion against the Papal authority, and the Rulers of Parma and Modena were deposed by their subjects. The provisional Governments of Emilia and Tuscany were established, and the unsatisfactory peace of Villafranca had driven Cavour from the political arena. Wild rumors of a revolutionary invasion of the Neapolitan territory by Garibaldi and his dreaded hordes began to circulate, while vague reports of Sicilian agitation reached the capital. Filangieri, realizing that not a moment was to be lost, boldly presented to Francis, on September 4th, the draft of the Constitution prepared by Manna; making its acceptance conditional to his retention of office. The King, timid and vacillating, fearing to risk a decision, yet harried by the threats of the " Camarilla," desired a further postponement, urging the peril of so radical a departure from the conservatism of his father. Whereupon Filangieri unhesitat-

ingly presented his resignation as President of
the Council and Minister of War. Although
Francis did not unconditionally accept the
tendered resignation, he signified his willingness that the Minister should temporarily seek
a much required rest, replacing him provi-
sionally with Raffaele Carrascosa, and nominat-
ing one of Murat's old Lieutenants, Gaetano
Garofalo, to take charge of the War Office.

Filangieri now betook himself to the seclusion of his villa at Sorrento, over the door of
which he caused the following placard to be
affixed : " This notice denies entrance to all ;
for it is either a proof that I am out, or that I
will receive nobody."

Although pleading advanced age and ill-
health, as an excuse for his withdrawal from
active participation in public affairs, it is probable that Filangieri at first contemplated no
more than a voluntary temporary retirement,
as a protest against the rejection of the policy
of reform and diplomatic negotiation he advocated. Thoroughly disheartened, however, by
the failure of his plans for the rescue of the
Throne from the perils he so keenly appreciated, as well as by the continual blunders of the
Crown, and those who had succeeded him in
the administration of affairs, he was gradually
led to the conviction that it would be impossi-

ble to retrieve the errors committed, and therefore continued to insist that he should be relieved of all official responsibility. It was not
until March 16, 1860, that Francis, yielding
to his persistent entreaties, finally and formally
exonerated him from the nominal discharge of
the duties of President of the Council and
Minister of War.

In the interval, blunder after blunder had
still further estranged the sympathies of the
nations an alliance with which offered the only
hope of salvation, and widened the gulf between the Government and People of the Kingdom of the Two Sicilies. Aiossa, a man whose
ignorance and violence were proverbial, had
been entrusted with the direction of the Police,
and had forthwith revived the excesses and
persecutions which had signallized the reign of
Ferdinand. The " Camarilla," again triumphant, was omnipotent in those branches of the
public service whose agents came in direct contact with the citizen, and as a natural consequence the friction and mutual animosity daily
increased.

Not satisfied with declining the friendly
proposals of France, England and Piedmont,
Francis had excited their suspicious resentment by the formation of a military camp on
the frontiers of the Papal States ; and by allow-

ing it to be surmised that the establishment of
the same was not merely intended for the defence of his territory, but also designed as an
efficient support to the Pontifical troops, should
the latter be assailed. This army corps, which
had left Naples on September 14, 1859, under the command of General Pianell, had been
preceded by profuse assurances of filial reverence for his Holiness, which were universally
interpreted as equivalent to an avouchment
of eventual co-operation with the forces of
the Holy See. The Piedmontese Government
promptly demanded an explanation as to the
scope of the military demonstration, and received in reply assurances that the expedition
was intended merely to insure the inviolability
of Neapolitan territory in view of existing
political conditions. Nevertheless, and in spite
of this plausible explanation, the incident
caused considerable annoyance, for it was generally conceded that the Neapolitan Government was not sincere in its protestations, and
that the troops were destined for a very different service should occasion present.

The Peace of Villafranca had apparently
left Austria but slightly disabled. With
Venice, the fortresses of Peschiera, Mantova,
and the other strongholds of the Quadrilateral,
she could still strike terror to Italian hearts.

Austrian influences at the Vatican were also still formidable in spite of recent loss of prestige. Cavour's resignation at Villafranca had been considered as a national calamity by the Liberals, although as a matter of fact, owing to his more complete individual liberty of action, the Count was enabled to inspire his personal agents throughout the Peninsula with greater freedom from restraint than when in office. His retirement was moreover universally recognized as temporary, and his return to power merely a question of expediency. In the meantime the onus of reconciling a discontented public opinion to the unsatisfactory peace negotiations fell upon the shoulders of Rattazzi.

In announcing his retirement to the Marquis d'Azelio, Cavour writes on July 16, 1859 : "Je suis la bête-noire de la diplomate. You have been able to convince yourself of this during your last visit to Paris. Walewski detests me for a thousand reasons, and above all on account of the sarcasms and 'quodlibets' we indulged in with Clarendon over the Treaty of Paris. Cowley has nervous spasms when he sees me. I think I would cause a nightmare to the Austrian Plenipotentiaries. In short, I am the man least calculated to obtain concessions from the diplomatists. These gentlemen would

11

refuse to the man what they might perhaps grant the Country, provided it were represented by a sympathetic person."

As evinced by the following letter from Lord Palmerston to Lord Cowley, then Ambassador in Paris, England was fully prepared for the inevitable changes in the political geography of Italy. Writing from London under date of August 22, 1859, the English Prime Minister says : "I know that all the partisans of arbitrary government in Europe represent me as the bitter enemy of Austria, and I wish whenever you hear this you would deny its truth. I am an enemy to bad government, to oppression and tyranny ; and, unfortunately, the Austrian rule in Italy, as elsewhere, has been marked by those evils. I am an enemy, therefore, to the bad system of Austrian Government, and heartily wish all Italians to be freed from the Austrian yoke. . . . Much is said at Paris of what are called the intrigues of Cavour—unjustly, I think. If it is meant that he has labored for the enlargement of Piedmont and the freedom of Italy from foreign yoke, and from Austrian rule, he will in history be called a patriot ; but the means he has employed may be good or bad. I know not what they have been ; but the end in view is, I am sure, the good of Italy. The people of the Duchies have as good a right to change their rulers as the people of England, France, Belgium, and Sweden ; and the annexation of the Duchies to Piedmont would be an unmixed good for Italy, and for France, and for Europe. I hope Walewski will not sway the mind of the Emperor to make the enslaving of Italy the end of a drama which opened with the declaration : 'Italy free from the Alps to the Adriatic,' and : 'l'Italie rendue à elle-même.' " *

Villafranca made it manifest that Italy must work out her own salvation ; and Italians were in no mood to passively await the adoption of the curtailed programme of national independence laid before the Congress of Zürich. In his letter of October 20, 1859, Napoleon III. had informed Victor Emmanuel that the demand would be made that Parma and Piacenza be reunited to Piedmont, that territory being strategically indispensable to it. But the rule of the Duchess of Parma was merely to be transferred to Modena, and Tuscany restored to the Grand-Duke Ferdinand, with provision for the introduction of certain liberal reforms. According to the ideas of the Emperor, as expressed in this letter, essential conditions for the regeneration of Italy necessitated the composition of several independent States

* Ashley's " Life of Lord Palmerston."

united by a federal organization, each of these
States being free to adopt its own Constitution
and reforms. This Confederation would, it
was asserted, consecrate the principle of Italian
nationality ; it would, moreover, be under one
flag, one Customs regulation, and one system
of coinage. The Central Government was to
be in Rome, and formed of representatives from
each State, under the Honorary Presidency of
the Pope. No mention is made in the letter
of the scheme for the partial spoliation of the
Holy See to the mutual advantage of Piedmont
and the Two Sicilies, and it is difficult to understand how Napoleon proposed to reconcile this
latter scheme with the political necessity of
retaining the support of the Catholic voters at
home. It is probable, however, that Napoleon
III. had as little faith in the power of the half-
measures propounded for the consideration of
the Congress of Zürich, to quench the dangerous fires he had fanned into flame, as he had
in the strength of the colorless Francis, to
withstand the fierce opposition of the clerical
element and "Camarilla" to a political venture
so at variance with the sacred traditions of his
Dynasty.

The Emperor's enigmatic "We shall now
see what the Italians can do by themselves,"
addressed to Victor Emmanuel at Villafranca,

was almost an incentive to push ahead and let
consequences take care of themselves. France
must temporarily wash her hands of an undertaking which unforeseen contingencies on the
Rhine frontier had dangerously complicated ;
but the fury of Italian Liberals to whose cause
the Emperor was personally deeply committed
must be appeased by some well-sounding, yet
not too substantial, sop. In other words, Napoleon found himself compelled to hedge ; and
to retrieve his lost popularity at home, while
he circumvented the baffled Italians by the aid
of a diplomatic paradox, which the laws of
Probabilities might be counted upon to render
innocuous. Cavour deeply chagrined, yet realizing the futility of further reliance or material
aid from France, readily grasped at the alternative, appreciating the advantages to be gained
by purely Italian initiative in a question of
national supremacy.

The rumor that Francis, even at this late
date, under pressure of the " Camarilla," and
released from the nominal restraint of the
presence of Filangieri, meditated an alliance
with the Pope, and the vanquished, yet still
formidable, Hapsburgs, was not wholly improbable, and justified the ruffled susceptibilities of Piedmont. While the perplexities
arising out of the projected annexations were

rife, Naples must be closely watched. The strict neutrality of the Southern Kingdom was absolutely essential to the furtherance of northern ambitions. Hence the uneasiness evinced at Turin by the news of the concentration of Neapolitan troops on the Papal frontier. That Francis only required to be given enough rope in order to hang himself was confidently anticipated; but the consequences of the suicide might be attended by considerable risk to those who had too complacently furnished the cord; while it was especially desired to avoid conflict with parties whose bonds of amity, or mutual interests, would give countenance to a claim in the disposal of the deceased's estate.

England was ready enough to lend a hand surreptitiously in schemes calculated to diminish French or Austrian prestige in the Neapolitan and Papal States. Sir James Hudson, Her Majesty's Envoy at Turin, personally a warm and trusted friend of Italy, and advocate of unity, frequently entertained political exiles from various Italian States, especially Mazzini. Lord Hubert de Burgh, at that time (1859–60), Secretary of the English Legation, jocosely remarked one evening to his French colleague d'Ideville : " I have just dined with Sir James. We were ten at table, and with the exception of the Minister and myself, *all* were under sentence of death. I still shudder!'' At the same time Her Majesty's Government was not prepared at that period to openly antagonize either of the Powers above mentioned by a frank and explicit declaration of policy in regard to Italian affairs. Mr. Henry Elliot, the English Minister at the Neapolitan Court, had received general instructions to urge the necessity of reforms, and to second the French Envoy in his endeavors to obtain such ; but this action was prompted rather by humanitarian than political considerations. No very definite line of policy had been established by either Whig or Tory Cabinets with regard to Italian affairs, beyond the traditional, although spasmodic, encouragement of Liberalism, or rather Constitutionalism, exacted by an indignant public opinion whenever any especially virulent outbreak of tyranny was forced into notice by the exiles who made London their headquarters. The moral support, or frown, of Great Britain, had, however, on more occasions than one influenced the destinies of Italy. The positive veneration entertained by Count Cavour for the political institutions of England, and his continued efforts to retain the sympathies and good-will of her leading statesmen, is demonstrated in his private correspondence with the Sardinian

Minister in London, the Marquis Massimo d'Azeglio. Although generally admired and esteemed in the English political world, Cavour never succeeded in gaining the confidence of Prince Albert, who entertained an invincible mistrust of the Italian statesman. "This feeling," writes Sir Theodore Martin in his Life of the Prince Consort, " seems in some degree to have prevented the Prince from making full allowance for the difficulties with which Cavour had to contend in accomplishing his great task. It would in all probability have been altered by the fuller knowledge of the secret history of the time, which has since become available. . . ."

The political bargain of Plombières by which the Princess Clotilde of Savoy was given in marriage to Prince Jerome, cousin of the Emperor, had produced a deplorable impression at the English Court, where also the intrigues between Cavour and Kossuth, lending countenance to the insurrections plotted in Hungary, and on the Danube, were viewed with suspicious aversion.

In spite of diplomatic squabbles, or compromising incidents, English public opinion was almost universally in sympathy with the great Italian Statesman who was making such a plucky fight, against what appeared overwhelming odds, for the diffusion of the Constitutional Liberties so dear to the Anglo-Saxon ; and was consequently disinclined to pry too closely into the possibly accessory schemes for territorial aggrandizement, which so troubled foreign politicians.

Critical moments there certainly were ; while delicate situations not infrequently arose, for the satisfactory solution of which no small credit is due both d'Azeglio in London, and Sir James Hudson at Turin. To the latter Nicomede Bianchi offers a well-merited tribute in his " Politique du Comte de Cavour de 1852 à 1861." " It will certainly not be superfluous," he writes, " to add that the diplomatic activity of Sir James Hudson, during the entire period that he occupied the post of English Minister near King Victor Emmanuel, was to Italy of eminently practical utility. Under all circumstances, and under the most difficult conditions, he always merited the esteem and confidence which the King, and the most Liberalist of his Ministers, placed in him ; as well as that of the most influential and most esteemed chiefs of the Italian National Party."

The Chevalier Canofari, Neapolitan Envoy to Piedmont, was fully aware of the diplomatic influences, and Nationalist ambitions, at work in Turin, ample details of which he forwarded to his Government.   But Filangieri alone read correctly the signs of the times, and recognized the urgency of concluding the proffered friendship before rapidly shifting interests should make it advisable for Sardinia to dispense with Italian alliances.   From his solitary retreat at Sorrento the old statesman gazed with mournful eyes on the apathetic indifference and besotted intolerance which were hurrying the Throne to destruction ; and the young Sovereign, he would so willingly have saved, to exile.

The Government of Piedmont, in spite of the failure of Count Salmour's mission, could not accept the refusal as final.   The diplomacy of Europe seemed at this moment to be in league against Victor Emmanuel's reaping any considerable material advantages from the late war. It is true the populations of the Duchies, as well as of the Romagna and Marches, clamored for admission into the fold ; but the Congress assembled at Zürich had under consideration eventualities which Piedmont could, in the present crisis, not openly ignore.   A period of uncertainty must be tided over—a period fraught with dangerous possibilities ; arising both from the patriotic zeal of the victors, and the subtle intrigue of disappointed ambitions. As an offset to these, as well as offering the surest guarantee against further foreign intervention in the purely domestic affairs of Italy, the Neapolitan alliance seemed the most satisfactory solution of the problem. Once such an agreement concluded by the two Great Powers of the Peninsula, the details of the partition and distribution of the minor States might form the subject for amicable mutual negotiation. Something must be yielded if aught were to be gained.

With this end in view, as well as for purposes of trusty observation, it was decided to confide the contemplated negotiations to the Marquis de Villamarina. The diplomatic experience and personal attributes of the late Sardinian Minister to Paris designated him as especially fitted to undertake the extremely delicate duties which were now assigned him. Although originally recalled from the Imperial Court to superintend the reorganization of the civil administration of Lombardy, the diplomatic services now required of him, ungrateful as they must have appeared, were nevertheless courageously, if reluctantly, undertaken. That the scope of the mission, organized in a spirit of loyal amity, and for the attainment of reciprocal advantages, became later liable to the accusation of duplicity, was due primarily to the inconceivable shortsightedness of the Bourbon Court. The relentless pressure of political combinations, unforeseen a few months previously, could not in fairness be construed as a reflection on the good faith of the Marquis de Villamarina in his dealings with the King of the Two Sicilies. In his documentary History of European Diplomacy in Italy, Nicomede Bianchi cites " in extenso " the instructions imparted to Villamarina by General Dabormida, at that moment Minister for Foreign Affairs at Turin. These enjoined on the Sardinian Envoy to conduct himself with dignity, prudence and tact, in his relations with the various political factions. While advocating the introduction of liberal reforms, no undue pressure was to be exercised, and no interference attempted in the domestic affairs of the State. Neither inciting nor restraining either political party, the Minister should use his influence towards fostering the natural and spontaneous development of principles more in accord with the altered conditions of social and political requirements, which necessarily affected all the Princes and all the States of Italy ; and induce the Bourbons to calmly and patiently accept the inevitable modifications of government demanded by the times. All this was to be accomplished without social disturbance or political revolt ; the example of Piedmont being constantly placed before the eyes of Ruler and subjects, as an object lesson of the benefits to be derived from Constitutional Government. Thus indirectly a parallel was to be drawn between the partisans of Austria and Absolutism, and the representatives of Italy and Liberty ; and the responsibility of the rejection of the alliance, and its possible consequences, laid at the door of King Francis and his Government.

In his eloquent refutation of the charges of duplicity, advanced by his political enemies, Villamarina writes in the " Opinione " of April 26, 1861 : " I do not speak of the most conciliatory dispositions I carried to Naples, in accordance with the orders and instructions I had received from my Sovereign and from his Government. I will not mention the honest, frank and sincere manner in which I executed those orders and instructions in the negotiations I had the honor to undertake with the Court of Naples : without ever attempting to shake the loyalty of others, I yet placed my own beyond the insidious intrigues of the ever-alert enemies and adversaries of Italy, who swarmed in the Councils of that King, and constituted the domestic influences which surrounded him."

Addressing the Senate on April 9 of the same year, Villamarina draws the following word-picture of the Neapolitan Administration : " Corrupt and corrupting, it was organized thus : a people debased ; held in ignorance and the most revolting brutality : a large army, well uniformed, well paid, of fine appearance, but inspired by absolutely anti-national senti- ments, and trained to look upon the foreigner as a friend, and to regard the fellow-citizen as an enemy, and as such to be oppressed and de- spoiled. No development of commerce ; none of industries, nor of agriculture : all doors closed to this unfortunate people, save one alone, that of official life : and that not for the formation of honest employees, but rewarding the bad and corrupting the good, in order to win over the greatest number of satellites to the ferocious despotism and cruel oppression practised. Each official received a modest salary, but each knew that he could steal with impunity, and for these reasons the offices were sought after : not in order to serve the State and benefit Society, but on account of the fat increment afforded by fraudulent con- tracts and malversions of all kinds."

The picture is a dark one, and some allow- ance should be made for the righteous indig- nation of the speaker. A glimpse at the ad- ministrative branches of the Kingdom under Ferdinand II. has been afforded in the earlier pages of this study : consequently the reader will be able to draw his own conclusions con-

cerning the accuracy of what appears a rather
sweeping statement ; reproduced here, however,
as exemplifying the sentiments prevailing
amongst a considerable number of persons high
placed in the official world.

CHAPTER IX.

Efforts to secure alliance.—Cavour returns to office.—His correspondence with Villamarina.—Prudential policy.—Cession of Nice and Savoy.—The reasons for same.—Villamarina's reports.—Distrust and opposition excited by cession of territory.—Cavour's relations with Kossuth and Hungarian patriots.—Cavour and European Diplomacy.—Victor Emmanuel's letter to King of Naples.—Determined opposition to alliance.

DURING the opening weeks of 1860—a year fraught with the direst consequences to the tottering Neapolitan Throne—the Marquis de Villamarina labored incessantly to bring about a mutual understanding between the Courts of Turin and Naples. Of the futility of his efforts to secure an alliance, or even a semblance of conciliation, the Minister was quickly persuaded. The intrigues woven at Court and directed against the principles of National Independence, together with the plots hatched in conjunction with the Vatican for the frustration of the Piedmontese negotiations, confirmed the diplomatist in his conviction that no lessons had been learnt from recent events in the States of Northern Italy, and the misfortunes of those Rulers who sought to oppose the manifestation of popular aspirations towards National Liberty. In addition his task was still further complicated by the agitation of certain enthusiasts whose noisy clamor alarmed the susceptibilities not only of Francis, but of European Diplomacy.

Count Cavour returned to power on the twentieth of January, and it was indeed fortunate for Italy that he again held the tiller.

In his letter to d'Azeglio of July 16, 1859, written on the day of his retirement from office, Cavour had said : " You are aware that the policy of the present Cabinet has always been frankly National ; that it had not in view the territorial aggrandizement of Piedmont, but the emancipation of Italy ; the establishment throughout the whole Peninsula of a wisely liberal system."

Was a modification of these views now advisable ? And must the obstinate refusal of Francis to come to terms with the generous Nationalist aspirations of the day, mean the removal of the chief obstacle to the establishment throughout the whole Peninsula of a " wisely liberal system " ? That Cavour already foresaw that his Royal Master must eventually occupy the Neapolitan Throne is incontestable ; but he was keenly aware that Europe, and first and foremost the French Emperor,

12

would strenuously oppose such ambitions. Just how far the Italian Statesman guided, or was guided, by the political events of the next three months it is hazardous to affirm.

That he was sincere in his desire for at least a temporary arrangement with the King of Naples there can be no doubt. "I strongly approve your prudence," he wrote Villamarina on February. 11, "and I agree with you that at the present moment it is of supreme importance to prevent any revolutionary movement in Italy." The old Italian proverb "chi va piano, va sano" fitted the negotiations he had in hand. The dread of undoing by the premature disclosure of inopportune ambitions the good work already fairly in course of accomplishment, was as strong as his desire to complete the mighty fabric of his dreams. None other but this past master in the arts of dissimulation—combining as he did the wile of the serpent and the boldness of the lion—could have safely steered through the perilous complications of the next few months. France had ceased active opposition to the annexation of Central Italy, now merely insisting that irrefragable evidence of the public sentiment should be forthcoming. This both Cavour and Ricasoli were determined to provide, and to carry their point in the face of the opposition of the French Emperor as well as the futile decrees of the Congress of Zürich, which had formally recognized the rights of the Sovereigns of Tuscany, Modena, and Parma, when it concluded its labors on November 10, 1859. Again, fortunately for Italian Unity, the Government of Lord Palmerston, now in power, was inclined to regard with benignity the spread of Constitutional liberties ; and this moral support, in conjunction with the inflexible persistency of Ricasoli, who would accept no compromise, or half-measures, finally turned the scales. Without the employment of force it was manifestly impossible for Napoleon to gainsay the decision of the Tuscan leaders, supported by unequivocal manifestations of popular sentiment.

True to the principles of his "politique de pourboire," as Bismarck had termed the Emperor's diplomacy, Napoleon, in spite of his voluntary renunciation of all such claims after the Peace of Villafranca, again broached the subject of the cession of Nice and Savoy as compensation for the territorial aggrandizement allowed Piedmont. Undoubtedly this was no surprise to Cavour ; and in anticipation of the immense eventual advantages to be gained he was fain to accede to the French pretensions with as good grace as possible.

Summoning what philosophy he can to his

aid, Cavour writes on February 12th to the Marquis d'Azeglio, in London : "Having persuaded France to undertake the Italian war in the name of the principle of nationalities ; having invoked for the last eight months the principle of deference to the wish of the people, especially when in harmony with the first ; we would not have contested on one side of the Alps what we upheld on the other. When France asked us what we would do if the great majority of the inhabitants of Savoy and Nice demanded union with the people speaking the same tongue, we answered that we did not traffic in populations : that we would neither sell nor exchange the smallest of our villages ; but that if the subjects of non-Italian races desired, as was said, to separate from us, we would certainly not restrain them by force."

On March 24th the treaty ceding Savoy and Nice to France was signed. As he took the pen from the hand of the French Plenipotentiary, Cavour cynically remarked : "Now you are our accomplices." In other words this signified that the price of the cession of territory to France was that Piedmont be allowed a free hand in the south. "The two principal men in Europe to-day are Napoleon and Cavour," said Monsieur Guizot. "The stakes are laid ; I back Monsieur de Cavour."

The French statesman was correct : that document bound the Emperor hand and foot, and delivered him into the power of his crafty ally. As a matter of form he might demur to the Sicilian expedition, and in the case of Naples, peevishly resent the unceremonious discard of Muratist ambitions, but beyond diplomatic protestations he was not likely to go.

Putting aside the purely sentimental considerations, in themselves of considerable importance, the loss to Piedmont was not of great material consequence. The abandonment of Nice seemed likely, however, to cause the Government embarrassment, as it aroused the furious resentment and violent opposition of Garibaldi, already a power to be reckoned with, who being a native of that town regarded the cession as a personal grievance.

Meanwhile Villamarina was patiently studying the situation in Naples, and slowly reaching the conclusions which proved of such inestimable value in the guidance of the policy emanating from Turin. To him Cavour appeals on March 30th for trustworthy information concerning the probable condition of public sentiment under certain political contingencies ; as well as regarding the relative strength of the Republicans, Annexationists and Muratists, throughout the realm. These are interesting as indicating a possible modification of policy, resulting from the signature of the treaty ceding Nice and Savoy, by which sacrifice it was hoped to commit the French Emperor to at least a tacit acquiescence in the purely Italian diplomacy of the Piedmontese Cabinet. "You know," he continues, "that I do not at all desire to force a premature issue of the Neapolitan question. I think, on the contrary, that it would suit us to have the existing condition of affairs prolonged some years. But I learn from a trustworthy source that even England despairs of the maintenance of the 'statu quo,' and it is, doubtless, in view of not improbable eventualities that she keeps her fleet in Neapolitan waters. I fear therefore that we shall soon be forced to adopt a plan which I would have liked to have had time to mature."

The reply forwarded by Villamarina, on April 14th, served as the basis for the subsequent diplomatic policy of Piedmont, until, owing to the bewilderingly rapid sequence of events, the studied policy of to-day gave way before the expediency of to-morrow. Viewed as such, a synopsis of the Envoy's opinions is pertinent.

The Marquis expressed himself deeply distrustful of the arguments advanced by Napo-

leon to secure Neapolitan intervention in the
Marches, and the consent of Piedmont to this
undertaking. In this scheme he thought he
recognized a double policy, the result of which
would prove a deception to his Government.
The guarantee of Austrian non-intervention,
except in the event of a revolution in Naples,
meant nothing, or rather meant everything, as
such revolution could be provoked at will by
the Austrian agents there, should it be deemed
opportune. Unless supported by armed intervention, an insurrection incited by French
agents could not result in the Emperor's favor.
Muratism, although not dangerous under existing circumstances, might become so should
the Emperor give that party frank and unequivocal support. In the event of such a
combination, the party would undoubtedly be
greatly strengthened by the adhesion of a large
body of indifferent or timid partisans who
would avail themselves of an opportunity to
cast in their lot with the strongest. To
Cavour's query concerning the possibility of
an annexationist movement such as had taken
place in Tuscany, Villamarina unhesitatingly
replied in the negative. He believed the army
to be with the King ; and the Government
amply strong enough to restrain the populace.
A revolution such as had recently broken out

in Sicily could alone dethrone the Bourbons of Naples. While Naples still held very generally to autonomy, the Sicilian revolt was purely annexationist : questions of Liberty, Reform or Constitution entering into it merely because synonymous with the doctrines of the House of Savoy. Should the Sicilian revolt prove successful, continental Naples might be drawn into the movement : the provinces leading, the capital following. Such a consequence, foreshadowing as it must Italian Unity, would undoubtedly prove most distasteful to Napoleon III. as also to non-Imperial France. Republicanism, the Marquis considers an insignificant element in the present crisis, the frank honesty of the Savoy Dynasty having disarmed the most energetic apostles of that creed. Turning to a consideration of the attitude of foreign diplomacy, Villamarina says in reference to Russia : " I must say that the Representative of this great Power has for several days past insisted, both with the King and with the Government, even putting great vivacity in his arguments, on the necessity, and even the urgency, of adopting a more conciliatory system. Aside from this advice, which is to-day perhaps rather tardy, he holds aloof, and maintains a strict reserve." This attitude is ascribed by Villamarina as due not to special friendliness for Piedmont, but to the desire to be revenged on Austria and wipe out the humiliations imposed by the Court of Vienna in 1856. As far as England was concerned there appeared no difficulty whatever. The Marquis placed no faith in the insinuations, fostered by Continental jealousies, that Great Britain aimed at gaining possession of Sicily ; nor did he anticipate any opposition on the part of that Power to the eventual achievement of Italian Unity. Her Majesty's Minister at Naples had frankly and openly declared to him that England would not repudiate, where Naples was concerned, the principles she had admitted in Central Italy ; provided the annexation be the result of universal popular suffrage, expressed with entire liberty of action, and without pressure or constraint.

The cession of Nice and Savoy had caused considerable discontent ; but Sir James Hudson, who thoroughly understood and appreciated Cavour's motives, was generously disposed to report the matter in the most favorable light to his Government, and to smooth over all diplomatic asperities ; while d'Azeglio, who possessed the esteem and confidence of many influential English politicians, labored incessantly to minimize the political importance of France's acquisitions, and was successful in turning the wrath of the British Cabinet against the greed of the French Emperor, who had thus ruthlessly exacted his pound of flesh.

To cripple Austria, and embarrass her military independence by encouraging the political fermentation in Hungary was an essential part of Cavour's general policy. The Italian statesman entertained more or less secret relations with the great Hungarian patriot and agitator, Louis Kossuth, as well as with his accredited agents, principally Klapka, Pulszky and Teleki, who spent much of their time in Turin, and kept their chief accurately and minutely informed on all questions of current interest. Kossuth, with whom the Emperor Napoleon III. was also in frequent and intimate communication, and who exercised an undoubted influence both in Paris and Turin, was tolerated, even sympathized with, yet distrusted, in official England. Moral encouragement had not been withheld the Hungarian agitator in London and Paris, while Turin had given more substantial support in the shape of funds and arms. In the complications resulting from the proposed annexations in northern and central Italy, and during the Neapolitan crisis the importance of the rôle Hungary might assume was clearly recognized. "The Hungarian question," wrote Cavour to Lorenzo Valerio,

Governor of Como (near which place Kossuth was staying in the spring of 1860), "is for us of supreme importance. It is closely allied with our own. Without the co-operation of Hungary the seizure of the Quadrilateral is an extremely risky undertaking ; nevertheless it must be attempted, not so much for the liberation of Italy from the Austrians as for our protection from anarchical revolution."

Pulszky, who obtained an audience with Victor Emmanuel shortly after Garibaldi's arrival in Sicily, in his report of the conversation to Kossuth, represents the King as answering his request for a fresh consignment of arms, with the significant remark that all available arms were sent to Sicily to be kept in readiness for use in Naples. "We are on the eve of great events," said the King. "It is possible that Austria will attack us : I should be glad of it : I would courageously resist the onslaught. I have still many accounts to settle with Austria ; the exile and death of my father are not yet avenged. I know they hate me, and they have good reason for so doing. . . . In a month we shall know if we are to have war this year ; ('preparez-vous') hold yourselves in readiness." *

* Chiala, Politica Secreta di Napoleone III. e di Cavour.

It was to this plotting Prince Albert objected, deeming it unworthy of a great statesman.
It would, however, be exacting too much of
any statesman, especially one situated as was
Cavour, to renounce the use of clandestine
weapons in combating a crafty foe of im-
measurably greater numerical strength ; or to
look for an over-scrupulous interpretation of
the rigid ethics of international obligations in
times of peace, pending the solution of a crisis
involving national existence. And especially
when it was patent that Austria neglected no
opportunity of opposing the full force of her
diplomatic and dynastic influences to circum-
vent the legitimate aspirations towards the Neapolitan alliance, and the adoption of a purely
national policy in Italy. If Cavour outwit-
ted European diplomacy he was merely the
winner in a contest of official duplicity in which
many of his competitors overreached themselves, and became the victims of their own
double-dealing. Yet notwithstanding the probability of England's complacence, and the conviction that the French Emperor, by virtue of
the recently concluded territorial bargain, must
needs "laisser faire" should an issue of the
Neapolitan question be forced upon him, Cavour
with true statesmanlike foresight, and the very
thorough knowledge he possessed of national

idiosyncrasies, preferred that evolution rather than revolution should be the means employed. Besides these prudential preferences, the political horizon beyond the Alps did not at this moment (April) appear sufficiently free from clouds to warrant a radical change of policy.

It was therefore under his advice that Victor Emmanuel wrote a carefully worded proposal (partaking somewhat of the nature of a warning) to his Cousin of Naples : "... We have reached a period when Italy can be divided into two powerful States ; one in the North, the other in the South ; two States which by the adoption of one and the same National policy, could maintain the great conception of our time : National Independence. The principle of Dualism, provided it be well established and honestly adhered to, may yet be accepted by Italians. ... If you allow some months to elapse without giving your adherence to my friendly suggestion, your Majesty will understand the bitterness of those terrible words, '*too late*,' as experienced by a member of your family in 1830 in Paris : perhaps Italians may concentrate all their hopes on a single head, and there are duties which, however painful, an Italian Prince must accept. Therefore let us devote ourselves jointly to so noble a task ; let us demonstrate to the Holy Father

the necessity of granting legitimate reforms ;
let us bind our States with a bond of real
friendship, whence will undoubtedly spring the
grandeur of our common country.   Grant
without delay a Liberal Constitution to your
subjects ; make appeal to the influence of the
men who are most esteemed on account of the
sufferings they have endured in the cause of
Liberty.   Efface all suspicions from the minds
of your people, and let us conclude a perpetual
alliance between the two most powerful States
of the Peninsula.   Thus shall we secure for
our country the inestimable advantage of being
the arbiter of its destinies. . . .   *

"Whom the Gods destroy they first drive
mad." Victor Emmanuel's personal appeal
was received in the same spirit of stubborn
antagonism as had been the advice of his
diplomatic representatives, and the counsels of
France and England.   Even the encouragement of Russia, which favored the proposed
alliance, was powerless against the opposition
of the Pope, who objected to Francis that intimate relations between the Neapolitan and
Sardinian Courts must unavoidably imply
acquiescence in the spoliations of which the
Church had been the victim.

* Victor Emmanuel to Francis II., April 23, 1860.

CHAPTER X.

Revolutionary plotting.—Morelli in Calabria.—Garibal·li and
Tennyson.—Preparations for Garibaldi's expedition.—Maz-
zini indorses Unity and Victor Emmanuel.—Conspiracy and
Massacre of La Gancia.—Risings in Sicily, their repression.—
Diplomatic protests.—Nunziante's mission.—Rumors of
Garibaldi's expedition.—Plans to frustrate same.—Garibaldi
lands at Marsala.—Lanza sent to Sicily.—His methods of
combating revolution.—Sicily welcomes Garibaldi.

DURING the early months of 1860 unparalleled activity reigned amongst the various revolutionary committees in Naples, the provinces,
and in Sicily. None believed in the maintenance of the political "statu quo"; and the
events in Upper Italy, and discouraging attitude assumed by the new King, left only a few
optimists, or dynastic enthusiasts, with any illusions concerning the stability of the Throne.

In Calabria more especially, the revolutionary organizations were plotting a general uprising, and unceasingly laboring for the dissemination of their doctrines amongst all classes.

As early as December, 1859, Donato Morelli,
one of the most ardent Calabrian patriots, and
an enthusiastic Unionist, opened a vigorous
campaign with the object to securing the co-

operation of Garibaldi in the revolutionary movements of the South. In his letters to the Committee at Naples, he advises that Garibaldi be urged to organize an expedition to the Calabrian coast. A couple of thousand men, well officered, and provided with efficient arms, munitions, and a dozen field-pieces, would, Morelli is confident, be successful. Everything is in readiness in the southern provinces, and only the initiative of Garibaldi is needful. "We dwell over a mine," he writes, "and must either fire the train or withdraw the charge ; otherwise there is imminent danger that it explode spontaneously ; " and the enterprise be thereby seriously compromised, for " the young men already champ the bits which restrain their generous impulses, and reproach us with the tremendous responsibility we assume in deferring action."

The Central Committee in Naples, in acknowledging Morelli's eloquent appeal, declines the responsibility of a resolution, and contents itself with cautioning the Calabrian chief to use extreme prudence in his relations with the various sub-committees throughout his district. Morelli, nothing daunted, redoubled his marvellous energy, and doggedly continued his propaganda, contributing inestimable services in the preparation of the political soil, and the planting of the seed which was to flourish so luxuriantly six months later.

But the cry for Garibaldi was soon taken up. The name of the popular hero exercised a potent fascination over the people of Southern Italy, and inspired even the Neapolitan troops with vague awe. The legends of his exploits in America acquired fabulous proportions in the minds of the ignorant and impressionable Southerners, while the traditions of 1849, and the memory of the precipitous retreat of Velletri when the Bourbon arms fled before the red-shirted warriors of the Roman Tribune, were still fresh in the recollections of the soldiers of Francis II. De Cesare says that even before the General landed at Marsala, or had entered Palermo, his invincibility had become legendary amongst the populations of the Two Sicilies. He was believed to be endowed with superhuman powers : in his presence the opposing forces melted away ; he had conquered all those who measured themselves against him, and only a few months ago the Austrians in Lombardy had been routed. His proud, and at the same time benevolent physiognomy, confirmed this belief, and was universally known by means of innumerable reproductions of his portrait.

During Garibaldi's sojourn in England, in

13

1864, he visited Tennyson, who " was charmed with his simplicity," but thought that in worldly matters he seemed to have the " divine stupidity of a hero." In a note to the Duke of Argyle the Poet refers to this visit : " . . . What a noble human being ! I expected to see a hero and I was not disappointed. One cannot exactly say of him what Chaucer says of the ideal Knight, ' As meke he was of port as is a maid ; ' he is more majestic than meek, and his manners have a certain divine simplicity in them, such as I have never witnessed in a native of these islands, among men at least, and they are gentler than those of most young maidens whom I know. He came here and smoked his cigar in my little room and we had half an hour's talk in English, though I doubt whether he understood me perfectly, and his meaning was often obscure to me. . . . I happened to make use of this expression, ' That fatal debt of gratitude owed by Italy to Napoleon.' ' Gratitude,' he said ; ' hasn't he had his pay ? his reward ? If Napoleon were dead I should be glad, and if I were dead he would be glad.' "

Donato Morelli's activity on the mainland was ably seconded in Sicily by Francesco Crispi and Rosolino Pilo, both natives of the island. As agent of the revolutionary committee Crispi

—who in spite of long exile was thoroughly in touch with the political aspirations of his fellow-citizens—made two expeditions throughout the island, and carefully laid down the lines for the new movement prepared by the exiles in Turin. At this period Crispi was an ardent Republican, and as a disciple of Mazzini, was looked upon with suspicion by Cavour, to whom he made known the result of his investigations and applied for material aid. With Farini, then Governor of Modena, he was more successful, however, receiving the promise of a million francs towards the organization of the projected expedition which he sought to induce Garibaldi to command.

Petty jealousies and dissensions amongst the leaders and instigators of the auxiliary expedition from Northern Italy, together with the hesitation of Garibaldi to assume the responsibility of the command, caused the miscarriage of expected co-operation between the exiles and their impatient brethren in the South when, on April fourth, the flame burst forth in Palermo.

Meanwhile public opinion was electrified by a renunciation, or modification, of creed coming from a most unexpected quarter. The action of Mazzini, who, in launching his soul-inspiring proclamation to the Sicilians, coupled the destruction of the Bourbons with the war-

cry of " Annexation " and " Long Live Victor
Emmanuel, King of Italy," overcame all hesitation, and rallied the independent parties to
the banner of Savoy. " Before I became a
Republican," he wrote, " I was a Unionist ; I
thought that the Republic alone could lead to
unity, I was mistaken. Victor Emmanuel has
carried Italy nearer this goal, and will lead her
thither if the people lend him their support.
For this reason I sacrifice old theories, and with
you, Sicilians, and with all the other Peoples
of the Peninsula, who in future will become
one People, with you I cry : ' Long Live Victor Emmanuel, King of Italy ! Sicilians, the
hour has come ; in the name of Italy, to arms !' "

Mazzini's formal and unconditional indorse-
ment of the revolutionary programme of Unity
under the House of Savoy, caused the wildest
enthusiasm throughout Italy. In Naples tricolor badges and ribbons made their appearance in the streets, or were thrown from the
galleries of the theatres, in spite of the redoubled vigilance and severity of the Police.

Twenty-four hours previous to the outbreak
in Palermo the Count of Syracuse addressed a
solemn warning to his nephew, pointing out
the dangers of the present policy and terminating as follows :   " One single course remains
open for the salvation of the country and the

dynasty, threatened with dire peril : namely, the adoption of a national policy which, having its foundation in the real interests of the State naturally indicates that the interests of the realm be amalgamated with those of Upper Italy."

Although there would appear to be a direct connection between the Prince's words and the almost simultaneous thunder-clap in Sicily, such is not really the case. That the Count of Syracuse, owing to his avowed sympathies with the Liberal Party, was aware that a rising was projected in the island is possible ; but the explosion in Palermo being due to fortuitous circumstances of which he could not have been cognizant at the time, precludes the supposition that he counted on its effect to augment the significance of his warning. Nevertheless the more bigoted of the "Camarilla" persisted in tracing the conspiracy to the Count, and, incredible as it must appear, persuaded Francis that the whole affair was a trap to frighten him into the acceptance of the desired alliance.

The conspiracy of La Gancia had been organized in accordance with the scheme for the uprising fomented by Crispi in his recent visits to Sicily, and was intended to co-operate with the expedition from Piedmont, promised by Crispi and Pilo. The monastery of that name situated on the outskirts of Palermo had been selected as a deposit for arms and ammunition, gradually collected for use at a propitious moment. Information having been furnished Maniscalco, a famous chief of the Sicilian Police, on April 3rd, by a treacherous inmate of the establishment, to the effect that arms were concealed in the building, and that it was the habitual meeting place of Liberalist conspirators well known to the Police, steps were immediately taken to raid the premises. In concert with General Salzano, Military Commander of Palermo, Maniscalco penetrated into the buildings and instituted a search, which, however, revealed nothing of a more revolutionary character than a dozen monks calmly performing their evening devotional exercises. Nevertheless, convinced of the accuracy of his information, the suspicious Chief of Police caused the monastery to be closely watched during the night, and aided by the soldiery completely surrounded the buildings. Trapped like mice the insurgents who had lain concealed in the vaults during the search, rashly opened fire on the Royalists at daybreak; the Church bells sounding a general alarm. Cries of "Viva l'Italia; Viva Vittorio Emmanuele" resounded on all sides, as the troops stormed the monas-

tery and breaking in the doors were soon engaged in a hand-to-hand struggle with the
inmates.   The defenders, few in number, were
quickly overpowered ; nineteen Liberals and
one monk were put to death, and many wounded.
Having gained possession, the soldiery completely sacked and devastated the premises,
carrying off even the sacred images and objects
of ritual.

General Salzano, fearing further disturbances, immediately placed the city under martial law, and demanded the consignment of all
fire-arms within a delay of twenty-four hours,
under penalty of death.   Maniscalco, in the
meanwhile, lost not a moment in placing under
arrest all citizens suspected of participation in
the conspiracy, or known as sympathizers with
the Liberalists.   Amongst those imprisoned
were Baron Riso, whose son had been wounded
at La Gancia ; Prince Niscemi, Prince Giardi-
nelli, Chevalier Sangiovanni, and many others
of social and political prominence.

In spite of the crushing defeat suffered by
their comrades in Palermo the insurrectionists
throughout the island rose against their oppressors, and joined in the cry for " Italy and
Victor Emmanuel."   Bloody encounters took
place at Bagheria, Misimeri, Carini, and Par-
tinico, and quickly spread to other towns and

villages of the provinces.   Rosolino Pilo, who had landed secretly just after the disaster at La Gancia, hastened to undertake the organization of the scattered bands ; at the same time urgently petitioning Garibaldi to no longer delay his expedition for the liberation of the unhappy island.   Through his instrumentality the following proclamation was circulated over the length and breadth of Sicily, and kept alive the flagging energies of the patriots : " The blood of the massacred martyrs cries out for vengeance.   Let all prepare to fight.   We will no longer have peace until Sicily be united to our common country, Italy ! "

In Naples the news caused intense excitement in the Liberal ranks, although the Court and official world made light of the incident. In the streets seditious cries for Italy and Victor Emmanuel kept the police busy with arrests ; while the sympathy openly expressed for the Sicilians might have been supposed to enlighten the most deluded optimists as to the trend of public sentiment.

None could fairly question the right of Francis to chastise his rebellious subjects. Unfortunately for the Neapolitan Monarch the zeal of his agents exceeded all bounds, and the barbarous punishment, and wholesale executions, aroused the humanitarian instincts of civilized Europe. The reign of Ferdinand II., so replete with shocking abuses and political persecutions as revealed in the widely-circulated letters of Mr. Gladstone nine years earlier, was not forgotten. Philanthropic legislators in foreign lands, recalling the descriptions of the atrocities perpetrated during those years, and aware that Francis refused to depart one iota from the mistaken policy of his father, now asked whether they were to be called upon to passively witness a repetition of those horrors. The Military Commission in Palermo organized for the trial of those suspected of participation in the recent outbreak appeared to have lost all sense of moderation in its thirst for blood. Both the English and French diplomatic representatives in Naples, horrified at the reports received from the Sicilian capital, protested to Francis in the name of outraged humanity. "I fear," wrote Brenier to his Government, "that the military justice of the King of Naples will cause more blood to flow than was shed during the actual insurrection, and that it will be even more effective in severing Sicily from the Throne of the Bourbons than the rebellion."

Francis finally yielded to the protestations of diplomacy, and, on May seventh, so far restrained the ferocity of his agents as to decree that no capital execution should be carried out without his personal consent.

Meanwhile the repressive measures instituted by General Salzano were vigorously prosecuted, the Royalist troops attacking, and in most cases routing, the insurgents, who disbanded only to form again in the mountainous districts where pursuit was attended by almost insurmountable difficulties. Again, unfortunately for the King of Naples, the officers in command of the Royal Troops allowed their men to commit excesses of such flagrant brutality, burning and pillaging towns and villages, and torturing the miserable victims suspected of collusion with the rebels, that the sympathies not only of liberal-minded foreigners, but of many loyal Neapolitans, were actively enlisted in the cause of the unhappy islanders, while the blood of the Liberals throughout Italy boiled with indignation.

Francis, rudely awakened from the rosy dreams of security in which the courtiers of the "Camarilla" sought to keep him by studiously belittling the importance of the insurrection, or its consequences, finally decided to despatch General Nunziante to examine and report on the situation in the island. The result of this investigation, which was reported

personally to the King by Nunziante, and cor-
roborated by Acton, who commanded the
steamer which carried him ; was most discouraging, amounting in fact to a thinly veiled
insinuation that under a continuance of the
existing official régime, the island must inevitably be lost to the Crown. The Prince of
Castelcicala, Lord Lieutenant and Commander
in Chief of the forces in Sicily, had on a recent
visit to the capital assured the King that the
utmost quiet reigned throughout the island.
Deeply chagrined by the lamentable failure of
his political insight, and dismayed at the proportions the conspiracy had developed (some
say doubting his competency to cope with it)
Castelcicala tendered his resignation on April
15th, together with the request that he be immediately relieved of the responsibility of office.
This request was not granted, however, until
a month later ; and in consequence the unhappy Lord Lieutenant suffered the additional
mortification of having heaped upon his head
the bitter reproaches of the Court for his
failure to prevent the first brilliant success of
Garibaldi's invasion. "The men who will
land in Sicily," wrote Francis a few days after
the proffered resignation, "will certainly not
be less than a thousand ; add to this number
those from the villages and outlying districts

who will rise after the landing, and those who will be furnished with arms and ammunitions brought by the expedition, and it is evident that one single battalion cannot stand against such a concourse. I leave for you to imagine the pitiable effect which would be produced, should the regiment be defeated in the first encounter, or worse still, be made prisoner, and transported abroad as a trophy. For this reason strong concentrations of troops should be arranged, that these may act in concert with the detachments destined to operate where the filibusters may land, in order to take them between two fires."

In spite of these military preparations the unpleasant revelations contained in the report of Nunziante and Acton respecting the degree of confidence to be reposed in the officers and troops in the island, decided Francis to essay a policy of opportunism, the propagation of which, however, earned him not gratitude but indignation, mingled with a feeling akin to contempt. Instructions were issued from Naples to raise the state of siege, and to deal leniently with the malcontents; for it was recognized that should Garibaldi's threatened expedition take place, and a landing be successfully effected, the Rebellion of to-day would rapidly be converted into the Revolution of to-morrow. Half measures of any description now came too late. The brutality of the military and police had snapped the last feeble link which bound the Sicilians to their legitimate Sovereign. Nor could it be expected that with the promise of aid in the immediate future from the renowned Garibaldi, in whose invincibility they firmly believed, the harassed and hunted bands of Rosolino Pilo, would passively surrender their arms and persons to the discretionary clemency of the Bourbon, the value of whose assurances the dread experience of the past had taught them to correctly appreciate. As a consequence, although the insurrection was apparently crushed in the towns of the seaboard, it burned fiercely in the mountainous districts where the organized bands had taken refuge, pending the advent of the long-awaited succor from over the sea.

At eight o'clock on the evening of May 6, 1860, in the midst of the Court preparations for a ceremonious visit on the morrow to the venerated shrine of San Gennaro, a telegram arrived from Chevalier Canofari, Neapolitan Envoy at Turin, warning his Government that Garibaldi had sailed. The uncertainty to the movements of the expedition prevented any concrete plan for the concentration or disposal of the naval and military forces of the Kingdom.

Would the two steamers seized by the filibusters attempt a landing on the Calabrian coast, or make directly for Sicily ? The fact that Garibaldi with his lieutenants, Crispi, Bertani, Bixio and Medici, were plotting and organizing the expedition at Genoa, was of course known to the Neapolitan police, but the secret of the choice of a landing place had been well kept, or was rather so entirely dependant on circumstances impossible to foresee, as to partake more of the nature of expediency or sudden inspiration. The vessels of the Neapolitan squadron had been given instructions as early as April twentieth to keep a sharp lookout ; and their commanders received a broad official hint not to hesitate to overhaul suspicious strangers flying a friendly flag.

Although the news was concealed from the public, it leaked out on the following day when the French mail steamer from Genoa reached Naples ; and the knowledge that Garibaldi had succeeded in evading the Piedmontese authorities, who it was feared might hesitate to carry complaisant near-sightedness to the length of an official cecity so manifestly a violation of international etiquette, caused the most frantic joy amongst the Liberals.

After attending the religious function, for which elaborate preparations had been made,

Francis sent for General Filangieri, and communicating the news to him without apparent emotion or appreciation of its significance, asked the old statesman's advice concerning the despatch of fresh troops to Sicily.

On the eleventh the telegraph brought the news of the landing of Garibaldi at Marsala, and the " Official Journal " which had ignored the report of the sailing of the expedition, in an issue a couple of days later laconically referred to the " flagrant act of piracy which was consummated on the eleventh instant, by the landing of an armed forced at Marsala."

While persisting in representing the expedition to his own subjects as of small importance ; the raid of a band of rapacious brigands, who burned and devastated the districts they overran ; threatening, bribing, or coercing the peaceful peasants to join their ranks, Francis now sufficiently realized the gravity of the situation to make an urgent protest at Turin, and to despatch the following circular to all Neapolitan diplomatic representatives abroad : " In spite of communications from Turin, and the promise of that Government to prevent the expedition openly organized and armed by brigands, it sailed nevertheless, under the very eyes of the Sardinian fleet, and yesterday landed at Marsala.   Inform the Government to which

you are accredited of this act of savage piracy
promoted by a friendly State."

At the Council of State held in Naples on
the fourteenth, to which Filangieri had been
bidden, and at which the Count of Aquila also
assisted, Sicilian affairs formed the sole subject
of debate.   The Cabinet were unanimous in
their desire that Filangieri, vested with plen-
ary authority, should go to Sicily.   The old
General, however, refused, putting forward his
advanced age, and the physical impossibility of
assuming at such a crisis so onerous a charge.
In vain did Francis plead that again the Monarchy would be indebted to him for the preservation of Sicily ; Filangieri persisted in his
refusal to undertake the operations, although
he suggested a plan of campaign, which was
accepted.   At the further recommendation of
Filangieri, General Ferdinand Lanza, an old
Sicilian, was appointed as the successor of
Prince Castelcicala ; and in spite of his remonstrances and discouraging prognostications,
was hurried off to Palermo, where, on the
seventeenth, he assumed the reins of government and the command of the troops in the
island.

Lanza presented himself to his countrymen
next day, armed with a proclamation redolent
with conciliatory sentiment, promises of moral

and material ameliorations, and the offer of a free and generous pardon, in the name of his Sovereign, to all misguided individuals who should now make act of submission to governmental authority. Once the pacification of the island accomplished, he was authorized to state that a Prince of the Royal Family had already been selected to reside in their midst as Viceroy. This functionary would immediately begin the construction of roads, railways, and other works of public utility ; and would devote all his energies to the development of the resources and industries of the country, as well as the adoption of every means suggested by experience for the increase of general prosperity. With a mild warning of those who heeded the dangerous teachings of crafty agitators, the promulgator called upon his compatriots to cast in their lot with the Royal Troops, under whose protection alone they would find salvation.

Lanza himself could have had but little faith that the anodyne of his well-intentioned but insipid appeal would convince the impenitent insurrectionists, flushed with the strong intoxicant of success ; and who had, moreover, in times gone by awaited in vain the execution of the provisions of so many similar documents. Now the revered Leader was actually in their midst, and his undertaking had from the start been crowned with tangible results. Even those who would fain have still hung back, or temporized, were drawn forward by the magnetism of the man, and the enthusiasm of their native leaders. The evening before the publication of his proclamation the tidings of the defeat of the Royalists at Calatafimi had reached the General. He forwarded the same to Naples in a gloomy despatch describing the condition of the island as most alarming, and the inhabitants "possessed by the delirium of revolution."

Nor could the "alter ego" of the King of the Two Sicilies pretend to ignore the very different conditions prevailing between the forces which now confronted each other. On the one hand wild enthusiasm ; bravery amounting to heroism ; an apostolic faith in the cause they served, and for which they cheerfully sacrificed their lives. On the other side an army numerically superior, but lacking an Ideal ; devoid of the stimulus of conviction : an army which bore arms professionally in the service of a Sovereign for whom they personally felt no enthusiasm, nor even the mingled fear and respect his father had inspired. Opposed to them was a leader surrounded with the halo of legendary invincibility, whose name evoked recollections of the fatal retreat of Velletri : a retreat which, as De Cesare justly remarks, "had imbued the Neapolitan army with the conviction of its impotency to combat an enemy who knew not the fear of death." Unlike their opponents whose commander's word was absolute and unquestioned law to his followers, the Neapolitan troops were led by officers whose jealousies, mutual recriminations and accusations of treachery, destroyed the confidence of their subordinates. Add to this the knowledge that the Neapolitan soldier stood alone, while his adversary enjoyed not only the good will of the native population, but felt himself backed by the moral approval of all Italy, and the sympathies of Liberal Europe.

The history of Garibaldi's astounding achievements is too familiar to require recording here. On May twenty-seventh the General astonished the world by his audacious capture of Palermo ; and shortly after demonstrated by the conclusion of an armistice, in accordance with the terms of which eighteen thousand Neapolitan troops evacuated the capital, that the loss of the island to the Crown of the Two Sicilies was henceforth inevitable, if not already virtually an accomplished fact.

CHAPTER XI.

Cavour and the Sicilian expedition.—His relations with Garibaldi.—Diplomatic perils.—Garibaldi a Republican.— His letter to Victor Emmanuel.—Cavour to d'Azeglio concerning expedition.—-He explains position of Piedmont.— Cavour is blamed.—His defence of his policy.—A Russian protest.—Cavour and European Diplomacy.—Anecdotes from his private correspondence.—His relations with French and English politicians.—Louis Napoleon's entanglements.

THE attitude assumed by Count Cavour towards Garibaldi's expedition, although not openly antagonistic, was one of extreme reserve, and had given great offence to the ultra-Liberals, while at the same time it failed to satisfy the Conservative element. The former made no allowance for the embarrassing exigencies of Diplomacy ; the latter witnessed with alarm the thinly concealed collusion of the King's Government in an undertaking, the startling illegality of which must needs offend the susceptibilities of Conservative Europe. The Minister's conduct of affairs was certainly open to misconception, and severe criticism : and if incomprehensible to Garibaldians, and as such condemned by their sympathizers, must be scored in unmeasured terms by scandalized

Conservative Chanceries. Certain it is the great statesman sailed dangerously near the wind on more than one occasion; while the dust he threw in the eyes of foreign diplomatists so blinded many of his own compatriots that they failed to credit him with the strict adherence to the fundamental principles he so adroitly juggled with. Considerable friction existed between the Minister and the General consequent on the recent territorial cessions to France, which Garibaldi had bitterly denounced. On his side Cavour mistrusted the generous impetuosity of the Free-Lance and self-constituted arbiter of the political destinies of Southern Italy; and was moreover unfeignedly apprehensive of the influence which might be exercised over him by associates, the orthodoxy of whose political creed was dubious, and who might be assumed to prove utterly callous to the irksome entanglements of the diplomatic obligations he himself was constrained to propitiate, if not strictly observe. To the Unionists at all costs the bid for the Neapolitan alliance seemed to destroy the only admissible explanation of the cession of Savoy and Nice; a sacrifice, they argued, might have been avoided had Cavour played off English susceptibilities against French ambitions; and it consequently became a matter of indifference whether they involved the Government in foreign complications through their machinations in the Papal and Bourbon States. Mazzini had written Garibaldi in January : " I appreciate the times : I yield to the Nation : I will not act against the King, I will not conspire for the Republic ; I only breathe the word 'Unity' ; I aim at annexation ; at successfully inciting revolt in Sicily and elsewhere, bargaining only for immediate acceptance." But he included in this programme Rome as the National capital and the ousting of the French ; and therein lay the peril. What Mazzini advocated in January, Garibaldi was prepared to execute in May. The "Vous voilà nos complices" gleefully uttered by Cavour when the French Plenipotentiary affixed his signature to the treaty of March twenty-fourth, might be interpreted as the implied recognition of a certain license in the Sicilian question, but could not possibly be stretched into a reference to Rome.

La Farina, who labored to allay the suspicions lurking in Cavour's mind, concerning the orthodoxy of Garibaldi's political creed and loyalty, informed the Minister on April twenty-fourth that his fears of Mazzini's influence were needless, since a "pronounced discord" existed between the General and the celebrated agitator. Yet this disagreement was but a passing one, and in spite of Mazzini's renunciation of his personal preferences, Cavour considered that he had good ground for his misgivings as to the depth and sincerity of the monarchical convictions of the late Republicans.

An anecdote related by Aurelio Bellisomi gives color to the suspicion of temporary subservience to a political expedient, entertained by Cavour. On April twentieth an applicant for enrollment in the proposed expedition, asked Garibaldi whether it would not be possible to omit the arms of the House of Savoy from the banner under the ægis of which it was designed to combat. "My son," he replied, " you are aware that I am as much of a Republican as you are ; but you must make the same sacrifice I do, because it is necessary for Italian Unity." That Garibaldi never wavered for an instant, his loyal allegiance once spontaneously offered, became evident in the sequel ; at the same time the above conversation, which is quoted by White Mario * affords partial justification of Cavour's misapprehensions, for which he has been so roughly handled by the more enthusiastic biographers of the Garibaldian heroes.

* " Agostino Bertani e i suoi Tempi."

Nothing more frank and loyal than Garibaldi's farewell address to Victor Emmanuel, as the expedition sailed from Quarto could well be desired.

"I did not counsel the insurrectionary movement of my brothers in Sicily," he wrote, "but the moment they rose in the name of Italian Unity, of which Your Majesty is the personification, against the most infamous tyranny of our epoch, I did not hesitate to place myself at the head of the expedition. Our war-cry will ever be : 'Long live Italian Unity : Long live Victor Emmanuel, its foremost and bravest soldier !'"

Two days after the departure (nominally if not effectively clandestine) of " *The Thousand*," Cavour forwarded to the Marquis d'Azeglio, his intimate friend and confidante, as well as official representative in London, a letter in which his position is so clearly outlined that it seems permissible to transcribe it in its entirety. Dated from Turin, on May eighth, 1860, whither he had hurriedly returned from Bologna on receipt of the news, Cavour writes : " The events in Sicily have decided me to depart from the reserve which I had assumed vis-à-vis the English Government in consequence of the sentiment of distrust which the affair of Savoy had unfortunately kindled

against us in England. Whatever the difference of views which manifested themselves on
this occasion between the Ministers of Her
Britannic Majesty and myself, a difference I
sincerely deplore, it seems to me indubitable
that England and Sardinia have, as concerns
Sicily, but one and the same interest. In
reality (as you have frequently had occasion to
repeat to Lord Palmerston and Lord John
(Russell) we have no other aim than that of
restoring Italy to the Italians ; of founding on
a real and durable basis the independence of
the Peninsula ; and of freeing it from all moral
as well as material subjection. We ceded
Savoy and Nice only because, rightly or
wrongly, we are convinced that those districts
cannot be considered integrally as of Italian
nationality. But (as I hastened to inform you
by telegraph) we would not yield one inch of
Italian territory no matter what advantages
might be offered with the exchange. You can
consequently absolutely deny the absurd rumor
relative to the cession of Genoa, or any other
portion of Liguria, to France. Lord Palmerston and Lord John have too much clairvoyance
not to believe in the sincerity of this declaration. *By the treaty of March 24th we sought
to deprive France of all pretexts for hindering
the furtherance of our policy in Italy. I hope*

to have succeeded : at least as far as Sicily is concerned, where nobody dreams of Muratism. * But if the agreement with France costs us such efforts and sacrifices, the understanding with England should be quite a matter of course and almost self-evident. I am too well acquainted with the existing principles in English politics to credit the old stagers who attribute to Lord Palmerston designs for the conquest of Sicily, and of the project of turning the island into a fief under an English protectorate. In Sicily, as in Central Italy, England can have but one object : to leave the Italians masters to decide their destiny ; to prevent any foreign intervention or influence. This is just what we desire ; for, I repeat it, I am first of all an Italian, and it is in order that my country may enjoy *" self-government,"* * * at home and abroad, that I have undertaken the arduous task of driving Austria out of Italy, without substituting the domination of any other Power. You will be careful therefore to explain to Lord Palmerston that, in the Sicilian affair, we desire first of all to put ourselves in perfect accord with England. *We did not encourage Garibaldi to embark upon this adventure, which appeared to us foolhardy.*

* The italics do not exist in the original text.
* * The words are in English in the original.

*We regretted the precipitation which causes us
the most cruel embarrassment, and which may
dangerously compromise the future of Italy.
Nevertheless we respected the highly honorable
motives which inspired his audacious resolution, and we did not consider ourselves authorized
to prevent by force efforts which aimed at amel-
iorating the fate of the Sicilians. If Garibaldi succeeds ; if the great majority of Sicilians
cluster around him ; we only ask for them the
full liberty of deciding their destiny ; of making
of the independence they have acquired the usage
which seems to them most advisable.* * I hasten
to give you these explanations. In communicating them to Lord Palmerston, and Lord
John, you will add, my dear Marquis, that in
order to satisfy the pressing solicitations of
Russia, I had inserted in the " Official Gazette "
of to-day an article which refutes the rumors of
the complicity of the Government of the King
in Garibaldi's expedition." * *

As was to be expected, however, European
Diplomacy saddled Cavour with the moral
responsibility of Garibaldi's action ; charging
the Piedmontese Government with tacit complicity, if not active participation in the enter-

---

* The italics do not exist in the original.
* * Nicomede Bianchi " La Politique du Comte de
Cavour."

prise. But although the various Cabinets stormed and vigorously protested, the policy of non-intervention was not departed from. It was speedily manifest, moreover, that public opinion throughout Europe (and especially in England) did not concur with the official world in its scandalized condemnation of so flagrant a breach of neighborly relations. Occurring between States of a common nationality, whose political division was considered by many an anomaly, and by those professing the sacred principles of consanguinity loudly proclaimed a detrimental anachronism, the "international" aspect of the incident appealed no more strongly to the general public than had the recent events enacted in Tuscany and the Duchies.

But if public opinion viewed with leniency an episode, the chivalrous character of which powerfully appealed to the imagination, the official world was less inclined to condone the triumph of a revolutionary movement, the threatened extension of which must inevitably entail a shifting of the existing political equilibrium, by the foundation of a new Great Power on the ruins of the petty sovereignties of Italy : a probability not to be contemplated without concern.

It is characteristic of the man that Cavour

unhesitatingly accepted a situation not of his own making, seeking the furtherance of his fundamental policy in spite of the new dangers and complications which surrounded him, with a skill and patience which compelled the admiration of the more broad-minded of his opponents. Without repudiating Garibaldi, an action which would have destroyed his personal influence with the Liberals and Nationalists, and unquestionably, in view of the rapid and complete success of the expedition, have lost Victor Emmanuel his popularity, while it might even have menaced the existence of the Dynasty, he contrived to turn the tables on the more importunate of his accusers, if not by convincing logic, at least by arguments, the magnificent audacity of which engendered plausibility. Cleverly brandishing the dread spectre of the Republic, or Anarchy, before the eyes of monarchical Europe, should Victor Emmanuel attempt to restrain the explosion of righteous indignation against the systematic tyranny of the Neapolitan Bourbons, he turned upon Austria and England with the sarcastic query: " By what right is Sardinia accused of not having prevented the landing of the audacious adventurer in Sicily when the whole Neapolitan fleet was incapable of doing so ? While Austrians and Irish embark without hindrance at

Trieste, in order to flock to the defence of the Pope ; how could the Sardinian Government, even if cognizant of it, prevent Sicilian exiles from aiding their own brothers in the struggle against their oppressors ? "

From distant Russia the voice of Prince Gortchakoff thundered forth the threat that, as the Government of Turin avowedly found itself dominated by the revolutionary element to the extent of being driven to the disregard of international obligations, all European States should combine for a mutual regulation of their relations with Piedmont : adding that " did the geographical position of his realm not forbid, the Tzar would lend armed assistance to the Neapolitan Bourbons, without regard to the policy of non-intervention proclaimed by the Western Powers." To these continued remonstrances and threats Cavour replied : " We cannot be less Italian than the English and French, who openly aid Garibaldi's expedition. Not one of the vessels sailing recently for Sicily was under the Sardinian flag : the greater number displayed the American ensign." The attitude of Prussia was hardly less alarming than that of Austria and the great Northern Empire, but to France and England Cavour looked with most anxiety for the possible checkmate in the game so boldly undertaken.   Appreciating that concertive action between the three first named States was an eventuality so remote that he could legitimately discount the risks, he continued to fence with such cleverly intermingled audacity and cunning, that before the bewildered diplomatists had unravelled the import of an ambiguous declaration, they found themselves confronted with fresh entanglements which kept them busy until the Minister's projects had become accomplished facts.

The progress of events was so rapid that, on June twenty-fifth, little more than five weeks after the landing of the expedition, Cavour, referring in a private letter to the proposed intercession to dissuade Garibaldi from crossing to Calabria, remarks: " We will second as far as the continent is concerned for the *Macaroni* is not yet cooked ; but as for the *oranges* which are already on our table, we are quite decided to eat them."

That the *oranges* were within his grasp was due to France and England. The attitude of England in regard to the annexation of Tuscany and the Romagna offered a reassuring guarantee as to her probable action in Southern Italy, which indeed Lord John Russell foreshadowed in the significant despatch of May fifth to the British Ambassador at Vienna, Lord Loftus. " If tyranny and injustice are the characteristic traits of the Government of Southern Italy," he remarks, "those of the Government of Northern Italy are liberty and justice. This being the case, sooner or later the populations of Southern Italy will be politically united to their brothers of the North, and will wish to be ruled by the same Sovereign. . . . " As a matter of fact England was deeply concerned with but two eventualities which might emanate from the existing, or future, complications in the Peninsula : firstly, the re-opening of hostilities between Austria and Piedmont ; and secondly, the temptation offered Cavour, by reason of the enormous difficulties surrounding him, to purchase the aid of France with further territorial concessions, especially that of the island of Sardinia. The Count's letters to D'Azeglio are full of fervent disclaimers of the reports crediting the Government with such intentions, and indignantly proclaim that, regardless of consequences, not another inch of Italian soil will be yielded. Once this suspicion satisfactorily dispelled, Great Britain was willing enough to allow matters to follow their natural course ; and not adverse, on occasion, to allowing it to be implied that Garibaldi enjoyed, within certain limits, the good-will of English statesmanship, as represented in Lord Palmer-

ston's Cabinet. Of the sympathy of British
public opinion there had been, and was, no
room for doubt.

With France the negotiations were of a more
delicate nature, in spite of the "complicity"
which Cavour assumed was created with the
signature of treaty of March twenty-fourth.
The Peace of Villafranca had imbued Italians
with an irresistible longing for National Unity,
and the Emperor, Napoleon III., was responsible for Villafranca in the eyes of all Italians.
He was, moreover, bound by subtle and numerous personal ties to the Italian cause. Although the political union of the Peninsula
must prove unacceptable to those statesmen
who foresaw with its achievement the inevitable decline of French influence, yet the
Emperor (whose politics were not by any
means always in harmony with those of the
majority) could not consistently retract a policy whose fundamental lines were based on
the extension of the principle of nationalities, and for the defence of which the blood
of his soldiers had been so recently shed. Of
this Cavour felt reasonably convinced ; yet the
vehement protestations from Paris called forth
by Garibaldi's action were disconcerting. Undoubtedly Napoleon III. viewed with disapproval this wholesale annexation, together with
15

the probable disappearance of the Southern Kingdom ; yet the current which threatened to sweep Victor Emmanuel and Cavour aside should they resist its impetus, had so entangled Louis Napoleon in its eddies and whirlpools that he too must needs follow the stream. "What can be done with a Government like that of Naples, which obstinately refuses to heed advice ?" he remarked evasively to those who sought his opinion on the situation. And later, when Francis in desperation sent his envoys to Paris to plead for intercession : "It is not to me you should have come, but to Victor Emmanuel. Sardinia alone can check the course of the revolution."

Under these circumstances, while Cavour groaned beneath their protestations, and discomfited the querulous diplomatists with enigmatic refutations, he plodded stolidly towards his goal ; always seeking to guide the tumultuous revolutionary flood into the quieter channels of Diplomacy, through which he was confident of accomplishing his ends, if more tediously, at least with greater immunity from the risk of possible shipwreck.

CHAPTER XII.

Anxiety at Naples.—Filangieri's counsels.—He leaves Naples.—
Francis sends De Martino to Paris.—His reception by French
Emperor.—The Emperor's advice and warning.—The "Camarilla's" accusations.—Francis grants Constitution.—The
Pope antagonistic to Piedmontese alliance.—The Franchise
coldly received by Liberals.—Riots in Naples.—The application for alliance.—Cavour's embarrassments.—His conditions.—Arrival of Neapolitan Envoys at Turin.—Their demands.—Victor Emmanuel writes Garibaldi.—The General
refuses obedience.—Cavour confides to D'Azeglio details
of his policy.

MEANWHILE at Naples Garibaldi's achievements were watched with growing concern,
while the revolutionary mutterings echoed
from Calabria and the southeastern provinces
of the continent became a source of further
apprehension in Court and Governmental cir-
cles. A Council of State assembled on May
thirteenth to study the situation and devise
expedients. Besides the King, several members of the Royal Family, and the regularly
accredited officials, Filangieri was present.
When called upon for his opinion, the old
statesman affirmed that his views had undergone no change, and that he could only reiter-
ate his former advice. His belief was that the

227

policy hitherto pursued must be reversed ; Austrian influences be discarded, and a "rapprochement" attempted with France ; a course he considered obviously dictated by the lessons of Magenta and Solferino. Furthermore, he advocated the concession of a Constitution and the acceptance of the proposal to occupy the States of the Church, as far north as Perugia and Ancona. He also proposed that an envoy be despatched to Paris to seek to obtain from the Emperor the necessary guarantees for the integral preservation of the Kingdom, or at least, as he prudently but significantly added, of the continental provinces. To General Carrascosa, who insinuated that had he, Filangieri, accepted the mission to Sicily, when so urged by the King on April fourth, the Royal cause would to-day have been triumphant in the island, the veteran sadly objected : "You are mistaken, General. When I left Sicily on September 30, 1854, I carried away with me the conviction that the system of government Cassini was endeavoring to enforce on that country would sooner or later entail its loss to the Neapolitan Monarchy."

During the heated debate which followed between the party which approved concessions and a radical change of policy (not from conviction, but by virtue of necessity), and the ultra-Conservatives, adverse to the slightest departure from the old system, Francis maintained the impassive fatalism so deeply rooted in his nature. Convinced that France, England, and Piedmont had decreed the extinction of his Dynasty, he saw in Garibaldi the tool, and behind him recognized the guiding forces which would encompass the ruin of his House.

Although Filangieri's proposals could not be accepted unanimously, they were favorably considered by a majority of those present, who perceived that in the execution of these previsions alone lay any reasonable hope of salvation. A diplomatic council, which followed immediately, was attended by the English, French, and Spanish representatives. Of these Carafa begged their good offices to induce Garibaldi to provide for an honorable evacuation of Palermo by the Neapolitan forces, then practically at his mercy.

Three days later Francis again summoned Filangieri, who then learnt that the strategical plans, prepared by him for the military operations in Sicily, had been discarded and another, preferred by Nunziante, adopted in its stead. This latter, which included the bombardment at Palermo, he emphatically denounced. Although again consulted by the King concerning the advisability of a return to the Constitution of 1848, which he advocated, Filangieri, convinced that his advice, although solicited, was unheeded, and unwilling to witness the catastrophe he felt was now unavoidable, left Naples and sought refuge in France.   While he returned to his native city shortly after the collapse of the Dynasty he had so faithfully served, he refused all honors or emoluments at the hands of the new Government ; not from animosity, or even regret for that which was lost, but prompted by a quiet dignity which gained him the esteem of all parties. He passed away in 1867, at the ripe old age of eighty-three ; to the last a noble example of the virtues of the ideal soldier ; steadfast to his allegiance, to his military oath, and to the obligations of patriotism, in spite of personal opinions, or preferences.

The deliberations of the Council of State of May thirtieth resulted in the decision of Francis to address himself personally to the Emperor of the French.   On June sixth he wrote declaring himself ready to grant a Constitution, provided the Emperor would guarantee the autonomy of the Kingdom and the preservation of the Dynasty.   Chevalier de Martino, at that period Neapolitan Envoy at the Papal Court, was selected to undertake this delicate mission, concerning the success of which even the most sanguine demurred. "If you allow some months to elapse without giving your adherence to my friendly suggestion, Your Majesty will understand the bitterness of those terrible words : ' *Too late,*' . . ." had been the prophetic utterance of Victor Emmanuel but a couple of months earlier. Francis was now about to drink of that bitterness to the dregs, and to reap the harvest of his own folly, and the years of persecution and barbarous oppression of his perjured predecessors.

On reaching Paris the Chevalier de Martino, together with the Neapolitan Envoy accredited to the Imperial Court, immediately sought an audience with the Emperor. This was granted next day (June 12) at Fontainebleau, and the prolonged conversation which ensued between Napoleon III. and his Minister, M. de Thouvenel, on the one side, and the two Neapolitans on the other, left no illusions in the minds of the unfortunate diplomatists as to the fate in store for their royal master.

The Emperor began by deploring the events which had taken place in the Kingdom, and expressed his regret that his disinterested advice had been so long unheeded. Having read the letter from the King to the Two Sicilies,

Napoleon III. echoed the words of Victor
Emmanuel : " It is too late." A month ago
I might have been able to arrange everything ;
now it is too late.   France is in a difficult position.   Revolutions are not restrained by words,
and, at this moment, the revolution not only
exists, but is triumphant.   The Italians are
cunning, and they realize full well that after
having given the blood of my children for their
National cause, I will never turn my guns
against them.   It is this conviction which has
brought about the revolution ; the annexation
of Tuscany ; in spite of me, and contrary to
my interests.   They will treat you in the same
way."

The Neapolitan Envoys, endeavoring to convince the Emperor that his interests were identical with their own, lost no opportunity of
painting the political future of the Peninsula
in the darkest hues.   They argued that Sicily
could not possibly be retained permanently by
Piedmont, and was consequently inevitably
doomed to be included within the sphere of
English influence—probably engulfed by Perfidious Albion, under the guise of a protectorate.   To all such prospects Napoleon remained
apparently indifferent, merely reiterating his
advice that Francis lose no time in accepting
the proffered alliance with Piedmont ; and

warning his hearers that only by adapting his policy to the National aspirations, could their Sovereign expect to stem the current, unless, indeed, he was strong enough to circumscribe and stamp out the revolution within his borders. In vain did the Neapolitans argue and protest ; Napoleon met protest and argument with the same objections : ''All this may be true enough, but we are now brought face to face with accomplished facts. The force of public opinion is invincible : the position of France is no longer that of 1849 : on this account we do not desire the annexation which is contrary to our interests, and we counsel the only practical means of avoiding, or at least retarding it. But an irresistible pressure is working against us : a force to which we *must* yield. Accede to the exigencies of the moment. The National cause must triumph. Sacrifice everything to this idea in one way or another. I don't discuss the means by which it may be found possible to solve all the objections which exist ; but I tell you to do it, and do it quickly. To-morrow it will be too late. In this case my loyal and sincere support will be assured you ; otherwise I shall be obliged to stand aloof and allow Italy to act by herself. The principle of non-intervention, sealed with the blood of France, will be maintained.''

These utterances, almost brutal in their frankness, were hardly capable of misconstruction, and the unfortunate Envoys fully realized that their cause was lost. Yet they pleaded that a word from the Emperor, if spoken with firmness and decision, could still arrest the revolutionary tide emanating from Turin ; and they further urged, not without reason, that if the principles of universal non-intervention be enforced, steps should be taken to prevent Piedmont from covertly aiding and abetting the revolution. Although the Emperor promised that he would use his good offices at Turin, he held out small prospect of success. " Of what use is it ! " he exclaimed impatiently, " Cavour himself is overwhelmed." In Napoleon's opinion Cavour was, in truth, most apprehensive lest the revolution, with its inevitable excesses and irresponsible plunges into the unknown, drag down to destruction the labors of his patient diplomacy.

In his detailed report of this most important conversation, Antonini, the Resident Neapolitan Envoy at Paris, adds that Thouvenel made no attempt to conceal his animosity. He further states that during a discussion as to the possibility of the royal arms achieving a re-conquest of Sicily, the French Foreign Minister gratuitously affronted them with the insinuation that,

were such a course attempted, it was " doubtful whether Europe could remain an impassive
spectator to the cruelty of our soldiers."

The contents of Antonini's despatches were
not calculated to re-assure the Neapolitan
Court ; yet, as had been the case with the reports from Sicily, the " Camarilla" accused
the diplomatist with coloring the tenor of the
Emperor's conversation, for the purpose of
frightening and coercing the King. Even
Antonini's disclaimer in his second report : " I
trust the justice will be rendered me that I
have never sought to arouse false hopes," was
characterized as gross and interested exaggeration, by the blinded adherents to the traditions
of the old régime. The intrigues, and malicious accusations of the " Camarilla," together
with the mysterious conferences between that
new-fledged Liberal, his uncle, the Count of
Aquila, and Brenier, the French Envoy, increased the doubts and perplexities of the
King.

All Europe awaited, with conflicting sentiments, the issue of the strange drama being
enacted at Naples. On the one hand, the
fierce and bigoted reactionary policy of the " Camarilla," headed by the Queen Mother ; on the
other, two of the King's uncles rivalling each
other in their spontaneous professions of a

Liberalism profoundly antagonistic to the traditions of their race. An hereditary Despot, distraught midst the counsels of foreign advisers ; the menaces of an increasingly strong political party ; half his Kingdom snatched from him by an audacious filibuster in the name of Greater Piedmont—of Italy ! and the dawning conviction that the other half was tottering on the brink, requiring but a touch to precipitate to destruction the Dynasty which had in spite of a century and a quarter of enforced allegiance held no place in the hearts of the people. By granting under the stress of disaster that which he ought to have inaugurated his reign by pontaneously proclaiming, Francis, like his relative Louis XVI. of France, showed his personal weakness and the rottenness of the obsolete institutions which alone upheld his Throne. The Constitution wrenched from him on June twenty-fifth now merely hastened the catastrophe, rendered inevitable by the suicidal policy persistently pursued during the first thirteen months of his reign.

The promulgation of the Sovereign Act, as the cession of liberal institutions was termed, was finally decided in a combined State and Family council held in the Palace at Portici, on June twenty-first, which included all those who had participated in the conference of May thirty-first, excepting Filangieri. This assemblage decided by a majority of eight out of fourteen votes, to recommend the King to follow the advice offered by Napoleon III., namely : a liberal Constitution for Naples ; special institutions for Sicily ; and the alliance with Piedmont.

The King had not assisted at the discussions of the Council. When informed of the result of its deliberations he signified his acquiescence, but, with characteristic vacillation, despatched the same evening De Martino, who had returned from Paris, to Rome to seek the Pope's sanction. While approving the proposed amnesty, and realizing the necessity for separate political institutions in Naples and Sicily, Pius IX. as a matter of conscience clung to his emphatic objection to the alliance with Piedmont, although, appreciating the perilous embarrassments of his neighbor, he did not insist on the abandonment of this essential point. As a result of De Martino's report, Francis, on the morning of June 25th, signed the important document which it was hoped would guarantee the preservation of the Throne. The Act embodied : a general amnesty for all political crimes committed prior to the date of its promulgation ; the formation of a new Ministry under Antonio Spinelli, charged with the elaboration of the articles of a Constitution modelled on a basis of Italian National representative institutions ; the conclusion of an alliance with His Majesty the King of Sardinia, for the common interests of the Two Crowns in Italy ; the granting of analogous representative institutions in Sicily, with a Prince of the Royal House as Viceroy ; and decreed, moreover, that the flag should henceforth be composed of the Italian National colors, red, white, and green, with the arms of the Reigning Dynasty in the centre.

On the morning following, the King and Queen drove into Naples in an open carriage. Although respectfully saluted by the populace as they passed through the crowded streets, there was no sign of the enthusiastic welcome they had been led to expect as a result of the proclamation of the previous day. This was due in great measure to the action of the Liberal and Revolutionary Committees in the capital, which had issued instructions that the Constitution be coldly received ; warning their members that the King had no intention of keeping faith with the Liberals, and that the measures now wrung from him would be revoked on the first favorable opportunity ; that to accept the same would be equivalent to treachery towards the Sicilians, who were at that very moment being butchered by the Neapolitan

Soldiery, besides dealing a death-blow to aspirations for Italian National Unity. As a consequence, while the men-of-war anchored in the bay, the forts, and public buildings, hoisted the new tricolor flag, greeting the same with the thunder of salutes from the artillery afloat and ashore; the official rejoicings awakened no response from the general public. To make matters worse riots broke out; and the following evening increased to alarming proportions. Bands recruited from the lowest scum of the population, their numbers swelled by agents of the secret Police, invaded the principal streets, yelling " Long live the King. Down with the Constitution. Death to the Liberals." The Police Offices, in various parts of the town were broken into; the archives burnt or destroyed; the Commissioners wounded or maltreated. In other quarters the infuriated mob attacked all those suspected of Liberal tendencies, and even insulted and struck the French Minister, Brenier, who was passing in his carriage. The fomentation, and enactment, of these outrages was generally attributed to the influence of the Queen Mother and the King's half-brother, the Count of Trani, both bitterly opposed to the proposed Constitution, and who hoped by these means to render its promulgation ineffective. It has been objected, however, that as Villamarina and the Unionists were equally anxious, although from very different motives, that the Constitution should not be successfully launched, or favorably received, it is unfair to hold one party responsible for the shameful scenes enacted. That the roughs and agitators were the paid agents of one or more political parties there is no doubt, while their indiscriminate attacks on Police and Liberals alike would seem to indicate the connivance of those interested in defeating, for one purpose or another, the proposed reforms. As a result of the disturbances the Constitutional Ministry initiated its career by proclaiming the state of siege, an unfortunate but imperative necessity, at least until measures could be devised for the preservation of order by the formation of the promised National Guard.

Under the Presidency of Antonio Spinelli, with De Martino in charge of Foreign Affairs, and the hitherto obscure, but soon all-powerful, Liborio Romano as Prefect of Police, the new Ministry lost no time in approaching Villamarina on the subject of the Piedmontese alliance. Count Talleyrand, French Minister in Turin, seconded the Neapolitan application, which now caused Cavour considerable embarrassment. The Marquis of Villamarina,

who had closely watched, and carefully studied
the development of the present situation, and
was thoroughly cognizant of its causes, expressed himself in his despatches to Turin as
not by any means satisfied concerning the sincerity of Francis, either in connection with the
concessions wrung from him, or the motives
which prompted the application for an alliance
so lately spurned. In his opinion, as in Cavour's,
the opportune moment for such a tie had passed;
while Garibaldi and his companions had
travelled too far on the road to success to brook
any attempt at direct interference, or suggestion tending to the restoration of the old order.
"If we yield now, and accept the Neapolitan
alliance," he wrote to Cavour, " we shall have
revolution at home as well as here in Naples :
and, moreover, the Bourbons will encourage
its explosion."

It was hardly to be expected that the astute
Piedmontese Prime Minister would willingly,
and in the face of recent developments, jeop-
ardize his Sovereign's National popularity by
formally binding himself to succor his found-
ering southern rival from the consequences of
his own blind folly. Yet the susceptibilities of
the European Powers demanded careful handling ; and especially France and England, who
now welcomed the proposed alliance as a possi-
16

ble termination of the vexatious Italian im-
broglio, which threatened to complicate international relations, and constituted a perpetual
menace to the equipoise of political combinations.   Consequently Cavour, while not declining to discuss the matter, began by insisting on three preliminary considerations, the
acceptance of which he held indispensable.   He
contended, firstly : that any formal bond between the two Governments was impossible
while civil war existed in Sicily, since Victor
Emmanuel could not become the ally of the
King of Naples, who was even now shedding
the blood of his subjects in the disaffected
island.   The second consideration called for
the immediate cessation of all intimate relations
with Austria, and the abandonment of obnoxious influences hostile or detrimental to the
principles of Italian Nationalism.   Thirdly,
Cavour laid stress on the necessity that the
policy of the two Governments towards the
Roman Curia should be identical.

European diplomacy could not openly take
exception to considerations so manifestly in accordance with the recognized interests of the
Italianism so loudly proclaimed; yet the subterfuge was too thinly veiled not to be clearly
perceptible to those gifted with an appreciation
of the probabilities, as evinced by existing real-

ities. The invalidation of the proposed treaty
owing to a possible breach of faith on the part
of the Neapolitan Government, would undoubtedly have entangled Austria, France and
the Holy See, and perhaps other European
Powers ; while the fruits of 1859 would certainly have been lost. It consequently behoved
Cavour, aside from dynastic ambitions, to proceed cautiously before committing his country
to a course which, whatever advantages it
might have offered a couple of months earlier,
was now viewed with sullen disapprobation by
an increasingly powerful party, spread over the
entire Peninsula.

On July third the Neapolitan Envoy at Turin
officially opened negotiations with the announcement that a special Embassy would shortly arrive
at the Piedmontese capital for the purpose mentioned, and two weeks later Commendatore
Giovanni Manna, and Baron Winspeare, reached
Turin. The former was well known as an authority on financial administration, and as an
ardent, if prudent, advocate of liberal institutions : the latter had gained a reputation as an
able diplomatist and administrator. The basis
on which negotations were to be carried on
were the following : An alliance between the two
Crowns, to consolidate and assure the independence of the Peninsula against foreign attacks

or influence ; a Customs and Commercial League ; Uniformity of coinage, weights and measures ; Agreement for postal service, and literary copyright, as well as for the railway systems. In fact, a general fusion of the material interests of the two States. The King of Naples, furthermore, consented that Sicily should be free to elect a Parliament in conformity with the Constitution of 1812 ; which body might decree a complete political separation from the Continental Kingdom, yet remain under the sovereignty of the Neapolitan Throne, which would be represented by a Prince of the Royal Family, as Viceroy. The Ambassadors were, moreover, empowered to treat concerning the recognition of the annexed provinces of Tuscany, and the Duchies ; but for the late Pontifical possessions a special arrangement was proposed, by virtue of which Piedmont was to exercise a limited sovereignty over the Legations, while the Bourbon King assumed similar functions in connection with the Marches and Umbria.

The Bourbon Envoys, however, very rightly and justly insisted, as a preliminary, on the cessation of hostilities in Sicily, and the formal assurance that neither Garibaldi, nor his followers, be allowed to cross over to the Continent, or to incite the continental population to revolt.

This last condition was warmly supported by
Russia, Prussia, France and England. Although
Cavour protested that the Government, as such,
had no authority over Garibaldi, who, having
severed every link of dependence on it by re-
nouncing his military grade, and his status as
Deputy, would undoubtedly turn a deaf ear to
any orders emanating from Turin ; he nevertheless considered it advisable to conciliate
diplomatic requirements by making an appeal
for prudent moderation on the part of the victorious filibuster, who still loudly proclaimed
his fealty to Victor Emmanuel. Under date
of July twenty-second the King of Sardinia
thus addressed the popular hero : " General,
you are aware that I did not approve of your
expedition, with which I have had absolutely
no connection. But to-day the difficult position in which Italy finds herself makes it my
duty to place myself in direct communication
with you. In the event that the King of Naples
concede the complete evacuation of Sicily by
his troops ; if he should voluntarily desist from
all intercession, and engage personally not to
exercise any kind of pressure over the Sicilians,
in order that they may have full liberty to select
that Government which best pleases them ; in
this case I think it would be more reasonable
to renounce all ulterior projects against the

Kingdom of Naples. If you are of a contrary opinion I expressly reserve to myself complete liberty of action, and abstain from expressing any opinion relative to your designs." The reply which reached Turin a few days later ran as follows : " Sire, Your Majesty is aware of the affection and reverence I entertain for your person, and how eager I am to obey you. Nevertheless your Majesty must appreciate the embarrassment I should find myself in, should I assume a passive attitude in face of the Neapolitan continental population which I have been obliged to restrain for so long, and to whom I have promised my immediate support. Italy would demand of me an accounting for such inaction, and would suffer immense detriment from it. On the termination of my mission I will lay at your Majesty's feet the authority which circumstances have conferred upon me, and shall be most happy to obey you for the remainder of my life."

An examination of his private correspondence with the Marquis d'Azeglio affords an insight into the perplexities and worries which harassed the Prime Minister during these days of uncertainty, and multitudinous entanglements. Writing to D'Azeglio on July 12th, in anticipation of the arrival of the Neapolitan Envoys, he professes to know neither the proposals they will advance nor the replies he will make. "If they really consent to the cession of Sicily, and will aid us to demolish Rome, I think we might come to an understanding : for a time at least." His estimation of Manna, after their first interview, is interesting. The Envoy struck him as a thoroughly honest man who had been forced into assuming a rôle which inspired him with profound repugnance, and whose confidence in the Government " he has been made to represent " is of the most limited. On the same day on which Victor Emmanuel penned the letter to Garibaldi which has been quoted above, Cavour informed his correspondent in London : " I am going to advise the King to write to him (Garibaldi) to accept a truce, on the basis of the concession to the Sicilians of their political future. I doubt very much whether Garibaldi will accept this advice. It would indeed be too stupid not to take advantage of the deplorable condition in which Naples finds itself. In the meanwhile the whole Diplomatic Corps here is down upon me ; Hudson excepted." After describing the attitudes of the various representatives, Cavour acknowledges that, while the diplomatists rail and storm he presses forward, and that the fleets and armies of the West alone can stop him. Referring to the proposed alliance, and the cowardly cession of

Messina to Garibaldi, he exclaims : "This measure proves that at Naples there is no longer an army, no longer a Government. Manna himself admits that the discredit into which his Government has fallen renders an alliance more difficult. One may ally oneself with an enemy one respects, even after having defeated him : one cannot sully oneself by a union with a Government which does not even know how to fall with honor." At Turin the surrender of Messina was considered as doing away with all possibility of preventing Garibaldi's descent upon the mainland, should such a course have been deemed advisable. Cavour in this connection writes explicitly : "Don't think that I look without serious apprehension on this coming event. It is no longer a question of the King of Naples : nobody in his capital wants him any more, and the good Villamarina (whose last despatch I forwarded) does not cease in his warnings to me that it would be an enormous blunder to attempt to prop up an edifice which is crumbling on all sides, and whose every support, Navy, Army, Administration, is undermined. But there is great danger in allowing Garibaldi to gain possession of Naples. Not being able to prevent his taking Naples, there is but one means of saving ourselves from being overwhelmed by him : it is to vie with him in boldness, and not allow him to monopolize the unitarian idea which now exercises an irresistible fascination over the popular masses. Certainly the dangers of this situation are not concealed from me ; but events are stronger than men. There would be no use in struggling against them." He then desires D'Azeglio to sound the British Government, with all due secrecy and circumspection, as to what aid would be forthcoming, should events in the South make the active intervention of Piedmont necessary or advisable. A week later Cavour furnished the Marquis d'Azeglio with a copy of the ultra-confidential instructions to Count Nigra, which outlined the proposed expedition of General Cialdini to Ancona. A postscript to this important document encloses a lock of Garibaldi's hair, as "a trophy to be dangled before the eyes of the female admirers of the hero of Sicily!"

CHAPTER XIII.

Promulgation of Constitution.—Preparations for elections.—
Amnesty of political prisoners.—Tumultuous reception of
exiles.—Action of troops.—Disorders in the capital.—Romano's influence.—Romano ; his character and antecedents.—The Queen-Mother goes to Gaeta.—Intrigues of the
"Camarilla."—Romano's further demands.—Insulting resignations.—The Press embarrasses the Government.—Schism
in Revolutionary Committees.—Romano's revelations.—His
political memoirs.—Cavour's opportunity.—His despatch to
Envoy at St. Petersburg.—His remarks to Nisco.—Disaffection in Neapolitan Army.—The Ministerial programme.—
The elections postponed.

THE newly-formed ministry in Naples, anxious to allay popular suspicions by a tangible
proof of the sincerity of the Sovereign Act promulgated on June twenty-fifth, strongly advised Francis to revive without delay the Constitution of 1848, which they argued " had only
been suspended in consequence of painful circumstances, which need not now be recalled,"
and had never been abrogated. The King
signed the decree re-establishing this Constitution on July first, and simultaneously convened
the Electoral Colleges for August nineteenth,
and Parliament on September tenth. Next
day the city was relieved of the oppressive
250

measures of martial law, which had been in force since the outbreaks which accompanied the promulgation of the Act.

The Ministry now became absorbed in the formation of committees for the preparation of laws and reforms, to be submitted to the consideration of the future Parliament.

The amnesty of political prisoners and exiles, promised by the Act, went into operation on July third ; not only for those whose trials were still in progress, but including all undergoing confinement, or under sentence of perpetual banishment from the Kingdom. The execution of this decree plunged the Government into fresh embarrassments and complications, for the bolder, and more irreconcilable, of these political agitators lost not a moment in inciting their adherents to continue a struggle, the first fruits of which were already theirs. The arrival of each popular martyr, such as Settembrini, Pisanelli, and Imbriani, was the signal for demonstrations of tumultuous sympathy, invariably accompanied by cries of " Viva Italia," and " Viva Garibaldi." Count Cavour had advised all the exiles who had taken refuge in Turin to return to their country, and to use their influence towards the propagation of National principles. Most were anxious to avail themselves of the facilities extended, but

Carlo Poerio significantly refused to return to Naples, as long as the Bourbons occupied the Throne.

It was rumored that the troops were opposed to the franchise lately granted, and naturally continual friction between the Liberal and Military elements ensued.   On July fifteenth the Grenadiers of the Royal Guard, exasperated by one of the aforementioned demonstrations, charged the Liberalist sympathizers, with the cry of " Long live the King ;" cut down those who resisted, and even sacked several shops in which terrified citizens had taken refuge.

The occurrence spread terror throughout the city, and caused consternation in the ranks of the Ministerial party.   Liborio Romano laid the responsibility at the door of the Reactionists, and claimed to possess documents in support of his accusation.   The Minister of War resigned, and was succeeded by General Pianell, while Liborio Romano took charge of the Ministry of the Interior vacated by del Re.   During his brief administration of the Prefecture of Police, Romano had surrounded himself with members of the "Camorra," numbers of whom had but just obtained their release from the prisons, by virtue of the recent amnesty.   This policy, which has been adversely criticised, was not without sound advantage at the moment, and although originally resorted to under stress of complex circumstances, was undoubtedly later the means of saving the capital from far more serious disturbances. The system gave rise to great abuses, it is true, and favored many individual acts of retaliation on Bourbon adherents; but the formation of the National Guard acted as a check to the over-zealous police, and moderated the evils of this temporary expedient, which became alarmingly apparent, however, when, after the fall of the reigning Dynasty, it was necessary to expurgate this element from the ranks of the local and National bureaucracy.

In the meantime Liborio Romano was the idol of those he had placed in positions of more or less importance. The police force, and the members of the National Guard, the ranks of which were also thronged with "Camorristi," affectionately styled him "Father." This latter body of men, which on July seventeenth consisted of six thousand men, was two days later increased to nearly ten thousand. Prince Ischitella, formerly a Minister of Ferdinand II., and a devoted friend of Romano, commanded this branch of the service, and was surrounded by officers equally attached to the new Minister of the Interior. The enthusiasm aroused by Romano's visit to the barracks of the National

Guard on July seventeenth, in company with Ischitella, was indescribable, and cleared away all doubts as to the influence at the command of the political star which had but so recently appeared above the horizon.

Liborio Romano, originally an obscure lawyer from Lecce, a town in the heel of Italy, has traced his political memoirs, or justification of the policy pursued during the few months he was in power. These are, however, unconvincing and susceptible to varied interpretation, leaving the impartial reader in doubt as to the real share, or responsibility, attributable to him in the disasters which overtook the Sovereign he professed to serve. He proclaimed himself a Federalist at a time when that doctrine was popular with political agitators ; and the expression of these views had gained him credit amongst a certain class of politicians, and even served, in conjunction with other qualifications, to bring him into more or less intimate relations with the Count of Aquila, who dabbled in Liberalism, and was eager to play a political rôle at any cost. Although Romano had suffered persecution, imprisonment and exile at the hands of Ferdinand II., and had been mixed up in various conspiracies from 1828 upwards (he was born in 1794), his political convictions were dubious and his talents hardly above mediocrity. If his phenomenal popularity was the result of a combination of circumstances, more or less beyond his control, it was also due in great measure to the man's special aptitude for intrigue, and the possession of what has been described as the Italo-Grecian cunning, at once ingenuous and caressing, characteristic in the descendants of the Greek colonists who settled on the shores of the lower Adriatic, and Ionian Sea. His immense popularity and undoubted, though brief, influence, were of advantage to the Bourbons and Liberals in turn ; for he possessed no vestige of political conscience, and from the outset played a double game. It is a significant fact that after the collapse of the Government he served, and an exceedingly brief career under Garibaldi, Romano was shunned by the Unionists, and was given no part in the reorganization of Southern Italy.

On assuming the administration of the Prefecture of Police, which office the Count of Aquila was instrumental in overcoming the King's hesitation to grant him, Romano insisted that the Queen Mother, whose influence he rightly mistrusted, should no longer reside in Naples. Francis, greatly impressed by the evident authority of the new Minister over the undisciplined elements of the population, as well as his power with the Police and National Guard, reluctantly yielded to this and other conditions hardly less humiliating. The Dowager Maria Theresa, accompanied by the King's half-brothers, and the more notorious of the "Camarilla," took their departure to Gaeta, but continued, nevertheless, from the shelter of that stronghold, to conspire against the Liberal institutions whose spread they witnessed with impotent rage and horror. Romano describes the "Camarilla" as more fatal to the Dynasty than any of the revolutionary factions. "This party, blinded by implacable hatred of the Liberal institutions, revived in spite of it, failing to appreciate the nature of the Italian movement or the strength of the revolution, did not recognize the fact that the Dynasty was abandoned by all Europe, by the country itself, and by those who had previously been its staunchest upholders. Counting on the hesitating, uncertain character of the King, who had no definite plans, they hoped to secure a facile victory, could they, by means of a 'coup d'état,' possess themselves of the Government, throw over the Constitution, and lay hands on the Ministry, and the chiefs of the various parties." Romano further states that he frankly told the King when he accepted the portfolio of the Interior, that, in view of the altered conditions throughout Italy as well as the triumphant progress of the revolution, it was now useless to expect Piedmont to agree to the alliance. He did not conceal from the Sovereign, he says, that the universal sympathy with the House of Savoy, the victories of Garibaldi, and the growing desire for National unity, offset by the recollections of an irreparable past, constituted almost insurmountable obstacles. In his opinion, the only possible salvation lay in the observance of the strictest legality, and the most loyal and broadest interpretation of the constitutional franchises. This, and this alone, could inspire trust in the Government, and faith in the sincerity of its intentions.

Not content with the banishment of the Queen Mother to Gaeta, and the dispersal of the " Camarilla," Romano demanded that the army be immediately required to swear fealty to the Constitution ; that the Royal Guard be disbanded, and the National Guard increased to twelve thousand men. Francis reluctantly consented that the oath be administered to the troops, and still more unwillingly yielded to the demand for an increase of a body of men manifestly hostile to his personal interests, but stood firm for the preservation of his Guard, although he compromised the difficulty by transferring the quarters of these regiments to Portici, outside Naples. By these measures Liborio Romano practically controlled the whole military and police force in the capital; while, thanks to the methods of recruiting already described, his influence rapidly extended throughout the provinces as well.

Another bitter humiliation and source of fresh anxiety awaited the unfortunate Francis after the promulgation of the Constitution. Alexander Nunziante, Duke of Mignano, the trusted and favorite General of Ferdinand II., as well as of his son, requested the acceptance of his resignation; and a few days later returned to the King all the decorations which had been showered upon him, with the insulting comment that he could no longer wear on his breast the insignia of a Government which confounded honest, straightforward and loyal subjects with those deserving only of contempt. Simultaneously, the Duchess of Mignano requested that she be relieved of her duties of Lady of Honor. In addition, Nunziante addressed an order of the day to the troops under his command, couched in terms which left little doubt of the political spirit which animated him.

The publication of these documents caused a profound impression throughout Italy, which was greatly increased when it became known that Nunziante had communicated his intentions to Count Cavour, together with declarations which virtually committed him to the Unitarian Cause.

Francis now received daily and significant indications of the growing isolation of his position. The Legitimist element of the aristocracy, deeply offended by the Liberal franchises embodied in the Constitution, held aloof, or manifested their indignation by refusing to salute the Sovereign in the streets.

Meanwhile, Romano vigorously pursued his system of official expurgation. In every branch of the public service the adherents of the old régime were retired, or unceremoniously turned out, being replaced by those in sympathy with the new order. Long lists were daily presented for confirmation to the King, who, although he might rebel on occasion, was, nevertheless, in the end obliged to yield to the inexorable will of the Minister he distrusted, but to whose supremacy he was forced to submit.

The liberty of the Press, accorded by the stipulations of the Chart, quickly degenerated into the most reprehensible license. Paltry sheets of every shade of progressive or reactionary opinion, anti-dynastic for the most part, some frankly Unitarian, others officious mouth-pieces of the Cavouriani, the followers of Garibaldi, or of Mazzini's more fanatical disciples, sprang up in all directions, the only loyally Constitutional and Federalist paper supporting the Ministerial programme being the " Italia." Although it was attempted to restrain the vituperative excesses of this ephemeral literature by means of bonds which each political publication was required to deposit, the measure raised such a storm of protest that its enforcement was rarely resorted to. The malicious misrepresentation of proposed reforms proved one of the serious embarrassments against which the Constitutional Ministry labored from the outset, and must even under less unfavorable auspices have constituted a source of danger and failure.

To add to the confusion occasioned by the heterogeneous politics of this unbridled Press, a schism was created in the Liberal Committee, the ramifications of which extended throughout the southern provinces. The split resulted in the formation of two Committees : that of Order, and that of Action. The former, composed of men devoted to Count Cavour, and convinced of the wisdom of the prudential policy he advocated ; the latter made up of the followers of Garibaldi. While both aimed at the triumph of the revolution, their methods and vehicles were divergent. The Committee of Order desired the success of the revolution on the Continént to be independent of the personal participation, or direct influence of Garibaldi, and worked to bring about this result by securing the co-operation of the Neapolitan military organizations. To this party the defection of General Nunziante, and its possible influence on the troops under his command, was of supreme importance. In the hope that a "pronunziamento," enhanced by his presence, might accomplish this end, Cavour summoned Nunziante from Switzerland, where he had retired, and entrusted him with a mission to Naples. The Committee of Action, on the other hand, desired for various reasons that the, no longer doubtful, overthrow of the Bourbon rule should redound to the credit of Garibaldi alone.

A third party, essentially reactionary and bitterly anti-Liberal, conspired under the guidance of the Queen Mother and Count of Trapani, against the existing Government, and aimed at creating a "coup d'état," which would throw the power into their own hands, and allow them to get rid, not only of the constitutional franchises, as has been said, but to dispense with the King himself. Romano

clearly states that the disorders of July
fifteenth were the beginning of a "coup
d'état" organized by this party, and that, although unsuccessful in its immediate object,
its effect on the negotiations pending in Turin
was far-reaching ; while the loss of prestige
to the Crown, both abroad and at home, was
incalculable. The Neapolitan Minister of the
Interior is not surprised that Cavour should
avail himself of the incident to abandon any
serious ideas of the alliance he may previously have entertained, although in order
not to prematurely provoke a crisis, the consequences of which could not then be foreseen,
he allowed it to be understood that the question was still under diplomatic discussion.
While, for very obvious reasons, it is not safe
to rely on the strictly historical accuracy of
many of the explanations of disputed points
advanced by Romano, it is nevertheless interesting to note that he, a prominent actor in
the drama, declares that the Spinelli Cabinet
opened negotiations for the alliance unwillingly, "coerced by Napoleon III., and by all
the European Powers, except Austria. . . ."
He adds that the Neapolitan Government, in
seeking the alliance, "had not only in view
the propitiation of foreign Diplomacy, but
hoped thereby to foist on Turin the responsi-

bility of the progress of the revolution, and of the civil war which might ensue." He absolves Cavour of the accusation of bad faith, hurled against him by the infuriated and disappointed supporters of a policy which aimed at the entanglement of Piedmont ; and is of opinion that the prudential dissimulation, and procrastination, of the Sardinian Minister, who was early aware of the real situation, served the double purpose of safeguarding the interests of his own country, and averting the untold horrors and excesses of a civil war in the southern Kingdom ; at that moment the theatre of the violent passions of contending political factions of all denominations.

The recent publication of much of the secret political correspondence of this period, has given us perhaps a clearer appreciation of the real motives of some obscure negotiations than the actors themselves possessed. In the case of Romano the fact should not be lost sight of that his memoirs, published after his death (1873), take the form of an apology, or an attempt at posthumous political rehabilitation ; and display in the most favorable light many actions generally considered difficult of satisfactory explanation. Nevertheless his estimates of the closing scenes of the remarkable drama in which he played so conspicuous, though unenviable, a part cannot fail to be instructive.

The disintegration of the Military and Naval forces of the Kingdom became daily more apparent, both in the field in Sicily, and amongst the reserves in the capital, and the continental provinces. General Nunziante boasted to Cavour that his personal influence with the army, and especially with the regiments of Chasseurs he had lately commanded, was sufficient to secure their adhesion to the banner of Victor Emmanuel and Unity. Cavour, now thoroughly convinced that the collapse of the Bourbon Dynasty was merely a question of time, and realizing the importance of being prepared for all eventualities, despatched the General on a Sardinian man-of-war to Naples, in order that he might ascertain the extent of his vaunted influence. At the same time Admiral Persano, under pretext of placing himself at the disposal of the Princess of Syracuse, a member of the House of Savoy, was instructed to station his fleet in Neapolitan waters, and hold himself in readiness for all contingencies ; being especially watchful lest, with the spread of disaffection, the Bourbon Marine come under the direct control of Garibaldi. The Admiral now placed himself in open communication with Villamarina, and the Committee of Order, which, as has been said, favored the cautious diplomacy of Cavour in preference to the audacious policy of the Garibaldians. On the squadron under his command, which was gradually increased as opportunity offered, Persano embarked several regiments of Bersaglieri in anticipation of the necessity of their presence for the preservation of order, or protection of the Sardinian Envoy.

In his despatch of July twenty-eighth to the Marquis Sauli, Sardinian Envoy at St. Petersburg, Cavour broadly hints at the probable action of the Government. After graphically describing the political and social conditions of the Neapolitan Kingdom, he adds : " As for us, if it were in our power to infuse a breath of moral regeneration in a body stricken with incurable decrepitude, we would not refuse our aid. But, under existing conditions, we must be careful not to wound the National sentiment." This intimation that the Government regarded the present issue as a reproduction of the principles of 1789 ; the opposing forces representing Absolutism and Liberty; Nationalism versus local autonomy ; one of which must destroy the other ; was undoubtedly intended for the edification of European Diplomacy, and as such produced its effect.

We have seen that his despatch to d'Azeglio,

dated three days earlier, was more explicit, and prognosticated a rivalry in audacity with Garibaldi as the sole means of counter-balancing the dangerous popularity of the hero of the Sicilian conquest. To Baron Nisco, a Neapolitan exile, whose collaboration with Nunziante was desired, he exclaimed : "We have now entered upon a phase when it is incumbent on us either to become conspirators in order to make Italy, or to perish with the Nation. Let us make this last sacrifice ; let us conspire ! "

The problem, which had now reached a dangerously acute stage, resolved itself into the query whether Piedmont should profit by the intrigues of the revolutionists at Naples (doubtful transactions perforce, and which could not always bear the light of day) or run the risk of seeing the prize slip between her fingers to the advantage of one of the ultra-radical parties, eager to filch the booty from the monarchists. Cavour, although certainly not a squeamish politician, still hesitated to declare openly, and in the face of European opposition, for the revolution ; but from this moment the mask was tentatively lifted, and Villamarina and Persano, while careful in the observation of international diplomatic conventionalities, nevertheless worked more or less openly in the cause of Unity.

The disaffection in the army grew apace as
the conception of National Unity waxed more
popular, owing in part to the astounding achievements in Sicily, and also to the incessant labors
of the Committees in the two Calabrias, and
other southern provinces. In spite of the
splendid bravery of Colonel Bosco and his faithful band at Milazzo, the insolent disregard of
orders from Naples convinced the King's advisers that many of the commanders of the
island were no longer worthy of implicit confidence. The feeling of uneasiness was greatly
intensified when the Count of Syracuse, in person, warned the Ministry that the loyalty of
the crews of the vessels destined for the transportation of three battalions which it was desired to send to the aid of Bosco, still beleaguered in the citadel of Milazzo, was not to be
counted on ; and advised the abandonment of
the proposed expedition.

The deluge, as it mounted higher and higher,
found the Government practically inactive ;
still hesitating as to the line of policy to be
adopted, and obviously incompetent to cope
with the complex problems of the situation.
Spurred on to a semblance of operative energy,
a Ministerial programme was finally issued on
August fourth. The belief that the Government seriously thought to arrest the invading

tide by the publication of this weakly-con-
structed document, seems incredible. Such
phrases as " Protection of the established Religion ; " " Institution of Communal Reforms
and Public Works " sounded well ; but to thinking men the promise of the " entire and sincere fulfilment of the previsions of the Constitution," seemed suspiciously superfluous, while
there was a decidedly false ring in the optimistic references to the negotiations in progress
for the Piedmontese alliance. Nor is it conceivable that Spinelli believed he could long
deceive popular sentiment concerning the doom
of negotiations the unsatisfactory reception of
which from their initiation was well known.
The announcement of the forthcoming opening of the polls for the election of the National
Representation in Parliament alone lent meaning to this programme. But the exaltation of
the public mind was too great to be calmed
with vague and indefinite assurances. The
Press seized upon the question of the representation in Parliament, and immediately began
the publication of lists of candidates, selected
from amongst the late exiles and political prisoners professing the most unequivocal Unitarian and anti-Dynastic principles.

Liborio Romano publicly denied that the
Government exerted any influence in the prep-

aration of the electoral lists, and stated that it merely "desired an honest, prudent, independent and Constitutional-Monarchial Chamber."

The Electoral Colleges were convened for August nineteenth, but the convocation was prorogued until the twenty-sixth, and again postponed to September thirtieth ; for the reason, as advanced in the royal decree, that "the disturbances in Sicily and in Calabria were unfavorable to a candid election."

CHAPTER XIV.

Garibaldi crosses the Straits.—Preoccupations of Cavour.—
Plan to neutralize Garibaldi's prestige.—The mission to
Chambéry.—Napoleon's encouragement.—Conspiracy of the
" Camarilla." —Seizure of arms.—Expulsion of Count of
Aquila.—Francis amidst conflicting counsels.—Romano's
memorandum.—Letter of the Count of Syracuse.—Francis
addresses himself to Garibaldi.—Indecision of King.—Energetic policy of Cabinet.—Resignation of same.—Garibaldi at
the gates.—Francis decides to leave Naples.

THE passage of Garibaldi, and what was now
known as the Army of the South, to continental Italy, was viewed with hardly less acute
alarm in Turin than in Naples.   Although the
personal loyalty of the Chief whose banner was
inscribed with the patriotic device, "Victor
Emmanuel and Italian Unity," was not questioned by the mass of Unionists throughout the
Peninsula, the political creed of many of his
lieutenants and henchmen was open to suspicion.   Cavour dreaded the influence of these
surroundings ; and while unwilling to renounce
the prudent policy thus far adhered to, fully
realized the blow to the national prestige of
the "Honest King" which would follow the
insinuations of pusillanimous inertia, should
Garibaldi be permitted to accomplish unaided

the conquest of the Southern Kingdom. Already the independent and brilliant achievements of the guerilla chieftain suggested disquieting possibilities, should he, flushed with even greater triumphs, give vent to the resentment he had felt at the cession of his native town of Nice, and embroil his country with France by an attack on the Eternal City.

Much as Cavour dreaded a departure from the diplomatic channels hitherto pursued, it was now apparent that, unless Piedmont was to reap merely odium, and possibly incur serious danger, from an enterprise entered upon in the name of the national cause her Sovereign impersonated, action could no longer be delayed.

Although the Piedmontese Government cannot be said to have been taken by surprise, yet, nevertheless, the rapidity of events in the South was unprecedented, and Cavour would have preferred more time to mature his plans. This, however, was denied him, and he consequently faced the dilemma with characteristic energy.

"I don't flatter myself," he wrote d'Azeglio on August first, "that England will particularly relish my plan; I think she would prefer to see Garibaldi reach Naples, even if he brought anarchy and revolution in his train.

She considers him as the enemy of France, and that is enough to render him dear in her eyes. But we cannot expose ourselves to destruction for the sake of pleasing England. . . . "

Needless to say, that the plan referred to aimed at reaching Naples in advance of Garibaldi. In determining upon this bold move the Piedmontese Minister laid great stress on the oft-proclaimed non-intervention policy of the English Cabinet. France he felt confident would not go contrary to British opinion in this matter, although the Emperor might deem it incumbent on him to bluster officially in order to propitiate the Legitimist and Clerical elements, which must necessarily take exception to any violation of the territories of the Pope.

The result of the mission of Farini and Cialdini to Chambéry, where they met the Emperor, who was visiting his newly-acquired possessions, was satisfactory in so far as it confirmed Cavour's conviction that Napoleon III. would not resent the passage of the Piedmontese forces through the Papal States, provided Rome itself were left untouched. The Envoys were greeted with the reassuring exclamation : " Well ! Why are you not more energetic ? Count Cavour hesitates to confront the scarecrow represented by the Legitimist volunteers which Pius IX. has gathered around

his banner ! Do you think that the whole of
France is ready to rush to the aid of these
discontented loafers ? " *

Yet, while raising no objection in principle
to the proposed expedition, the Emperor
deemed it more prudent, in view of the suspicion in which he and the Piedmontese Government were regarded by the Diplomacy of
Europe, to await the inevitable result of the
revolutionary movement on Naples. "Let
Garibaldi go there first," he insisted, "and
you can go afterwards." A month earlier he
had written to Count Persigny, his Ambassador
at the Court of Saint James : " I am anxious
that Italy should obtain peace, no matter how,
so that I can withdraw from Rome, and that
foreign intervention may be averted."

The presence in Rome of General Lamori-
ciére, a brilliant, but anti-Napoleonic, officer
whose record in Africa had been a most
glorious one, and who now commanded the
Pontifical troops, constituted an undoubted
menace to the success of Cavour's proposed
undertaking. A bigoted Legitimist, bitterly
hostile to Napoleon III. and his policy, while
correspondingly devoted to the fanatical and
ultra-conservative faction at the Roman Court,
his influence would, it was feared, inevitably

* Farini and Cialdini to Cavour, August 29, 1860.
18

tend to involve France in any quarrel between the Pope and the Piedmontese Government. The dream of the Papal See was the reconquest of the Romagna, lost owing to the enforced withdrawal of Austrian support after Villa-franca. With the handful of troops at his disposal General Lamoricière could naturally not undertake this task ; yet a skilful manipulation of the threatened political chaos might make such an enterprise feasible at any moment.

The assurances given Cavour's envoys at Chambéry were consequently of the utmost value to Piedmont. If left alone to deal with the Papal troops and their French commander, General Cialdini was confident of success. It only remained to await the advent of a pretext, the seizure of which would not too violently shock the jealous susceptibilities of European Diplomacy.

Meanwhile the perplexities of the Nea-politan Government were aggravated by the petty and continual annoyances devised by the members of the " Camarilla," who seized every juncture to embarrass and vilify the Constitutionalists. The reactionary move-ment of July fifteenth, misunderstood by the masses, while it failed to yield any substan-tial profit to its promoters, had undoubtedly increased the popular suspicion of the Court

Party ; and public opinion included Francis
in this faction, failing to understand how
one could be more royalist than the King.
The Clergy, naturally reactionary and ultra-
conservative, perceiving that Francis was being
forced by the revolutionary tide to the cession
of liberties prejudicial to their interests, threw
the enormous weight of their authority into
the scales, and through the manifold secret
channels at their command, urged the abandonment of the Constitutional pledges, even
though such a course entail the deposition of
the King, bloodshed, and all the horrors of
civil war. The Count of Aquila, who aspired
to the Regency, was supported by this party,
as well as by the " Camarilla." The conspiracies of this Prince, as well as that of his
henchman, the French Legitimist priest de
Sauclières, although abortive, and under less
critical circumstances insignificant, were, nevertheless, indications of the disintegration of the
Dynastic principle. Under the specification of
hardware, the Count of Aquila had secretly
imported from France a quantity of uniforms
and weapons, identical with those used by the
National Guard. The plan was to equip a
number of the adherents of the " Camarilla "
with these uniforms, and to simulate disturbances between the populace, or rather mob of

suborned "lazzaroni," and this fictitious National Guard, on the one hand; while other bodies of traversied troops mingled with the real Civic Corps, creating confusion, and giving the semblance of mutiny in the ranks of the upholders of the Constitutional privileges; thus discrediting the Government, and evincing the popular aversion to the liberal leaders. This decidedly clumsy plot was easily unearthed by Romano's police, the arms and accoutrements confiscated, and documents, clearly compromising the Count, placed in the hands of the Government. The affair was immediately considered by the Council of Ministers, in special session; and after mature deliberation the arrest of the Count was decided on. This very proper decision was, however, not carried out, owing to the repugnance of certain members of the Cabinet, who feared to provoke a crisis by such extreme measures, and was commuted into an order of expulsion from the Kingdom within twenty-four hours. Francis, although cognizant of the nature of the accusation, and of the contents of the incriminating documents, refrained from taking part in the deliberations of the Council. He, however, approved its decisions, and yielded to Spinelli's emphatic demand that should the Count of Aquila re-

quest an audience of his nephew, this favor
should be denied. Owing to the weakness of
the Government, or the insistence of the credulous Francis, the threatened disgrace was
still further mitigated, and the Count left
Naples on August 14th on an improvised mission to England ; nominally for the purchase
of two frigates for the royal navy.

The details of the propaganda undertaken
by the priest de Sauclières, provided for a second Saint Bartholomew, in which the Liberals
were to have assigned them the unenviable
part of the Huguenots. De Sauclières, when
arrested, confessed that the conspiracy, which
he stated was in favor of the King, included
in its ranks " the highest in the land." That
Francis was cognizant of the conspiracy before
its discovery by the police is maintained by
certain writers, but the extent of its ramifications will never be known, for the Provisional
Government of Garibaldi quashed the proceedings against its participants, by virtue of the
decree of September 11th, granting full amnesty for all political crimes.

The moral condition of the capital when it
became known, on August 19th, that Garibaldi
had actually passed the fleets stationed in the
Straits of Messina, and successfully landed at
Melito, is indescribable. The fall of Reggio,

and the military promenade through Calabria, struck terror into the souls of the Reactionists, while it intensified the frenzied enthusiasm of the jubilant Liberals.   The King, distraught by the conflicting opinions of his official counsellors, hesitated to adopt a line of conduct. The Diplomatic Corps beseeched Francis to spare the Capital the horrors of a siege, culminating with the inevitable excesses attending a triumphant revolution.   Spinelli advised energetic action, although he did not conceal his apprehension of the contamination, and general demoralization, of the royal troops. He expressed the conviction, however, that should the King place himself at the head of his regiments, confidence and discipline would be restored.   "At least," he urged, "if it is our destiny to succumb, we would fall with honor, and would be free from the reproach of fleeing before a handful of men whose only strength lies in the prestige of their chief." It was argued that this prestige rested exclusively on previous abnormal achievements, and that a single defeat would destroy the popular credence in the infallibility of the hero.   The "Thousand" who had landed at Marsala had, it is true, increased to fourteen times that number ; but these were badly armed, wretchedly equipped, and, from a military point of view, undisciplined, besides being deficient in artillery, cavalry and commissariat, and with no reserve to fall back upon in case of serious reverse. Francis, on the other hand, had still nominally at his command some forty-four thousand men, efficient artillery, and (it was asserted) abundant ammunition and provender for man and beast, besides the substantial sum of six millions of ducats in the treasury. The Minister of War had prepared a plan of resistance acceptable to a majority of his colleagues, and approved by Ischitella. Francis read the document, listened to the counsels of his military advisers, and with characteristic but fatal irresolution continually postponed his decision.

On August 20th, Liborio Romano handed the King his famous memorandum. This document, not having been indorsed by the majority of the Cabinet, was presented privately, and on the personal responsibility of the Minister of the Interior. After summarizing the political situation at home and abroad, and dwelling on the lack of discipline, and consequent scant trust to be reposed in the army, and the even more deplorable conditions prevailing in the marine forces, Romano advances the belief that "a return of the confidence of the people in their Prince has become not only

difficult but impossible." Therefore he proposes, and counsels, that the King leave the
country for a time at least, placing the temporary Regency in the hands of a Minister
worthy of confidence.   The Regency of a
Royal Prince would not serve the purpose, as
it would not command public confidence, or
" offer any guarantee for the interests of the
Dynasty." Public opinion demanded a prompt
decision—on all sides, among the masses, as
well as in the ranks of those natural supporters of the Crown, the Army and Navy, there
existed profound distrust.   The Ministry could
do nothing to avert, or reconcile, this universal
scepticism of the good faith of the Crown ; nor
could they pretend to ignore it.   The Minister
then advises that Francis, at the moment of
his departure, " address the People with loyal
and magnanimous words, which shall bear witness to the kindness of your paternal heart,
which has taken this noble resolve in order to
spare your subjects the horrors of civil war.
Your Majesty will then have recourse to the
verdict of Europe, and will await from time,
and the justice of God, the return of confidence,
and the triumph of your legitimate rights."
Should the King, in his wisdom, decide to reject the counsels of his Minister, Romano adds
that no other course would be open to him but

to resign the high office with which he has been entrusted, in the belief that he no longer enjoys his Sovereign's confidence.

On a first reading of this extraordinary document we are inclined to brand Liborio Romano as a consummate hypocrite, but a more careful perusal discloses the fact that he exaggerates, conceals and promises nothing. It is patent that he, as other thinking men, realized that once the Bourbon Throne was vacated, either by spontaneous renunciation, or the forcible ejection of its occupant, no foreign or domestic power could, or would, restore a Dynasty so thoroughly unsatisfactory, not only to the country itself, but also in the eyes of progressive Europe.

Romano has been stigmatized as an arch-traitor by those writers who sympathized with Bourbon rule in Naples, and as has been said, the Italian Government showed no desire to retain his services after the fall of the Dynasty, although Garibaldi availed himself of his co-operation for a while. He was undoubtedly instrumental in avoiding unnecessary blood-shed in the capital, and subsequent events amply justified his estimation of the crisis. That he believed the advancement of his personal ambitions to be compatible with the best interests of his country, is a supposition which would be considered hazardous by many, but is not contradicted by facts.

The startling propositions contained in the Minister's memorandum were rciterated four days later in a document which, considering the source from which it came, must be acknowledged as infinitely more significant. The Count of Syracuse addressed his royal nephew in unequivocal terms, leaving no room for doubt as to the extent of the sacrifice demanded of him.

" SIRE :

" When I raised my voice to avert the perils which threatened our House, I was unheeded ; see to it that now, when I prophesy still greater misfortunes, I find access to your heart, and that I be not refuted by short-sighted and baneful counsel.

"The conditions of Italy which are completely changed ; the, ideal of National Unity which has assumed gigantic proportions during the few months following the fall of Palermo ; have deprived Your Majesty's Government of the strength which upholds States, and rendered impossible an alliance with Piedmont.

" The populations of Upper Italy, horrified by the reports of the Sicilian massacres, repulsed the Neapolitan Ambassadors; and miserably abandoned to the hazards of arms alone, deprived of alliances, we are the prey of the resentment of the multitudes which rise up in all parts of Italy demanding the extermination of our House, which has become the target for general reprobation. Moreover, the civil war, which now invades the continental provinces, will overwhelm the Dynasty in the supreme ruin which the crafty manœuvres of perfidious counsellors has long since prepared for the descendants of Charles III. of Bourbon. The blood of citizens, uselessly shed, will again inundate the thousand cities of the Kingdom, and you who were the hope, and the object of the affection of the people, will be contemplated with horror as the sole cause of a fratricidal war. Sire! Save our House while there is yet time : preserve it from the maledictions of all Italy; imitate the example of our royal relative of Parma, who released his subjects from their allegiance, and made them the arbiters of their own destiny, as soon as civil war had broken out in his Duchy. Europe, and your People, will credit you for your heroic sacrifice ; you will be enabled to serenely lift your face before God, who will reward the magnanimous action of Your Majesty. Your soul being regenerated through misfortune, your heart will expand to the noble aspirations of the Fatherland, and you will bless the day when you sacrificed yourself for the greatness of Italy.

" With these words, Sire, I simply fulfil the duty imposed by my long experience, and I pray God that He guide you, and render you worthy of His benedictions."

Abandoned by Ministers and family alike, the unfortunate Francis, in desperation, is said to have made a supreme appeal to the wielder of the avenging sword which threatened to sweep away his Crown. The following almost incredible proposition is vouched for by several contemporaneous writers, amongst others Signora White-Mario, who accompanied her husband during Garibaldi's southern campaign, and Maxim du Camp, who relates it in his personal experiences.* After the capitulation of Soveria, Garibaldi received, from the hands of M. J. La Cecilia, a letter written by the order of Francis, and dated August seventh, by the terms of which the King offered the successful General, on condition that he refrain from any attempt to overturn the Bourbon Government: (1) The abandonment of Sicily, which should be allowed to de-

* " Expédition des Deux-Siciles." Paris, 1861.

cide its own destiny by universal suffrage. (2) The free passage for himself and his army through Neapolitan territory, without, however, traversing Naples. (3) Three millions of ducats in cash. (4) The co-operation during six months of fifty thousand men of the royal troops, as well as the fleet, for the purpose of attacking Austria in Venetia, or the Papal troops at Ancona. (5) The right of raising volunteers throughout the Kingdom.

As there exists no official documentary evidence to substantiate their assertions, the burden of proof, as well as the responsibility of historical accuracy, must rest with the above-mentioned authors. Neither Liborio Romano, who would presumably have been cognizant of the transaction, owing to his subsequent official relations with Garibaldi, nor the victorious General himself, make any reference to the letter which, clearly branding Francis a traitor to country and traditions alike, would have been eagerly fastened upon by his enemies to stigmatize him as such in the eyes of the world, and especially those sympathizers who considered he had been unfairly dealt with.

Although Romano had warned the King, in his " Memorandum " of August twentieth, of the futility of resistance, or serious reliance on the loyalty of the troops still nominally at the disposal of the Crown, he did not hesitate to support his colleagues in the Cabinet in their demands for immediate and energetic action. Neither did he apparently deem it inconsistent to retain his official position, in spite of the threat of resignation should Francis disregard the advice given. The myterious conduct of Liborio Romano has been commented on by writers of all shades of political opinions. It is difficult to explain the object of his numerous intrigues with Royalists, Liberals, and the adherents of Cavour, Mazzini, and Garibaldi, unless we admit that he sought for himself, by virtue of his undoubted popularity with the masses and National Guard, the position of Regent, or Dictator, pending the settlement of the vexed question of the future of the Realm. His immediate acceptance of office under Garibaldi does not destroy this hypothesis, for the victorious General had loudly proclaimed his intention of at once passing on to the conquest of Rome, and the deliverance of Venetia ; the attempted realization of which projects was alone prevented by the unexpected stand of the Royalists at Capua, combined with the opportune appearance of Cialdini in the Papal States.

To the ever-nearing flood, which must infallibly overwhelm him, Francis opposed the same listless fatalism, the same mystic resignation, or vacillating concurrence with the proposals of his advisers, which had caused the despair of his well-wishers since the beginning of his troubles. The energetic decision which alone could arrest, or at least postpone, the cataclysm, seemed impossible to his unstable character, so fatally ready to yield to every new influence. Each day brought tidings of the defection of adherents whose fidelity was reckoned incorruptible ; while many of those nearest his person now forsook their allegiance, and openly joined the ranks of the revolutionists. All moral authority of the Government appeared to have vanished. Suspicion, bad faith, malign accusations, and petty self-seeking intrigue, invaded the Palace, the offices of the Government and the Civil and Military Associations. The southern provinces, the Calabrias, Puglie and Basilicata were in open revolt. On all sides Provisional Governments sprang into being, and placed their resources of men and money at the disposal of Garibaldi, or the Dictator, as he was already styled. Grossly exaggerated reports, and the wildest rumors, were spread about the capital, dangerously inflaming the imagination of the already overwrought and terrified populace. Yielding to the malicious insinuations of the ever active "Camarilla," and in direct violation of the advice of his Cabinet, Francis nominated General Cutrofiano, a noted reactionist, and advocate of drastic measures of suppression, as Governor of Naples.   His pernicious counsels were, however, annulled or rendered innocuous, by individual members of the Cabinet, who warned the King that the slightest provocative measure would hasten the explosion of popular fury, and involve the city in defiant revolt, resulting in carnage and plunder.

In the council of August twenty-ninth, the Cabinet, alarmed at the persistent intrigues of the " Camarilla," and enigmatical attitude of the King, resolved that decisive action must be forced upon him.   Spinelli, President of the Council, and Pianell, Minister of War, in spite of the uncertainty of the loyal support of the troops, were in favor of the adoption of a plan of resistance, and so solemnly informed the King ; making it clear that not a moment was to be lost.   Francis as usual agreed with them, and promised to give the matter his attention.   Next day, no action having been taken, the Minister of War declined further responsibility and tendered his resignation. The name of General Ulloa, whose previous offers to combat Garibaldi had been declined, again came under consideration, but met with

insurmountable opposition. On the evening
of September first, Pianell, in spite of his equivocal official status, again sought the King,
and urged that Francis concentrate the forces
at his command in some well chosen position
which would cover the capital, and there make
a stand against the enemy. He declared his
conviction that should the King place himself frankly at the head of these troops, which
included the mercenary regiments largely composed of Bavarians, and men from the Austrian
Adriatic provinces, his presence would inspire
fresh ardor, and re-establish the discipline,
weakened by systematic neglect, and the discredit into which the officers had fallen, owing
to personal jealousies and dissensions.

Francis appeared inclined to accept this advice, and ordered a Military Council to assem-
ble at the Palace next day.

Although the meeting took place at the appointed hour, its deliberations came to naught ;
in consequence, it is claimed by some, of the
treacherous attitude assumed by several of its
members. General Pianell, irritated beyond
endurance by the continual rejection of his advice, and deeply mortified at the evident lack
of confidence displayed, insisted on the acceptance of his resignations as statesman and military commander, accompanying the same with

a letter setting forth his reasons for so doing. He left for France the following morning, not being willing to witness the humiliations in store for his Sovereign.

On September third, having exhausted every means of inducing the King to attempt to save himself and his country, the Cabinet, following the example of Pianell, insisted on the acceptance of their resignations. Francis, while complying with their wishes, requested the Ministers to remain at their posts until their successors had been. selected. The formation of a new Cabinet which could cope with the overwhelming odds, and yet adhere strictly to the spirit as well as the letter of the Constitutional guarantees, was, however, obviously impossible. Garibaldi, without firing a shot, or striking a blow, was within a few days' march of the capital ; and for widely different reasons, Cavour and the " Camarilla " were anxious that disturbances should break out before his arrival. Rumors were actively circulated that the forts were about to fire upon the city ; the lowest element of the populace being reported as eagerly expectant of the plunder which must fall to their share in the ensuing confusion. To the vigilance and authority of the National Militia during these days and nights of unreasoning panic and universal intrigue, great credit is due, and whatever stigma may be attached to the political fame of Liborio Romano, his salutary influence over this body for the preservation of order cannot be disputed.

On the morning of the fourth, the alarming news that considerable reinforcements for Garibaldi had been landed not far from Salerno, brought together a hastily summoned council of war, attended by all the Generals available. The unanimous opinion expressed by his military advisers convinced the King that effective opposition to the entry of Garibaldi into Naples was now impossible. Should the troops about Salerno be called upon to attack the popular idol, it was averred, they would either disband, or go over in a body to the revolutionists. It was agreed that the only efficient line of defence now lay between Capua and Gaeta, to the north of the capital ; and Francis was advised to evacuate Naples, leaving small garrisons in the three forts, and intrusting the maintenance of public order to the National Guard. There being no longer a Minister of War, the Generals assembled in council signed the report, which was handed to the King. The venerable General Carrascosa alone, when consulted privately by his young Sovereign, disapproved the abandonment of the capital. " If Your Majesty leaves

Naples," he muttered, "you will never return again." General Prince Ischitella, although he signed the report with his colleagues, emphasized his disgust at his perfunctory action by flinging away the pen, and leaving Naples the same evening.

Spinelli was again summoned by the King early on the morning of September fifth, when Francis informed him that he had decided to leave Naples for Gaeta, and from the shelter of that stronghold vindicate his claims. After instructing the Premier to prepare a farewell proclamation to his Neapolitan subjects, Francis and Maria Sophia, accompanied by two gentlemen of their suite, went for a drive in an open carriage. They were greeted formally, even respectfully, by the passers-by. When opposite the Foresteria, so soon to be occupied by Garibaldi, an humiliating evidence of the altered spirit of the times was cruelly, though unwittingly, thrust upon the unfortunate Sovereign. At the corner stood the Royal Pharmacy, the signboard of which was decorated with the Bourbon lilies. A ladder, placed against the side of the shop, so encumbered the street that the carriage was brought to a momentary halt. Glancing up Francis beheld a couple of workmen busily engaged in effacing the Bourbon emblems. Smiling sadly, but otherwise unmoved, Francis drew the attention of his Consort to the prudential measure of the politic apothecary ; and ordered the coachman to return to the Palace.*

The remainder of the day was passed in transacting the official business necessitated by the King's departure. Receiving the chiefs of the National Militia, with their new Commander, De Sauget, at their head, Francis communicated to them his decision to leave the capital temporarily, and intrusted them with the maintenance of order during his absence, which he asserted would be of brief duration. In the course of the afternoon a Council of State was held, during which decrees of minor importance appertaining to the routine of the various Departments were presented and signed. Before dismissing his Ministers Francis instructed De Martino, who was in charge of the portfolio for Foreign Relations, to prepare a protest to the European Powers, and to submit the draft for his approval during the course of the evening. Spinelli handed the King the draft of this document, as well as that of the farewell proclamation, late that night. Francis signed both with but a passing comment on the style of their composition, which he recognized as that of Romano.

* Memor " La Fin di un Regno."

CHAPTER XV.

Farewell proclamation and protest.—Suspicions of treachery.—
Preparations for departure.—The gunboat "Messagero."—
Reception of Ministers and Diplomatists.—The Sovereigns
leave the Palace.—Refusal of Neapolitan war-ships to
follow King.—The voyage to Gaeta.—The King and Queen
during journey.—Arrival at Gaeta.

SEPTEMBER sixth dawned bright and fair.
On the street corners groups of excited
citizens discussed the farewell proclamation,
which had been published during the early
morning hours, and was conspicuously placarded over the town.

In language impregnated with deep resignation, singularly free from resentment, and not
devoid of a certain dignity, Francis informed
his subjects that, although at peace with all
Europe, "an unjust war contrary to the rights
of Nations" had invaded his realm, forcing
him to absent himself from the capital. "My
governmental reforms : my adhesion to the
great National and Italian principles could not
avert it : moreover, the necessity of defending
the integrity of the State provoked incidents

which I always lamented. I solemnly protest against this unjustifiable hostility, on which the present and future ages will pronounce severe 'judgment." In order to spare his Neapolitan subjects the horrors of war, as well as to insure the preservation of the National edifices, museums, and collections of priceless value, Francis states that, together with a portion of his army, he now goes forth to defend his rights. The remainder of his troops will be left in the city to watch over, in concert with the National Militia, " the security and the inviolability of the capital." To the Ministry, the Syndic of Naples and the Commander of the National Militia, is intrusted the task of avoiding the evils of civil disorders, and the disasters of war, to which end the fullest powers are conferred upon them. In taking leave of his fellow-citizens Francis adds : " I recommend to them union, peace, and the fulfilment of their duties as citizens. Let not an excessive attachment to my Crown become a source of trouble. If the chances of the present war should lead me back amongst you ; if on some future day, which it may please Divine Providence to determine, I regain the Throne of my ancestors, rendered more illustrious on account of the liberal institutions with which I have surrounded it, my sole desire

will be to find my people united, powerful and
happy."

This proclamation was accompanied by one
from the Prefect of Police, calling upon all
citizens to maintain strict order, and not
"rashly compromise the glorious destinies
now dawning" over their country.

Naples was in a state of mingled curiosity,
stupor, and terror. The mysterious preparations at the Palace, and the departure of large
bodies of troops, encouraged speculations of
the wildest nature. It was asserted that the
wording of the proclamation was ambiguous :
that its fair speaking was a snare to lull the
suspicions of the Liberals, in order the more
readily to overwhelm and destroy them. The
fact that some six thousand men, exclusive of
the National Militia, were left to garrison the
forts of Carmine, the Egg, and that of St.
Elmo, as well as to guard the Arsenal, gave
substance to the fears entertained by many
that Garibaldi's advent would be the signal
for a general bombardment, which must inevitably result in a rising of the "lazzaroni,"
and lower strata of the plebs, and the sack
of the city. Many families notoriously connected with the old régime left Naples, not
trusting in the ability of the Militia to over-
awe and restrain the infuriated populace,

under circumstances which seemed now un-avoidable.

During the night of September fifth numer-ous baggage vans, escorted by soldiers, left the Royal Palace, and turned in the direction of Capua ; while on the following morning large quanties of luggage were hurried on board the two small steamers, " Messagero " and " Del-fino," anchored in the Military Port, under the guns of the Arsenal. Although Francis carried with him considerable personal prop-erty, little or no treasure, or articles of intrin-sic value, were removed. The enormous ac-cumulations of gold and silver plate belonging to the Royal Household were left in Naples, and integrally turned over to the Government established by Garibaldi by those in charge. Nor did Francis attempt to withdraw from the Banks his private treasure, amounting to nearly eleven millions of ducats. In accord-ance with the special instructions of the King, none of the valuable pictures, or furniture, decorating the Palace, and forming the private property of the Crown, was removed ; with the exception of two portraits by Van Dyke, and Raffael's Madonna, to which latter picture he was particularly attached.

Orders had been issued to the Commander of the " Massagero," a small gunboat of 250 tons, to hold his vessel in readiness to sail for Gaeta at six that evening.   Although the personal devotion and loyalty of the Captain, Vincenzo Criscuolo, was beyond question, the same could not be said for all the members of his crew, and it transpired later that threats were employed to compel the firemen to remain at their posts.   Another panic was created shortly before the departure of the Sovereigns, by the action of the Piedmontese frigates, " Maria Adelaide " and " Maria Pia," which suddenly slipped from their former moorings, and took up positions directly opposite the Military Port, almost blocking the narrow channel.   This was interpreted as indicative of an attempt to be made to prevent the departure of the royal party ; and Francis was earnestly pleaded with to leave the city secretly, or under the protection of a foreign flag.   Criscuolo was, however, successful in prevailing on the King not to leave his capital as a fugitive, but to depart openly on board his own vessel, and under his own flag.

The Ministers took leave of the King shortly before the hour fixed for his departure.   Francis received them courteously, and addressed a few words of thanks, or admonition, to each in turn.   Although the King affected indifference, the great effort he made to control himself was evident to all. In taking leave of Spinelli and De Martino, he displayed affectionate regret : to Liborio Romano, after recommending him to watch ceaselessly that public order be not disturbed, he remarked with warning significance : "But look out for your head, Don Liborio." To which Romano replied : "Sire, I will see to it that it remain on my shoulders as long as possible."

The Diplomatic Corps was not received officially, although most of the members, to whom De Martino had communicated the King's protest addressed to their Governments, went privately to bid the Sovereign farewell. With the exception of the English, French, and Piedmontese Envoys, all the diplomatists accredited to the Neapolitan Court eventually received instructions to follow the King to Gaeta, where many of them remained during the greater part of the subsequent siege.

Besides the officials accompanying the Court, hardly twenty persons assembled at the Palace for the final hand-kissing. The numerous courtiers, and beneficiaries of the royal favors had melted away with the first indications of approaching calamity.

The Sovereigns left the Palace on foot for the landing stage, Maria Sophia leaning on her husband's arm, calm and outwardly cheerful.

The members of the suite, and those of the Military Household who still preserved their functions, followed the royal couple through the gardens and passages leading to the water gate.

Before leaving the harbor, Francis instructed Commander Criscuolo to signal orders to the Neapolitan war-vessels anchored in the roads, to follow him to Gaeta ; but these signals were ignored.   When hardly out of sight of the city a squadron of four vessels of the Royal Marine was met ; these also refused to obey the royal commands.

The voyage was a mournful one.   No refreshments had been prepared : indeed all were too absorbed by the anxieties of the moment to think of food.   About ten o'clock the Queen retired to a small deck-cabin, and rested on a sofa.   Francis passed the night alternately pacing the deck, plunged in solitary meditation, or in fitful conversation with the devoted Criscuolo.   About two in the morning he asked if the Queen had retired, and on being informed that she still slept in the deck-house, entered noiselessly, and threw his own mantle over the recumbent form of his unfortunate young consort.

At six in the morning the " Messagero " steamed into the harbor of Gaeta ; and the last act of the drama was begun.

CHAPTER XVI.

Naples remains calm.—Offer to land Piedmontese troops refused.—Commission appointed to meet Garibaldi. — His communications with Romano.—An officious Provisional Government.—Garibaldi enters Naples.—His reception by populace.—Evacuation by Royalist troops. — Garibaldi's loyalty suspected at Turin.—Romano's attempts at reconciliation.—Mistakes of Dictator's Government.—The Piedmontese ultimatum to the Pope.—Cavour's justification.—Piedmontese troops enter Papal States.—Diplomatic protests.—Napoleon privately approves.

MEANWHILE Naples remained outwardly calm. The theatres and other places of amusement were open, although less frequented than usual. The busy street life of the great city preserved its every-day animation, yet the multitudes which thronged the Toledo and principal thoroughfares wore an air of general expectancy and anxiety foreign to the pleasure-loving populace of the southern metropolis.

The offer of the Marquis Villamarina to land troops from the Piedmontese war-vessels to assist in the maintenance of order was refused by the Ministry, which called on the

301

Syndic and Commander of the National Guard to concert the measures to be taken to hand over the material resources of the city to Garibaldi. As a consequence of these deliberations the Syndic, Prince of Alessandria, and General de Sauget, were charged with the duty of negotiating with Garibaldi at Salerno next morning. Special messengers were despatched immediately to announce the departure of the King, and to acquaint the Dictator with the plans of the authorities in the capital, and of the arrangements proposed for his reception.

The messengers delivered their communications to Garibaldi late the same evening, and before seven o'clock on the morning of the seventh, the following telegram was received by Romano :

"As soon as the Syndic and Commander of the National Guard, whom I await, shall have arrived, I will come to you. During these anxious moments I recommend you to maintain the order and calm befitting the dignity of a People about to enter upon the possession of their individual rights.

"The Dictator of the Two Sicilies,
"JOSEPH GARIBALDI."

Romano instantly replied as follows :

"To the Invincible General Garibaldi, Dictator of the Two Sicilies. Liborio Romano, Minister of the Interior and Police.

"With the greatest impatience Naples awaits your arrival in order to salute you as the Redeemer of Italy, and place in your hands the reins of Government, and the direction of its destinies. While awaiting this I will firmly preserve public order and tranquillity; your authority, already made known by me to the populace, is the best guarantee of the success of this task. I await your further orders, and am with unlimited respect, Most Invincible Dictator, yours,

"LIBORIO ROMANO.

"NAPLES, September 7, 1860."

While Romano insists that instantaneous and unconditional annexation to the Kingdom of Italy was desired by the Committee of Order, he yet states that the Ministry considered such a course "fraught with perils and complications." He asserts in his memoirs,* that, in the estimation of those left in authority by Francis, Naples should retain untrammelled possession of her rights, and that the fusion with the rest of Italy, if desired, should result, not

* "Memorie Politiche di Liborio Romano," Naples, 1873.

as the compulsory annexation of a conquered
people, but as the outcome of free option, and
with the recognition of the rights of an equal ;
the conditions and nature of the compact being
determined, as in the instance of many of the
smaller States, by a Plebiscite.   This explanation is not in absolute harmony with the text
of Romano's enthusiastic despatch to Garibaldi,
wherein the Minister of the Interior proclaims
Naples' impatience to place in the hands of the
Dictator "the reins of government, and the
direction of its destinies."

That unconditional surrender as in the case
of a conquered foe was distasteful to the late
Ministers is conceivable ; yet as Garibaldi came
in the name of Italian Unity, and of Victor
Emmanuel, the objection to the co-operation
of that Sovereign's accredited representaitve
appears contradictory.   The explanation is to
be found, in part, in the jealousies and friction
which existed, and had for some time existed,
between the more ardent Ministers of the
Crown and the Marquis de Villamarina, who
was for political considerations (not to say personal ambitions) anxious to wrest from them,
and from Garibaldi, as large a part as possible
of the prestige attaching to the annexation.
Romano has stated that his earnest desire was
to bring about a reconciliation between Gari-

baldi and Cavour, and it is admissible that he feared the possible consequences should the Dictator find the fruits of his victories snatched from him, the city practically in the hands of Cavour's agents, and occupied by the Piedmontese troops.

Certain of the Cavouriani, with Pisanelli at their head, notwithstanding the fact that the Ministry still remained nominally in office, and that the National Militia was prepared to enforce its commands, determined to establish a Provisional Government pending the arrival of Garibaldi, and forthwith issued a decree calling upon all good citizens to assist in preserving order. Ten minutes after the promulgation of this decree, it became known that the General was actually on his way to the city, and this self-constituted Assembly promptly issued another, officiously creating him "Dictator." When informed of these proceedings Garibaldi, deeming himself slighted, and his dignity as conqueror offended, ordered the arrest of the presumptuous politicians. Romano, however, realizing the danger of friction, or desirous of being serviceable to Cavour, was instrumental in so arranging matters that the order of arrest was revoked, and Pisanelli actually became a member of the Dictator's Government.

20

Meanwhile, ignorant of the dissensions amongst the annexationists, or more probably conscious that he could afford to ignore them, Garibaldi started for the capital. Leaving Salerno by train on the morning of September seventh, the conqueror, accompanied only by General Cozenz and Doctor Bertani, without escort or following, alighted at the railway station in Naples at noon. Romano and a vast multitude were there to greet him ; the former ready with a discourse impregnated with fulsome flattery and extravagant optimism ; the latter with an enthusiasm born rather of relief at the escape from unknown danger, than of an intelligent appreciation of the altered political conditions symbolized in the person of the red-shirted warrior. Entering an open carriage, the Dictator and his friends drove slowly through the densely crowded streets, under the forts garrisoned by the Bourbon troops, and past the guard-houses of the Bavarian mercenaries, to the palace of the Foresteria. Garibaldi modestly refused to occupy the Royal Palace, so recently vacated by Francis, declaring that it should remain untenanted until Victor Emmanuel's advent. Yielding to the frantic entreaties of the multitude assembled beneath the windows of the Foresteria, the Dictator, in a few words thanked the people,

" in the name of all Italians and of Humanity, for the sublime deed which has this day been accomplished ; " and submitted to an embrace, which the donor, General d'Ayala, magniloquently assured him was "the kiss of five hundred thousand Neapolitans." Again entering his carriage, Garibaldi and his companions proceeded to the Cathedral to do homage at the shrine of Saint Gennaro, and assist at the Te Deum and solemn benediction. At the Dictator's request, Romano now seated himself beside him, and drove, amidst scenes of the wildest enthusiasm, to the Angri Palace, where the headquarters of the Government and the General's Staff were established ; and where he shortly received the chiefs, military and civil, who had renounced their allegiance to the Bourbon Dynasty.

Among the astounding incidents of this unparalleled appropriation of the capital of a great Kingdom, must be noted the orderly and unmolested evacuation by the Royalist troops of the forts and garrisons. Their march through the streets, re-echoing with joyful acclamations for Italian Unity and Victor Emmanuel, on their way to join their comrades on the Volturno to fight under the banner of the King whose overthrow the inhabitants were celebrating, resembled a parade rather than a retreat. Yet fidelity to the Bourbon Prince was by no means unanimous amongst those who had remained passive spectators of the Dictator's entry : many officers and men now availed themselves of the freedom afforded to throw in their lot with the new régime, while others, less martially inclined, abandoned the struggle and sought the seclusion of their native villages.

Hardly less anomalous was the spectacle offered devout Neapolitans when Garibaldi, on the day after his arrival, made his way in a hired vehicle to the shrine of the Virgin, at Piedigrotta, which the Bourbon Monarchs were accustomed to visit annually on this same date, attended by great pomp and military parade, in commemoration of the accession of their Dynasty to the Throne of Naples.

Once in possession of the capital, Garibaldi's first official act decreed that all vessels of war, arsenals, armaments, and marine supplies, belonging to the State of the Two Sicilies, be transferred to the fleet of the King of Italy, Victor Emmanuel, and placed at the disposal of Admiral Persano. (Considerable apprehension had existed that Francis might be successful in prevailing upon the Commanders to hand over their vessels to Austria.) Although this spontaneous and tangible token of the loyalty

of the victorious freebooters was calculated to
reassure those who had questioned the purity
of his intentions, it did not, strange as it may
appear, completely allay the suspicions of the
authorities in Turin. Not that the personal
oyalty of the chief was seriously doubted, as
has been already stated, but surrounded by such
political agitators as Mazzini, and urged forward by Bertani, and others, who had seconded
him in the Sicilian venture, it was felt that his
ambitions, or those of his counsellors, might
yet provoke European intercession, aud jeopar-
dize the fruits of previous successes. That
substantial cause existed for this is evinced by
the fact that on September tenth, three days
after his arrival in Naples, Garibaldi told Mr.
Elliot, British Minister at the Court of the Two
Sicilies, that he intended to push on to Rome,
and when that city was in his hands, offer the
Crown of United Italy to Victor Emmanuel,
upon whom would then devolve the task of the
liberation of Venetia. He spoke of the Emperor of the French with contempt and defiance.*

The organization of the first Ministry was
left virtually in the hands of Liborio Romano,

* Despatch September 10. Mr. Elliot to Lord John
Russell.

and Agostino Bertani, Garibaldi's trusted and
able Lieutenant, and "alter ego," during the
preparation of the Sicilian expedition.   Romano
claims that his principal preoccupation in the
selection of his colleagues was to surround the
Dictator with men devoted to Cavour, and thus
establish a link between the two great factors
of Italian Unity.   This chimerical opportunism
was foredoomed to failure.   Bertani strenuously
contested the influence of the Constitutionalists, urging that a Ministry responsible before
the Nation for its actions was incompatible
with the dignity and prerogatives of a Military
Dictator.   He was, in fact, desirous of seeing
his chief legally vested with powers as auto-
cratic, and absolutist, as those wielded by any
of the detested tyrants whose unfortunate successor had just been dethroned.   The consequence was immediate friction, and bitter animosity.   Three days after their nomination, the
members of the Ministry felt constrained to
tender their resignations ; while within fourteen
days of its formation the struggle between the
Cabinet and the Secretariat of the Dictator,
presided over by Bertani, had become so acute
that the Ministers were, at their urgent demand, relieved of office.   The retiring statesmen
handed the Dictator a document setting forth
the perils of a policy which ignored the Consti-

tutional Guarantees vouchsafed by the late Government, and vested with illimitable powers the representatives of the new régime in the various provinces ; some of which already began to display symptoms of a reactionary character which demanded the most delicate and judicious handling to prevent blazing forth in frank and open acclamation in favor of the deposed Dynasty.

Meanwhile Cavour, who had foreseen the Roman difficulty from the moment that Garibaldi proposed to cross the Straits of Messina, had, as we have seen, made preparation to meet it with a stroke of policy as audacious as any conceived by the red-shirted hero of the Pampas. His agents secretly canvassed the Marches and Umbria, and encouraged the disposition to revolt against the Papal authority, with promises of the co-operation of the Italian troops at the opportune moment. This crisis Cavour deemed to have occurred when Francis fled from his capital before the Garibaldian advance.

Consequently, on September seventh, the Piedmontese Government sent an ultimatum to Cardinal Antonelli, Papal Secretary of State, calling for the immediate disarmament of the mercenary forces levied by the Pope, alleging that their existence constituted a continual menace to the peace of Italy. The Papal Administration was furthermore unequivocally informed that, unless its forces were disbanded at once, the Sardinian Government would consider itself justified in "preventing any attempt which might be made to repress the manifestations of National feeling in Umbria and the Marches." But twenty-four hours were allowed the Papal authorities to extricate themselves from this awkward predicament. In his Circular, addressed to the European Courts, Cavour describes this action as "necessitated by the interests of the new Italian Kingdom, and the welfare of the Peninsula;" and recalls the fact that some years before, the Sovereign Pontiff had himself been the revered advocate of this great National movement, which had now passed beyond the control of Princes and States alike.

Writing to Baron Stockmar from Balmoral on September fourteenth, the Prince Consort says : " Here joy at the fall of the Neapolitan dynasty is universal. Sardinia gives out that she will be compelled to incorporate the Kingdom, and to send troops into the Roman States, in order to prevent anarchy, as Garibaldi is surrounded by Mazzinians."

The cry raised by Cavour that Garibaldi would certainly, if left to his own devices,

march upon Rome, and allow Mazzini to proclaim the Republic there, had its weight with
the European Courts for whose benefit it was
raised.   The Sardinian Cabinet contended,
with no small show of reason, that foreign intervention, from whatever quarter it might
come, must inevitably mean a renewal of the
chaotic struggles of preceding years ; and
argued that in this connection Piedmont, and
the Piedmontese army, constituted the only
safeguard for the peace of Europe.   Reference
has already been made to the mission of Farini
and Cialdini to Chambéry, where they ascer-
tained the views of the Emperor of the French
concerning the proposed official intervention of
Sardinia in the Neapolitan drama.   That the
personal policy of Napoleon III. on this occasion was not in accord with that of his official
entourage has been frequently advanced.
France professed herself interested in the formation and maintenance of three independent
States in the Peninsula : the Kingdom of Italy,
the Papal States, and the Kingdom of Naples.
In view of the uncertain political conditions
prevailing in the Peninsula, and in deference
to the solicitude expressed by the powerful
Catholic party, the French Government maintained a garrison in Rome, apparently for the
defence of the Pope.   The nomination of Gen-

eral Lamoricière to the command of the Papal forces had been considered by many, who foresaw the complications likely to arise out of the Neapolitan controversy, as a grave error ; the more especially as the General's authority was not restricted to the immediate precincts of the Eternal City, but ranged over the provinces which were in a state of ferment, and already showing irrefutable symptoms of sympathy with the Unitarians.

As was expected, the advance of the Sardinian troops into Papal territory, in accordance with Cavour's ultimatum, was defiantly opposed by Lamoricière. The Sardinian victory of Castelfidardo, and the total defeat of Lamoricière, and the Papal forces under his command at Ancona, after a brave but ineffectual resistance, placed the French in an anomalous position. Count Persigny, Napoleon's Ambassador in England, and one of his earliest and most devoted followers, condemns this policy with the severest strictures. In his opinion the consequences of Castelfidardo were ruinous to French prestige. By making possible the encounter, and allowing the subsequent spoliation of the Holy See, and the annexation of the Kingdom of Naples to that of Italy, the Emperor plunged his policy into inextricable complications and contradictions.

"In the eyes of all Europe," says Persigny, "his Government was discredited. He had desired to prevent the union of Italy, and Italian Unity was accomplished in spite of him. He pretended to protect the Holy See, and the Pope lost his richest provinces."

It is hardly to be wondered that Catholic France, and especially the Legitimist opponents of the Empire, cried out in horror at a policy which amounted in their eyes to sacrilege. The application of some balm to soothe the susceptibilities of the outraged victims of the Emperor's duplicity became imperative. A great cloud of diplomatic dust was consequently kicked up between the Foreign Offices of Paris and Turin, and in sign of protest; Count Talleyrand, French Minister to the Sardinian Court, was instructed to demand his passports (September 18th). Within a few weeks the Russian and Spanish Envoys received similar instructions, and left their posts, protesting loudly against this official violation of international obligations.

Notwithstanding this diplomatic bluster, when, a couple of weeks later, Victor Emmanuel decided to assist in person at the passage of his troops into Neapolitan territory, and so advised the French Emperor by telegram, stating that he was "leaving for Naples in order to prevent the proclamation of the Republic," he received the unofficial congratulations of Napoleon III. on the adoption of this "energetic resolution."

CHAPTER XVII.

Francis at Gaeta.—He forms a Ministry.—Instructions to local officials.—Address to the Army.—The battles of the Volturno. — Garibaldi's submission. — Political excesses in Naples.—Piedmontese troops enter Neapolitan territory.—Cavour's audacious counsels.—His belief in non-intervention of France and England.—Austrian hostility.—Victor Emmanuel at Ancona.--His proclamation to Southern populations.—The "Times" on situation.—Appointment of Pro-Dictator at Naples.—The Plebiscite.—Meeting of Victor Emmanuel and Garibaldi.—Fall of Capua.—Victor Emmanuel in Naples.—Departure of Garibaldi.—Honors and rewards offered him.—Alexander Dumas in Naples.—His opinion of Garibaldi.

AFTER consultation with the members of his family, and the military authorities assembled at Gaeta, Francis modified his previous intentions of passively awaiting in that stronghold the developments of Diplomacy, and decided, pending the arrival of reinforcements from Naples and the South, to concentrate the forces at his disposal at Capua, and on the line of the Volturno and Garigliano, in anticipation of circumstances which would permit of an attempt being made for the reconquest of the capital.

317

His first act was the constitution of a Ministry, which included not only a Minister of War, one of Marine, and a Secretary for Foreign Affairs, but provided for the portfolios of Finance, Public Works, Public Instruction, Grace and Justice, Interior, the inevitable Police, and Ecclesiastical Affairs. At the same time the Prefects and Magistrates throughout the realm were warned that the state of siege was proclaimed, and instructed to obey the Military commanders of their districts.

Although we may smile at what appears pure " naïveté " on the part of the dethroned Monarch, the motives for the adoption of this course were not devoid of ingenuity. Francis and his advisers were well aware that none of the former Crown officials thus addressed would pay the slightest heed to the instructions of a Government no longer in a position to enforce its mandates ; nevertheless, the proclamation was calculated to mislead the European Powers, and make it appear that the Government of the King still wielded authority throughout the provinces, in spite of the successful raid of the filibusters ; and in this wise partially retrieve, in the eyes of foreign diplomacy, the error committed in abandoning the capital. It is easy to discern the hand of the Queen Mother and " Camarilla " in this, and many subsequent schemes, the futility of which were manifest. Left to his own devices, Francis would certainly have abandoned a struggle, the hopelessness of which he appreciated, and have retired to Rome, or Bavaria, in obedience to the dictates of the fatalism which underlay his nature. Guided and influenced by stronger minds into the adoption of a course of obstinate resistance in the face of overwhelming odds, he and his faithful consort displayed a heroism on the ramparts of the beleaguered citadel, and an abnegation during the privations and sickness attending the siege, which compelled the unstinted admiration of his most bitter opponents.

General Ritucci was intrusted with the supreme command of the remnant of the army which occupied Capua and the surrounding districts, and to which the King addressed from Gaeta a desperate appeal :

"Soldiers : " (he cried) "It is time that the voice of your King should be heard in your ranks : the voice of the King who grew up with you ; who has lavished all his care upon you ; and who comes now to share your lot. Those who, by allowing themselves to be deceived and seduced, have plunged the Kingdom in mourning are no longer amongst us.

Nevertheless, I appeal to your honor and your
fidelity, in order that by glorious deeds we may
efface the disgrace of cowardice and treachery.
We are still sufficiently numerous to annihilate
an enemy which employs the weapons of deceit and corruption.   Up to the present I have
desired to spare many towns, but now that we
are relegated to the banks of the Volturno and
Garigliano, shall we allow ourselves to still
further humiliate our fame as soldiers ?   Will
you permit your Sovereign to abandon the
Throne, and leave you to eternal infamy ?
No !   At this supreme moment let us rally
round the flag to defend our rights, our honor,
and the fair fame of Neapolitans ; already
sufficiently discredited."

With the addition of the contingent from
Naples, and the arrival of many detachments
which had found themselves isolated and
scattered throughout the provinces, the military gathering on the banks of the Volturno
mustered some forty thousand strong.   These
forces were generally well equipped, amply
provided with artillery and munitions of war,
and were, moreover, strongly intrenched and
flanked, while their rear was protected by the
practically impregnable fortress of Gaeta.
Unfortunately for the Royal cause, the treach-

ery and deceit by which Francis was surrounded continued to be manifest even in the
face of the enemy. Desertions of Generals,
officers and men became daily occurrences;
while the prestige of the Crown was still further
weakened by the ill-advised absence of Francis
himself from the front on the eve of the first
encounter with the enemy.

Before returning to Gaeta, Francis, in an
order of the day, dated September twelfth,
confided the ramparts of Capua to the "valor,
fidelity and honor" of his soldiers, whom he
again exhorts to banish all ideas of treachery.
The King's half-brothers, the Counts of Trani
and Caserta, remained with the troops, and
took part in the battle of Caiazzo, when the
Royalists successfully engaged the Garibaldians
under General Türr. Had the advantages then
gained been promptly followed up, the consequences would undoubtedly have been
serious for the defeated Garibaldians. This
reverse, the first suffered by the invaders, and
which caused a feeling of uneasiness as to the
possibility of a movement upon the capital,
decided Garibaldi, who had returned in all
haste from a temporary absence in Palermo,
whither he had gone to reconcile the conflicting interests prevailing there, to concentrate
his troops, scattered along the coast from the

Gulf of Policastro to that of Salerno ; and to limit operations to the left bank of the Volturno, and the defence of the approaches to the capital.

The battles of the Volturno, which took place a few days later (October first and second), in which the Bourbon troops gave evidence of unqualified pluck and determination, being finally repulsed, thanks to the timely arrival of the Piedmontese regulars (Bersaglieri) despatched by Villamarina, at the earnest request of Garibaldi, convinced the latter that the task of dislodging the Royalists from their strongholds was beyond the unaided strength of his red-shirted volunteers. The proud independence of the victorious Dictator did not prevent his realizing the perils of his position, and the dangers which might result therefrom to the cause of Unity. Laying aside his former bombastic pretensions, he addressed Victor Emmanuel, on October fourth, in simple and loyal terms. Taking advantage of the opportunity offered by the recent victories of Cialdini over the Papal forces, he congratulated the King on these feats of arms, and modestly referred to his own successes on the Volturno, adding significantly : "I know that Your Majesty is about to send four thousand men to Naples, and it will be wise. Your Majesty will acknowledge that I am heartily his friend, and that I merit confidence. It is much better to welcome all honest Italians, no matter what parties they may have belonged to in the past, rather than favor the formation of factions, which might become dangerous in the future. Being at Ancona, Your Majesty ought to make an excursion to Naples, either by sea or by land. If by land, which would be preferable, Your Majesty should be accompanied by at least one division. Advised in time, I would effect a junction with my right, and would come in person to present my homages, and receive orders for subsequent operations."

The tone of this letter justifies the boast of the Marquis de Villamarina in his despatch to Cavour : "The political battle is won. I know that I acted contrary to my instructions in conceding two battalions of Bersaglieri in aid of the Garibaldians, but I also know that when the Dictator had news that our soldiers had arrived, he exclaimed with joy : 'This time I clearly see that Piedmont is sincere, and that the Piedmontese are our real brothers.'"

The news from Naples had recently been such as to cause Cavour the keenest anxiety. Excesses, political and military, marked the reign of the red-shirted followers of Garibaldi, or rather that of the adventurers and hangers-on, warriors in name only, who terrorized the town with their swaggering and disorderly conduct. Mazzini, Alberto Mario, Cataneo, Bertani, and others ; Republicans, Federalists, conditional Annexationists, and the advocates of an indefinite Dictatorship, each in turn made assault on the loyalty of the popular hero, and essayed to undermine his allegiance to his Sovereign, and envenom his personal quarrel with the wily diplomatist and statesman at the head of the Government in Turin, on whose dismissal from office he was urged to insist.

It was to counteract this pernicious influence, and check the exorbitant pretensions, which jeopardized the fair fabric of unity to as great an extent as the diplomatic opposition of Europe, as well as to officially place the " Re Galantuomo " at the head of the movement undertaken in his name, that Cavour now counselled Victor Emmanuel to complement one audacity with another by joining his forces at Ancona, and marching on Naples. The step was a bold one, and although undoubtedly necessitated by the situation at Naples, might readily have complicated an already sufficiently perilous predicament. It is now known that Bertani telegraphed the chief of a small force stationed near the Papal frontier, to " oppose the entry of the Piedmontese troops coming from

the border ; " * and that the patriotic action of
the commander of the National Guard of the
district, Count Acquaviva, alone prevented a
collision, the consequences of which must have
been almost irreparable.

Castelfidardo had deeply shocked European
Diplomacy, but the intelligence that Victor
Emmanuel was about to march his forces upon
Naples, and co-operate with those of the success-
ful filibuster, fairly staggered the Chanceries
of the Powers.

When counselling his Sovereign to partially
throw off the mask and unite, or, if necessary,
oppose, his forces to the unofficial legions oper-
ating in the South, Cavour played a dangerous
card. The notification to the various Courts
that the Piedmontese went to restore order in
the Neapolitan Realm, and to avert the impend-
ing proclamation of a Republic, could hardly
be expected to satisfy an already overtaxed
credulity. The ground had, however, been
carefully prepared, and no essential neglected
which might contribute to assuage, or checkmate, the jealousies, national and international,
which such action must arouse. In England
public opinion was overwhelmingly in favor of
Garibaldi's enterprise. While Her Majesty's
responsible Ministers might officially frown

* Nisco. "Francesco II."

ominously at so flagrant a violation of the
sacred rights of nations, they were individually
in sympathy with the Italian cause, and consequently disinclined to risk popularity by active
intervention in a question offering no prospect
of material advantages.   Of the personal good-
will of the Emperor of the French there had
been ample and tangible demonstration, and at
this time the will of Napoleon III. still constituted the law of France, although his opinions
might not be indorsed by the members of his
Government, or shared by a large portion of
his subjects.   With the latter the assurances
that the Eternal City should be respected and
protected from the proposed aggression of the
Garibaldians, and the Pope left in undisturbed
possession of the Patrimony of St. Peter, carried weight, especially with the Catholic Legitimist element, the long-standing umbrage of
which the Emperor expected still further to
propitiate by the Syrian expedition undertaken,
nominally at least, for the purpose of avenging
the massacres in the Lebanon.   Moreover,
France and England were at this moment
united for the protection of mutual interests in
the Far East, and consequently the less disposed to quibble over Italian politics.   Austria, undisguisedly and menacingly hostile,
might have to be reckoned with at any moment ;

in which case Russia and ¦Prussia would probably lend her moral support, if no more.

To his life-long friend, the Comtesse de
Circourt, Cavour admitted in his letter of
September twenty-third, 1860, that : "Italy
finds herself in a very critical position. What
with Diplomacy on the one side, and Garibaldi
on the other, it is not by any means pleasant.
I hope nevertheless that we shall succeed in
disengaging ourselves from our embarrassments, and in establishing our country on the
solid foundations of order and liberty, in spite
of the defiance of the Absolutists, and the
follies of the Republicans."

A month later he informs the same correspondent that "we shall possibly soon be
called upon to undergo a severe trial. Austria
it seems proposes taking advantage of the absence of the King, and of our best troops, to
attack us. We are preparing for a desperate
resistance. Although Cialdini and Fanti are
at Naples, we have with us La Marmora and
Sonnaz, who don't allow themselves to be in-
timidated by Benedeck and the Archduke
Albert. We are prepared to risk our all.
The country is as calm as if the outlook were
cloudless. While realizing the danger which
menaces them there is no panic, for all appreciate that the cause at stake is great enough to

warrant the most tremendous sacrifices for its attainment."

Victor Emmanuel, whose ardor had more frequently to be restrained than encouraged by his Minister, eagerly seized the opportunity for throwing off the wearisome yoke imposed by Diplomacy, and embarking on the adventurous activity his soul craved.

On his arrival at Ancona, the King received deputations from the Abbruzzi and Naples, presenting petitions, covered by many thousands of prominent names, clamoring for immediate annexation, and urging that he proceed at once to the capital.   Although nothing loath to comply with such request, diplomatic etiquette, and the amenities of international intercourse, forbade that such a step should be taken while the accredited representative of the King of Naples remained in official residence at Turin.   Cavour therefore informed Baron Winspeare in a curtly worded despatch, dated October sixth, that civil war, and the absence of a regular Government constituting a grave peril, Naples had had recourse to Victor Emmanuel to afford the needed protection. "It is with the object of fulfilling this high mission," he continues, "that His Majesty Victor Emmanuel sends his soldiers to Naples; they will safeguard Italy and Europe by crushing anarchy and disorder, and preventing bloodshed."

The Neapolitan Envoy replied with a vigorous protest; but realizing the futility of further effort, immediately left Turin.

Before crossing the river Tronto, which divided the Papal and Neapolitan States, Victor Emmanuel addressed a proclamation to the populations of the Two Sicilies. In this document, intended rather as a justification of his action before the European Courts than as an explanation of his presence amongst the obviously delighted subjects of the Bourbon King, the Sardinian Monarch dwells upon the political and social conditions which render his personal intervention imperative. The use of his name in the recent political changes effected throughout the Kingdom had given rise to serious misinterpretations. While the glorious deeds and popularity of Garibaldi were duly eulogized in the King's proclamation, and his personal probity compared in its disinterested purity to that of ancient times, the mistrust of those surrounding the hero was clearly indicated in a reference to the universal "dread that a factional attempt would be made to sacrifice the dawning National triumph to the chimera of an ambitious fanaticism." Again, he asserted that while holding himself respon-

sible before Europe for the recent events undertaken in his name, in the face of the undoubted peril to the National cause, occasioned
by the presence of hordes of adventurers of
every nationality in the Papal States, and
which constituted a veritable foreign intervention of the most dangerous type, he had proclaimed "Italy for the Italians," and would
never permit that the Peninsula become a hotbed for the intrigues of cosmopolitan sects
tending towards the universal spread of the
doctrines of the Demagogue.

The Conservative-Liberal elements throughout Europe, although perhaps shocked at the
apparent duplicity of Piedmontese diplomacy,
were, nevertheless, with the spectre of Revolution, or Anarchy, dangling before their eyes,
inclined to accept this vindication of a principle, dangerous in its essence, and to agree in
substance with the opinion expressed in the
"Times" of October nineteenth.   In this article the writer avers that : "In our eyes the
only defence for the conduct of the King (of
Sardinia) lies in those natural laws which lie
unwritten in every code and unnamed in every
form of Government, but which intolerable
oppression calls forth from latent existence
into active force.   It is the unbearable tyranny
of the two Sovereigns of Southern Italy, it is

the massacres of Perugia, the prisons of
Palermo, and the dungeons of St. Elmo, which
have given to the people of Southern Italy the
right to call for a deliverer, and which have
given to Victor Emmanuel the same excuse for
assuming the Crown of Naples which William
of Orange had for accepting that of England.
Upon this principle and upon no other, Victor
Emmanuel can vindicate his own presence in
Southern Italy, and upon this title he will be
fully justified in putting an end to the war by
one decisive movement."

If the intrigues at Naples had resulted in the
resignation of the Ministry originally formed
by Liborio Romano, these very excesses had
benefited the National Cause by necessitating
the appointment of George Pallavicino as Pro-
Dictator. Pallavicino, although a warm and
faithful friend of Garibaldi, was equally trusted
by the adherents to Cavour's policy, while his
devotion to the person of his Sovereign, and
his identification with the National Cause, was
above suspicion. To his energetic action, and
firm yet tactful perseverance in the face of per-
tinacious, and often malignant, opposition,
was due the eventual discomfiture of the dangerous faction whose policy aimed at an indefinite prolongation of the Dictatorship, even
should such a course necessitate open hostility

with Piedmont. His appeal to Mazzini to make a further sacrifice of his personal convictions by leaving Naples, where his presence and influence were a cause of serious embarrassment to the Government, was, it is true, ineffectual ; nevertheless the firmness of the stand he made in dealing with Cataneo, Bertani, Crispi, Mario, and others, whose policy was in open contradiction to the clearly expressed desire of the populations of the continental provinces and Sicily, prevailed ; the specious reasoning of his adherents being made apparent to Garibaldi himself.

The formula of the Plebiscite of October twenty-first was simply as follows : " The people desire Italy one and indivisible with Victor Emmanuel, Constitutional King, and his legitimate descendants." The yeas, polled in the metropolis and continental provinces amounted to 1,302,064, against 10,312 nays : in Sicily, 432,053 voted in favor of the island being politically merged with the common Fatherland, while 667 held a contrary opinion.

The same formula when offered to the populations of the Marches and Umbria, on November fourth and fifth, resulted in 134,847 yeas as against 1,592 nays.

Victor Emmanuel did not await the result of the Plebiscite, which indeed was only proclaimed officially on November fifth, but after defeating the Papal garrisons of Perugia, Spoleto, and S. Leo, crossed the Tronto, amidst the acclamations of the Abbruzzesi, whose deputations welcomed his troops as they marched through their province. The news that Garibaldi had yielded, and decreed the Plebiscite, reached the King at Grottamare. The necessity for immediate action thus removed, and being disinclined to enter Naples before the result of the solemn manifestation of the will of the people had been promulgated, Victor Emmanuel now continued his journey by easy stages.

Garibaldi, who had himself cast his vote in favor of annexation, now marched forward to meet his King. On the morning of the twenty-sixth, at the little village of Caianello, the commanders came face to face. Victor Emmanuel, on discerning the red-shirted warrior by the aid of his field-glasses, gave spur to his horse: Garibaldi did the same. Followed by their escorts, the King and the Dictator drew rein within a few feet of each other. To the cry of "Long live Victor Emmanuel" raised by those present, Garibaldi, lifting his sombrero, added significantly: "King of Italy." "Thank you," was the simple reply, as Victor Emmanuel stretched forth his hand and grasped the rough palm of the soldier of fortune.   Side by side, still hand in hand, the two continued their way, earnestly discussing the military operations both foresaw as inevitable.

Cordial and hearty as the meeting was, Victor Emmanuel clearly evinced his determination to brook no interference with his sovereign prerogatives, or any attempt to overshadow the prestige of his troops.   To the General's request that he be accorded the honor of leading in the advance against the Royalists intrenched on the Garigliano, the King gently but firmly objected : " You have been fighting for a long while past ; it is now my turn.   Your troops are exhausted, mine are fresh.   Your place is now with the reserves."

The meaning implied by these words was not lost upon the Dictator, who despondently remarked to Signora Mario : " They have placed us at the tail ; " and who, when two days later General della Rocca with the Fifth Army Corps began the regular siege of Capua, took leave of his troops and retired to Naples.   From thence he despatched a letter, impregnated with noble sentiment, to the King, resigning into his hands the powers, political and military, he had temporarily usurped.

Capua capitulated on November second.   On the following morning the seven thousand men which constituted the garrison marched out, stacked arms, the officers being allowed to retain their swords, and as prisoners of war were eventually transported to Genoa.

With the fall of Capua the sovereignty of Francis was restricted to the fortress of Gaeta and dependent village of Mola, the citadel of Messina, and the insignificant but practically impregnable little mountain stronghold of Civitella del Tronto, on the Papal frontier, which, after a memorable siege of seven months, only capitulated at the express command of the dethroned King from his exile in Rome.

Leaving Cialdini in command on the Garigliano Victor Emmanuel hastened to Naples. On the morning of the seventh, just two months after the flight of Francis, the King of United Italy entered the capital, amidst demonstrations of enthusiasm described in the chronicles of the period as bordering on delirium. In the carriage at his side sat Garibaldi, clad in his red shirt and wide sombrero ; while the Pro-Dictator Pallavicino and Andrea Colonna, Syndic of Naples, occupied the opposite seat. Next day Victor Emmanuel, surrounded by all the pomp and military splendor of his Court, after having received the official notification of the result of the Plebiscite of October twenty-first, gave solemn audience to Garibaldi and the members of the Government of the Dictator.

This was the last official function in which the ex-Dictator was to take part. Sore and chagrined at what he considered the ingratitude of his Sovereign, he left Naples next day on the "Washington," which was under orders to bear him to his island home at Caprera. The great leader who had won for his King the fairest provinces of Italy, and brought ten million subjects beneath his sceptre, carried with him as the fruits of his victories a bag of seeds for his garden, some vegetables and salted fish, and about three hundred dollars in a purse handed him by a friend as he embarked, for he had forgotten to provide himself with money.

The impression caused in Naples by this departure, which closely resembled banishment, was most painful. Yet, as Cavour wrote to the Marquis d'Azeglio, "We wished at all costs to avoid appearing ungrateful. . . ." The King and Farini made the most magnificent offers to Garibaldi. Not only was he appointed to the rank of Field Marshal ; ample provision made for his eldest son ; the title of aide-de-camp to the King bestowed upon his second son ; and a dowry provided for his daughter ; but to this was added the grant of one of the royal estates ; the offer of a steamship, as well as the highest

decoration in the gift of the Sovereign, the
Collar of the Annunziata, conferring upon the
holder the privileges and title of a cousin of the
King. Garibaldi refused all, demanding the
Lieutenancy of the Kingdom of the Two Sicilies for a year, and free control of the administration during that period. "To have yielded,"
adds Cavour, "would have been to submit forever to the domination, not of Garibaldi, but of
those surrounding him." The King replied
curtly : "It is impossible !" and Garibaldi left
for Caprera.

In his final audience with the King, the General begged that his companions, and officers,
be appointed to grades in the regular army corresponding to those they had held in his service,
and that his regiments be incorporated with
the troops of United Italy. Unfortunately even
this unselfish request, owing to the complications and professional jealousies which must
result therefrom, met with violent opposition.

Although at heart a republican, Garibaldi
never swerved from his allegiance to the Sovereign in whose name he undertook the expeditions which made his own of world-wide fame,
and the synonym for courage and chivalry.
The wiles and quicksands of Diplomacy were
to his straightforward but impulsive nature as
utterly incomprehensible as they were distaste-

ful.   In matters political, frankly ignorant and underestimating his own natural sagacity, he became an easy prey to the fanatical adventurers who fastened upon him and dogged his steps, playing upon his vanity by cunningly encouraging his ambitious dream of the liberation of Rome and Venetia, in order to forward their own selfish party, or personal ends.

Alexander Dumas, the elder, was amongst the horde of foreigners who attached themselves to the Dictator.   Eminently practical, in spite of his eccentricity, he managed during the confusion attending the administration of the capital, to secure a minor official sinecure, and, until turned out by the Piedmontese, dispensed Neapolitan gold with lavish hands in the charming Chiatamonte Palace which he had caused to be allotted to his use.   To his friend d'Ideville, Secretary of the French Legation at Turin, the great author exclaimed with vigorous enthusiasm : "The man is a hero ; a sublime adventurer ; a character of romance !   He is a fool, a simpleton, if you will, but an heroic simpleton ! "

Smarting under a sense of individual wrong, his heart ulcerated by what he considered the hostility and ingratitude of the Government, Garibaldi laid aside all personal rancor, and in his farewell address to his companions in so

many perilous adventures, refers to Victor
Emmanuel as the " Gift of Providence to Italy ;
the Honest King around whom every Italian
should **rally** ; under whose banner every rivalry
should **cease,** and every hatred be set aside."

CHAPTER XVIII.

Operations on the Garigliano.—Failure of fleet to co-operate.— Napoleon's enigmatical policy.—Conference at Varsovie. —Defeat of Royalists.—Retreat on Gaeta.—The fortress of Gaeta.—Its garrison.—Members of Royal Family assembled there.—Early days of the siege.—Napoleon proposes armistice.—Francis writes Emperor refusing to capitulate. —Action of Powers.—Cavour's influence over English statesmen.—Lord Palmerston's assertions.

GENERAL CIALDINI crossed the Garigliano on October twenty-ninth, Victor Emmanuel being present, and attacked the forty thousand Neapolitans intrenched beyond the river, with the pre-arranged design of enclosing the enemy between his own fire and that of Admiral Persano, whose fleet hovered off the estuary. The encounter proved a severe and obstinate one, the Neapolitan artillery causing terrible havoc in the ranks of the Piedmontese, who found themselves unaccountably deprived of the expected support of their ships. Both parties finally claimed the advantage, if advantage there was : although authorities differ on this technicality, all are agreed in eulogizing the undaunted pluck of aggressors and defenders alike.

The failure of Admiral Persano to co-operate with the land forces was due to the action of the French Admiral, Le Barbier de Tinan, whose fleet was stationed in the waters of Gaeta, and who interposed his vessels between those of the Piedmontese commander and the shore; intimating at the same time that his instructions constrained him to prevent any attack from the sea on the forces around Gaeta.

When the reason for the silence of Persano's guns transpired the indignation and fury of the Italians knew no bounds. Greatly incensed, and not a little mystified, Victor Emmanuel despatched a telegram to the Emperor complaining of the extraordinary conduct of the French Admiral. Garibaldi had, on October sixth, declared the blockade of Gaeta and Messina, the citadel of which latter port was still in the hands of the Royalists. Francis protested not without cogency, against the recognition of a blockade decreed by an usurped authority which thus presumed to control the commercial liberty of maritime Powers. He argued that the action of Garibaldi was that of a pirate; and that in passively accepting the decree civilized Europe tolerated piracy in the Mediterranean. The blockade

was, however, neither recognized in principle
nor enforced, the French mail-steamers calling
regularly during the siege, until after the departure of Napoleon's warships, when the
operations of the Italian fleet precluded a continuance of commercial intercourse.

That Le Barbier de Tinan misinterpreted
the instructions he had received, would seem
sufficiently evident from the following extract
from the despatch of November sixth, in which
Monsieur Thouvenel, French Minister of Foreign Affairs, communicated the occurrence to
the Duc de Gramont : " I regret that Admiral
de Tinan, although his instructions prescribed
that he limit his action to preventing the
attack of Gaeta from the sea, should have extended his operations further afield.   King
Francis will have been led to believe that we
intended to defend his cause, whilst our intentions were merely to leave a door open for him
to avoid becoming a prisoner of Victor Emmanuel.   This unfortunate mistake of the
Admiral will cause a great outcry ; and a
measure inspired by the Emperor's sentiments
of humanity will be represented as a fresh
example of duplicity."

In this, as in other cases, it remains to be
proved that Napoleon's policy, obscure, vexatious and humiliating as it often appeared to

Italians impatient for the immediate political redemption of their country, was not in reality in accord with his oft-expressed assurances of sympathy with their cause. A vacillating and uncertain policy it must necessarily be, based as it was on purely personal sympathies unsupported by either National or Dynastic interests. As has already been said, Napoleon III. never intended to go as far as the overwhelming revolutionary tide, combined with unforeseen and fortuitous circumstances, now carried him; the interests of France being distinctly at variance with those of a United Italy. It was owing to this conviction that Cavour never ceased to mistrust the apparent disinterestedness of his dangerous yet, for the time, indispensable ally.

In the present instance the exercise of diplomatic pressure on foreign Courts effectually discouraged the intervention of Austria, as well as the formation of a coalition for the reinstatement of Francis, as contemplated by the abortive conference at Varsovie (October 22, 1860), between the Tzar, the Emperor of Austria, and the Prince Regent of Prussia. On this occasion the much maligned and ridiculed treaty of Zürich, clumsily dragged in by Austria at the intimation from the French Emperor that he would not tolerate a new Holy

Alliance, served a purpose by reviving the principle of non-intervention.

The result of the Plebiscite of October 21st, the entry of Victor Emmanuel into Naples, together with the retirement of Garibaldi, terminating what had been regarded by the Legitimist Courts as a revolutionary incident, now lent a new aspect to the Italian question, simplifying it in one sense by the achievement of that possession which constitutes nine points of the law, yet complicating it in another with potentialities of far greater import than the dethronement of the King of Naples and banishment of the petty Sovereigns of the Peninsula.

After the withdrawal of the French fleet to the immediate vicinity of the fortress, the operations were resumed on a more extensive scale, the Neapolitan forces being simultaneously attacked by the divisions of Cialdini and Sonnaz on land, while raked on their flank by the guns of Persano's ships.

The retreat on Gaeta, begun in good order, rapidly degenerated under the murderous crossfire to which they were subjected into a hopeless rout, the panic-stricken Neapolitans breaking their ranks in wild confusion to seek shelter under the walls of the fortress. The village of Mola, hitherto held by the Bourbon troops, was now abandoned, enabling Cialdini to advance his outposts to within three thousand metres of the fortifications. But for the presence of the French fleet, and the fear of the international complications which must result should Persano disregard the injunctions of the Emperor, there is little reason to doubt that the Italians could have followed up their signal success, and at one blow have annihilated a foe, temporarily paralyzed by the magnitude of this irretrievable disaster.

To add to the misfortunes which overwhelmed the Bourbon Cause news reached the beleaguered citadel that the army corps commanded by General Ruggiero, an old and trusted officer, had fallen back, without opposing resistance, on Terracina, where, having been disarmed by the French in spite of the earnest supplications of the Pope, 16,686 men and 641 officers were disbanded and scattered over the States of the Church.

Relieved of the anxiety of a possible attack on his flank, Cialdini now began operations for the siege (November 6, 1860).

It was, of course, evident, in face of the overwhelming odds against him, that the Neapolitan King must now look to the aid of Diplomacy rather than to the achievements of the forces still at his disposal for the furtherance of his Cause.   Nevertheless the siege promised to be a protracted one owing to the obnoxious circumstances which hampered the Italian operations, and the very considerable natural and artificial strength of the fortress itself.

Gaeta had been a renowned stronghold in the days of the Norman invaders, its foundations dating from ancient times : successive generations fortified and improved its natural advantages, Ferdinand II. devoting special study to the adaptation of its defences to the requirements of modern warfare, while lavishing care upon the adornment and commodity of the royal palace within its walls.   The fortress and town perched upon the rocky promontory jutting out into the Mediterranean were consequently admirably calculated to hold in check an enemy advancing from the land, while in this instance the sea front, also provided with modern batteries, was guaranteed from assault by the presence of the French fleet.

At the beginning of the siege the place was garrisoned by twenty-one thousand troops, fully equipped and provided with munitions of war in vast quantities.   Food supplies continued to arrive from the neighboring Papal ports of Civita Vecchia and Terracina, the French Admiral abetting the liberty of communication by water.

In addition to Francis and Maria Sophia, and their suites, the Royal Palace gave shelter to the Queen Mother, the half-brothers and sisters of the King, his uncles, the Court officials, Ministers of the Crown, and those members of the Diplomatic Corps who had followed the Sovereign from Naples. Amongst these were the Papal Nuncio and the representatives of Austria, Prussia, Russia and Spain. It will be remembered that the British and French Ministers received instructions from their respective Governments to watch the progress of events from their Legations in Naples; as a consequence, in his personal communications with Francis, the French Emperor now had recourse to the services of his Admiral, who combined with the duties of his regular profession those of a plenipotentiary within the waters surrounding Gaeta.

No fighting of importance took place during the remainder of the month of November; but on the other hand Diplomacy was frantically active in its conflicting efforts to envenom or amend a situation all sides felt to be intolerable. Desultory attacks on the part of the assailants, accompanied by comparatively harmless shelling of the batteries, marked the weary monotony of the days. On the twelfth an ineffectual sortie took place, a half-hearted attempt being made to destroy the entrenchments which the Piedmontese were laboriously. constructing. The same day a number of Garibaldian prisoners confined in the Castle were exchanged at Mola for the Neapolitans in the hands of the enemy. The same date witnessed the abandonment of the Bourbon Cause by several of the most prominent Neapolitan officers, including Generals Barbalonga, Colonna, and Salzano, the latter ex-Governor of Capua. The defection of these last named, in whom he had placed implicit confidence, was a bitter mortification to the sorely-tried Sovereign. Hardly less significant was the departure on November twenty-first of the Queen Mother, the younger members of the Royal Family, and the whole of the Diplomatic Corps, with the exception of the Spanish Minister, Bermudez de Castro, devotedly attached to the person of the King. Even the Archbishop of Gaeta availed himself of this opportunity to abandon the sinking ship.

On the nineteenth Colonel Bosco, having now purged the six months enforced idleness stipulated in the parole granted him by the Italians after his distinguished defence of Milazzo, arrived at Gaeta, and offered his services to Francis. The King welcomed this gallant officer with enthusiasm, practically placing in his hands the entire supervision and organization of the military operations.

Count Cavour had in the interval lost no opportunity of protesting against the continued presence of the French fleet, and of impressing upon the Emperor the grave prejudice caused by this overt intervention on behalf of the Bourbon King. Acting under his advice, Victor Emmanuel sent Count Vimercati to Paris with a personal letter to the Emperor. After considerable delay, during which pressure was brought to bear on the defender of Gaeta, Napoleon informed Vimercati, through M. Thouvenel, that if Victor Emmanuel would consent to an armistice of eight days' duration, he would signify to Francis that the further defence of Gaeta was useless, counsel him to abandon the struggle, and, in case of refusal, withdraw his fleet.

That satisfactory results were expected from these negotiations is demonstrated by the following extract of Cavour's letter of December 9, 1860, to the Marquis d'Azeglio : "A telegraphic despatch from the King, received last night, informs me that His Majesty adheres to the Emperor's proposals, trusting that in eight days either Gaeta will have surrendered, or that the French fleet will have retired."

In the meanwhile Napoleon wrote privately

to the Neapolitan King urging him to abandon a struggle which could have but one termination, and intimating that he would be constrained at no distant date to recall his squadron.

To the Emperor's advice and warning, Francis replied in dignified terms, thanking him for the support afforded by the presence of his fleet, but declaring his determination to defend his rights to the end. " You are aware, Sire," he continues, " that Kings who descend from their thrones remount them again with difficulty, unless their misfortunes be illumined by a ray of glory. Here I am a Sovereign in principle, but a General in reality : I no longer possess a State ; I rule over but a sandy beach and faithful soldiers. Can I abandon, on account of the probability of personal risks, an army eager to preserve the honor of its flag ; a fortress on which my ancestors lavished their greatest care in order to make of it the last bulwark of the monarchy ? As a Prince, and a soldier, I must fulfil my duty to the end. I may succumb ; I may be taken prisoner ; but Princes must know how to die if need be. Francis I. was a prisoner, and yet History has not denied him praise for his valorous feats of arms, and the dignity with which he underwent his captivity. No evanescent exaltation inspires this language. It is the outcome of sober reflection, and Your Majesty possesses the heart and the intellect wherewith to appreciate my sentiments."

An offer from Great Britain of a war-ship to convey the King to any port he might select, was declined in like manner.

Undoubtedly the entreaties of the enthusiastic young Queen, seconded by the optimistic, at times even bombastic, assurances of Bosco, influenced Francis in the adoption of a decision, the suicidal if heroic nature of which was patent to all. Moreover, in spite of the disillusions experienced when Admiral de Tinan, in accordance with the limitations imposed upon his actions from headquarters, impassively assisted at the defeat and rout of his troops on the Garigliano, Francis still clung pertinaciously to the belief that Napoleon III. would continue to befriend him. Notwithstanding his brave words, and the proud stand he had taken, the inevitable consequences which must overtake him should the Emperor carry out his threat, haunted the unfortunate King, and spurred him to make every effort to secure the intercession of those foreign Courts avowedly friendly to his cause. At his earnest supplication the Tzar, Prince Regent of Prussia, and Austrian Emperor, sought, through their representatives in Paris, to persuade Napoleon to

maintain his squadron at Gaeta.   M. Thouvenel, when acknowledging the personal intercession of these Sovereigns, explained to their
Ambassadors that, in view of certain consummated facts which could now neither be un-
done nor ignored, the only means of relieving
the King's position was by facilitating the arrangements for an armistice ; and that Admiral
de Tinan had been instructed to use his good
offices to that end.   The French Minister for
Foreign Affairs added unequivocally, however,
that whether the propositions be accepted or
rejected " the moment for the recall of squadron, although not yet definitely fixed, would
not be long delayed."

The negotiations undertaken during the armistice failed to achieve any satisfactory result ;
yet Napoleon still hesitated to enforce his
threat.   " The miserable question of the fleet
does not progress," writes Cavour on January
fourth.   " The Emperor, while well disposed
towards us, puts us off from week to week,
never reaching a decision."

Meanwhile Cavour was straining every nerve
to induce the Cabinet of St. James to bring
pressure to bear on the French Emperor, particularly amenable at this juncture to suggestions from across the Channel.   Lord Palmerston and Lord John Russell were gradually

being won over to the views of the astute statesman in Turin as represented to them by the
Marquis d'Azeglio.   Under date of November
28, 1860, Lord Malmesbury enters in his enter-
taining Diary : "Lady Tankerville called and
told me she went to see Lady Palmerston this
morning.   Whilst she was there Lord Palmerston came in in a furious passion with the
Emperor of the French for preventing the
bombardment of Gaeta, and saying the atrocities committed by Francis II. were dreadful ;
that he had ordered people's eyes to be put out,
their noses cut off, etc., and that it was necessary to put an end to this state of things.
Lady Tankerville expressed her disbelief of this
story ; at which Lord Palmerston got more
angry, and said it was official and therefore
must be true."

The influence which the Marquis d'Azeglio
had gained over the English Premier is still
further demonstrated by a later entry in the
Diary of the ex-Minister.   On December first,
Lord Malmesbury notes : "Saw de Persigny
(the French Ambassador to the Court of St.
James), who abused Palmerston, saying he is
not at all the man he used to be ; that he was
completely led by d'Azeglio, and believed
everything he told him. . . ."

CHAPTER XIX.

The Siege of Gaeta.—Bombardment.—Diplomatic interference.
—Cialdini makes unexpected attack.—Francis rejects proposals for capitulation.—His letter to the Emperor Napoleon III.—Departure of French fleet.—Action of Royalist
officers.—Heroism of Queen Maria Sophia.—Typhus Epidemic. — Negative results of bombardment. — Series of
catastrophes.—Renewed attacks.—Terrific explosions.—A
truce.—General Milon negotiates surrender.—Conditions of
capitulation. — Departure of King. — Francis addresses
troops.—He goes to Rome.—His wanderings and death.—
Surrender of Messina and Civitella.—Victor Emmanuel
proclaimed King of Italy.—Conclusion.

ALTHOUGH there had been some sharp fighting, combined with a desultory but comparatively innocuous bombardment, since the in-
vestiture of the fortress of Gaeta, the embarrassing presence of the equivocally neutral
fleet, and the frequent interruptions necessitated by the diplomatic negotiations in process
between the Cabinets of Turin and Paris,
materially retarded Cialdini in the preparations
necessary for the concentration of his resources
for a decisive and effectual attack.

During the first days of January (1861) the
354

firing became more active, and on the seventh,
Francis and the Queen, accompanied by their
suites, abandoned the palace, and for greater
safety took up their quarters in the armored
casemates. The parallels, constructed with
great difficulty under the incessant fire of the
enemy, had now been carried within efficacious
range, and all was in readiness to begin conclusive operations, when orders again arrived
from Turin to cease firing, the French Emperor
being desirous of arranging another armistice.
While anxious to avoid bloodshed, and minimize the casualties of what he recognized to be
a fratricidal war, Cavour, in view of the prejudice, political, diplomatic and material,
which must result from a prolongation of the
abnormal situation, yielded unwillingly to
Napoleon's suggestion. In his despatch to
d'Azeglio of January 11, 1861, he explains
his position ; "The suspension of operations
for two weeks seemed inacceptable to me : all
the more so as a few days' rain would suffice to
seriously damage the earthworks constructed
at the cost of such sacrifices. On the other
hand, Hudson (British Minister at Turin) himself urged me not to reply to the Emperor with
a point-blank refusal. I therefore made a
counter-proposition limiting the armistice to
eight days, while letting it be understood that

if the fleet did not retire, Cialdini would, notwithstanding, storm Gaeta." *

Although Francis was unwilling to avail himself of the proposed armistice, Admiral de Tinan, acting under personal and urgent instructions from the Emperor, took upon himself the negotiations by which it was ultimately agreed that all operations should cease between January 9th and 19th—the date fixed for the departure of the French war vessels.

On the 8th, Cialdini, presumably desirous of protesting before Italy and Europe that the acceptance of the armistice was due solely to a courteous desire to gratify the Emperor, and refute in advance disparaging insinuations which would inevitably be levelled against the prowess of Italian arms, in the event of the Imperial intercession resulting in a capitulation, took advantage of the intervening twenty-four hours for a combined attack on the fortress with all the resources at his disposal. The firing on both sides was heavy and destructive. Cialdini, although deprived of the co-operation of Persano's ships on the water-front, a co-operation he would depend upon after the departure of the French, had, nevertheless, impressed upon him by the negative results of this improvised and unlooked-

* "La Politique du Comte de Cavour." Bianchi.

for attack, the immense strength of the fortress and the undaunted courage of its defenders.

It is difficult to comprehend the motives which prompted Francis to reject all consideration of the proposals now made to him, which provided for an honorable and advantageous capitulation, unless we assume that he was unduly elated by the spirited defence opposed on the 8th, and exaggerated the importance of the havoc created by his guns on the Italian works. This could, however, hardly warrant the assumption that the Italians would abandon an enterprise which would be greatly facilitated in its military aspect, and simplified politically, with the departure of the so-called neutrals. It is more probable that the dethroned Sovereign overestimated the issue of the organized "brigandage," as the guerilla warfare, waged by thousands of his former soldiery, was termed ; and misinterpreted the significance of the purely local reactionary movements which disturbed isolated portions of his former dominions. It is also certain that he was cruelly deceived in his appreciation of the essentially platonic, or sentimental, nature of the sympathy accorded him from abroad. His letter of January 15th to the French Emperor demonstrates very clearly the extent of the illusions he entertained ; but the simple dignity of its language, impregnated with an impassive resignation, not far removed from heroism, testifies to the influence exerted by the courageous woman at his side, rather than any transformation of the weak and yielding fatalism of his character.

"Monsieur mon Frère :" he writes, "Your Majesty's fleet will depart in a few days, and all communication between this place and the rest of the world will be interrupted. Permit me to avail myself of this last opportunity to write and thank you again for the interest you have so nobly evinced.

"I promised Your Majesty that when I had adopted a definite resolution my first care, an obligation dictated by loyal gratitude, would be to inform you of it. I now fulfil my promise. After the declaration of the French Admiral I hesitated long, I confess : on every side I recognized serious objections, and the opinions of those I felt bound to consult were divided concerning this supreme alternative.

"If, on the one hand, by remaining here, abandoned by the whole world, I expose myself to falling in the hands of a disloyal foe, and run the risk of compromising my liberty, perhaps my dignity and my life ; on the other hand, I should by withdrawing surrender a fortress still intact, thus tarnishing my military honor, and renounce, by an excess of prudence, all eventualities, all hope of the future.

"And how could I yield when in all the provinces of my Kingdom, my subjects rise with one accord against the domination of Piedmont? How can I surrender, when on all sides I am encouraged to resist; when from all parts of Europe private individuals or Governments incite me to persevere in the defence of my Cause, which is also the Cause of Sovereigns; of the rights of Nations; of the independence of Peoples? If political considerations give the appearance of temerity to my resolution, Your Majesty's great and noble heart will distinguish and appreciate my motives.

"I am the victim of my inexperience; of the cunning, of the injustice and audacity of an ambitious Power. I have lost my Kingdom; but I have not lost my faith in the protection of God, and in the justice of man. My rights are to-day my only inheritance, and it is necessary in their defence to bury myself, if needs be, beneath the smoking ruins of Gaeta.

"It is not this prospect which caused me to hesitate for a moment. My only fear was that in becoming a prisoner I might witness the royal dignity debased in my person. But should this last trial be in store for me; should Europe consent to this final outrage, be assured, Sire, that I will utter no complaint, and that I will meet my fate with resignation and firmness.

"I have made every effort to decide the Queen to separate herself from me, but I have been conquered by her gentle entreaties, and by her generous determination. She has desired to share my fortunes to the end, devoting herself to the direction of the hospitals, and the care of the sick and wounded. From to-night Gaeta is the richer by another sister of charity.

"Not knowing whether Your Majesty will recognize the blockade, and being doubtful if the Imperial mail-steamers will be able in future to bring me news of Your Majesty, I have hastened to write in order that the last news which reaches you from the interior of this fortress should carry assurances of the profound esteem, of the sincere gratitude, and of the true friendship, with which I have the honor to be, Monsieur mon Frère, Your Majesty's Good Brother ; Francis."

Before the expiration of the truce Cialdini commissioned General Menabrea and Colonel Piola-Caselli to parley with the enemy ; offering terms for an honorable and advantageous capitulation.   These were courteously but firmly rejected, with the somewhat pretentious allegation that it would be an outrage on the honor of Neapolitan arms to surrender a fortress capable of a vigorous resistance. When informed of this retort Cialdini paid a glowing tribute to the valor of his opponents by exclaiming : " If they were not Italians, I should be proud to fight against such men ! "

Yet in spite of this haughty demeanor the precarious conditions prevailing within the narrow and over-crowded limits of the town had made it necessary to reduce the garrison. During the previous days numerous bodies of troops had been embarked on vessels sailing under the French flag, and landed at various points along the coast ; whence most of them found their way to the mountains, or into Papal territory, there to be amalgamated with the bands of " brigands " recruited for the purpose of continuing the struggle and inciting reactionary revolt throughout the dominions of the ex-King. Owing to these departures, and to numerous desertions, the garrison at the moment of the recall of the French fleet had been reduced to less than twelve thousand men.*

With the expiration of the armistice the French squadron weighed anchor, at half-past four on the afternoon of January nineteenth, and sailed out of the harbor. Three Spanish vessels which lay under the shelter of the fort-

---

* " Rattazzi et son Temps." Madame Rattazzi.

ress yielded to the peremptory intimation of Cialdini, and took their departure, in company with the Prussian corvette "Ida," which had conveyed several members of the Diplomatic Corps to Gaeta during the armistice.

Deprived of the support of the French, and with the certainty of suffering and cruel privation before him, only to be relieved at the cost of his Crown, the heart of the unfortunate young Prince was cheered in this dark hour of anguish by the spontaneous action of his officers, who presented an address renewing their homage and allegiance to their King, and declaring : "Whether our fate is about to be decided, or whether a long period of struggle and suffering still awaits us, we will face our destiny resignedly and fearlessly : we will go to meet either the joys of triumph or the death of the brave with the proud and dignified serenity befitting soldiers."

Admiral Persano lost no time in stationing the fourteen vessels of various tonnage which constituted his fleet before Gaeta, and officially proclaiming the blockade.

And now began a drama the enactment of which called forth a chivalry and courtesy more in accord with the fabled narratives of the Crusades than the grim realities of modern warfare.   While the Queen was abroad on her visits of mercy, a black flag indicated her whereabouts, and there the Italians refrained from pointing their guns. Maria Sophia, however, despised this courteous discrimination, and was often to be found on the ramparts in the thick of the smoke and din of battle, encouraging the gunners; heedlessly exposing herself midst a rain of flying shells and bullets. To the horrors of war was added the hardly less ghastly spectacle afforded by the virulent outbreak of typhus, which quickly overcrowded the hospitals, and paralyzed the insufficient medical resources. To the fever-stricken fortress Cialdini sent supplies of ice and medicines; volunteering also surgical aid for the sufferers, or facilities for their transportation beyond the zone of active hostilities.

The combined bombardment from land and sea had begun on the 22d. During the eight hours this furious attack lasted the land batteries hurled about 11,400 projectiles against the doomed fortress, which responded with over 10,600. The damage done by the guns of the fleet was less extensive than had been anticipated. This was partly due to the inexperience of the gunners, but more particularly owing to Persano's timid hesitation at exposing his ships, and bringing them within effective range. Feats of daring and courage signalized the attack as well as the desperate defence. Maria Sophia, attended by the Swiss General Schumacher the regimental bands gaily playing the royal anthem, visited the batteries, her presence exciting the enthusiasm and redoubling the valor of the men. The horror and confusion of the scene was intensified during the afternoon by the bursting of a shell in the powder magazine of the " Cappuccini " battery, causing a frightful explosion, and the death of nearly all the brave fellows serving the guns, besides reducing the works to a heap of shapeless ruins.

Nevertheless the negative results of the naval bombardment decided Cialdini to adopt other means of attack, and suggested the employment of a species of torpedo, or powder-ships. These vessels, containing about one hundred thousand pounds of powder, were designed to be run ashore against the sea-batteries, and there exploding with terrific force, shatter the works and their defences, tearing open a breach. During the construction of these terrible engines of war, which necessitated careful calculations and somewhat intricate machinery, Cialdini continued to push forward the work on his trenches. It may be mentioned, however, that occasion for the use of the " fire-ships," as they were termed, was fortunately avoided.

With the opening of February the attack was resumed with increased impetuosity. A series of misfortunes and catastrophes, calculated to damp the ardor of the most sanguine advocates for uncompromising resistance, still further contributed to the horrors of the situation. The rapid, all pervading, epidemic of typhus spread consternation : in a single night the fell disease carried off ninety-three victims, amongst others the Abbé Eichellzer, the Queen's confessor, and several officers of the King's Staff, who died in the armored casemates within which the royal couple had taken refuge. The feeling of general despondency was further increased by the receipt of a letter to Maria Sophia in which the Empress Eugénie very clearly implied that all hope of the possible intervention of France must be abandoned. On February third the "Cappelletti" battery blew up : two days later a shell fell in the Sant' Antonio bastion, exploding the magazine, completely wrecking the works, killing two hundred and twelve soldiers, including General Traversa and Colonel di Sagro, and burying beneath the débris nearly a hundred sappers. The same explosion practically destroyed the defences surrounding the drawbridge leading to Porta di Terra, or the land gate, and cut off communication with that quarter. Admiral Persano, perceiving that an attempt was in progress to repair the breach, sent the gun-boat "Garibaldi" during the night to shell the ruins. In spite of the terribly destructive fire kept up by this war-ship, Major Afan de Rivera, accompanied by a handful of volunteers, went to the assistance of his comrades, and succeeded in extracting many who, though crushed and pinioned beneath the smoking ruins, still breathed.

The terrible effects of this explosion, or rather series of explosions, induced Francis to send General Ritucci with a petition for a truce of forty-eight hours, in order that a more thorough search might be undertaken for those still buried beneath the fallen walls. Cialdini not only willingly acceded to this request, but received a hundred of the wounded in his hospital at Mola, and forwarded an equal number to the infirmary at Naples.

During these operations it transpired, however, that the Neapolitans, in violation of the express stipulations governing the truce, were employing the materials extracted from the ruins in repairing the damage, created by the explosion. Cialdini, indignant at this unjustifiable breach of faith, now rejected further proposals for an armistice of fifteen days; refusing even to consider the prolongation of the present cessation of hostilities, beyond an additional twelve hours. In consequence, on the morning of the 9th, the combat was resumed with such energetic determination, and under conditions so disadvantageous to the besieged, that even those amongst his advisers whot had been most uncompromisingly firm in their counsels for resistance, now warned Francis of the futility of further efforts.

Preliminary negotiations for the surrender were opened on the evening of the 11th, just as the Piedmontese were preparing to storm the fortress, after having opened a breach in the Philipstadt bastion, which commanded the isthmus connecting the promontory of Gaeta with Mola on the mainland.

Francis, realizing that favorable terms would with difficulty be obtained by General Ritucci, who had incurred the personal animosity of Cialdini by his disloyal conduct during the recent truce, now transferred the command of the fortress to General Milon, intrusting him also with the negotiations for the capitulation. The discussions were carried on in the Piedmontese camp at Mola, and, owing to frequent interruptions, occupied the greater part of three days. Pending the conclusion of negotiations, and the ratification of the various articles, no cessation of hostilities had been granted : the plenipotentiaries consequently held their sessions amidst the roar of artillery and rattle of musketry. On the third day a shell fell on the magazine of the Transylvanian Battery, containing over three hundred and sixty thousand pounds of powder. The explosion was terrific : 56 soldiers and two officers lost their lives, while the material damage created by the disaster, and the continuous battering of the Italian artillery, so impaired the defences that further resistance became well-nigh impossible, and decided the courageous but disheartened Neapolitans to accept the terms offered them.

The conditions regulating the capitulation having been finally drawn up and duly signed, the order to cease firing was given. The conditions imposed were honorable and liberal : the surrender of the fortress with all the material of war, property of the State, and provisions it contained, was insisted upon. The honors of war were accorded to the garrison, the officers being allowed to retain their swords. All were to be treated as prisoners of war until the fortresses of Messina and Civitella del Tronto had surrendered, after which the Neapolitans were to be disbanded and the foreign mercenaries returned to their respective countries under parole not to take service against the Italians for a year. The King, accompanied by the members of his family, the Swiss Generals de Riedmatten and Schumacher, as well as General Bosco, was to be allowed to embark on the French corvette "Mouette," which Napoleon had instructed should be held in readiness for this mission after the recall of his squadron, and which was now summoned from Naples.

On the morning of the 14th, while the Piedmontese troops occupied the land batteries, the King, accompanied by his valiant young consort, the members of his family, and the Generals above mentioned, descended to the water front, and passing through a double line of his faithful regiments, embarked on the "Mouette," amidst the cheers of his soldiers and the thunder of a salute of twenty-one guns —the last homage of those who had so valorously upheld his Cause during the ninety-two days the siege had lasted. Not until the "Mouette" rounded the point and headed for Civita Vecchia was the Bourbon standard lowered and the tricolor of Italy run up in its stead.

On the day of his departure Francis issued an eloquent proclamation to his troops, thanking them for the unselfish support they had accorded him. "Thanks to you," he wrote,

" the honor of the army of the Two Sicilies is intact : thanks to you, your Sovereign can still lift his head with pride ; while in the exile where he will await the justice of Heaven the remembrance of the heroic fidelity of his soldiers will ever afford the sweetest consolation in his misfortunes."

Francis went directly to Rome, where he was warmly welcomed by Pius IX., anxious to reciprocate the hospitality he himself had received at the hands of Ferdinand when a fugitive at Gaeta twelve years previously. At Rome, in the magnificent Farnese Palace, or in his villa at Castelgandolfo in the Alban Hills, the ex-King continued to reside until, with the destruction of the Temporal Power in 1870, and the occupation of the Eternal City by the troops of United Italy, he became a wanderer. Drifting over the surface of Europe, now in Bavaria, now in Paris (where the ex-Queen Maria Sophia still (1899) makes her headquarters), Francis never renounced the hope of an eventual reinstatement on the Throne of his ancestors. A sufferer for many years from diabetes, he passed away during a sojourn at Arco, a small watering place in the lower Tyrol, at the head of the lake of Garda, on December 27, 1894.

On taking possession of Gaeta the victors

found 700 cannon, 56,212 rifles, 10,858 side arms, 209,859 projectiles, and over 200,000 cartridges, large quantities of powder, and provisions for twenty (some say fifty) days.

Prince Carignano, who had been appointed Lieutenant General of the new provinces by Victor Emmanuel, arrived from Naples the day after the departure of the dethroned King, and passed the Bourbon troops in review.

Messina capitulated a month later (March 15th), and the phenomenal defence of the stronghold of Civitella del Tronto was brought to a close on the 27th of the same month, in consequence of a letter dated from Rome, in which their late Sovereign, thanking the brave garrison for their loyalty and splendid courage, signified that further resistance was now useless.

With the capitulation of these last strongholds of Bourbon rule the conditions of the surrender of Gaeta were scrupulously complied with, and the soldiers of the late Dynasty were disbanded, those who desired being re-enlisted in the Italian service, and the others assisted to their homes.

On March 17, 1861, the Italian Parliament assembled at Turin, proclaimed Victor Emmanuel II. King of Italy, with only two dissentient votes : the Monarchy of the Two Sicilies being thus officially merged in the Kingdom of United Italy.

England recognized the new dignity conferred on the Head of the House of Savoy at once : France only in the following June.

　·　　　　·　　　　·　　　　·　　　　·

" The story of the collapse of the Neapolitan Government in the hour of need would (says Professor Dicey in his study of the life of Victor Emmanuel II.), if it were told honestly, point a moral how States fall to pieces when people, officials, ministers, and rulers are alike corrupt, degraded and demoralized. But low as Naples had sunk, the Government would, I am convinced, have been strong enough to withstand the onslaught of the Garibaldian invasion, if behind Garibaldi there had not stood the Kingdom of Italy."

THE END

X 51917

UC SOUTHERN REGIONAL LIBRARY FACILITY

A 000 741 556 5

ImTheStory.com

Personalized Classic Books in many genre's

Unique gift for kids, partners, friends, colleagues

Customize:

- Character Names

- Upload your own front/back cover images (optional)

- Inscribe a personal message/dedication on the

  inside page (optional)

Customize many titles Including
- Alice in Wonderland
- Romeo and Juliet
- The Wizard of Oz
- A Christmas Carol
- Dracula
- Dr. Jekyll & Mr. Hyde
- And more...

Lightning Source UK Ltd.
Milton Keynes UK
UKHW020232300620
365757UK00019B/5170